REVISED
AND
UPDATED

DAVID CAMPBELL

MYSTERY
EXPLAINED

A SIMPLE
GUIDE TO
REVELATION

LEGEND

FOREWORD
ANDREW FOUNTAIN

There are few commentaries, in my experience, that have such a depth of scholarly underpinning as this one, and yet can be read almost as easily as a novel. This did not happen by accident, or by a flash of genius, but by a long and disciplined process — a journey. When I first met David Campbell, he was on the initial leg of the journey. Like me, he had a love for the book of Revelation, and we shared a deep appreciation for the magisterial commentary by G.K. Beale. It had long been my go-to commentary whenever I taught courses on the book. The great strength of Beale's commentary is the way in which it uses other parts of Scripture, particularly the Old Testament, to shed light on the imagery of the Apocalypse.

The first part of David's journey was the massive endeavor of transforming this work into Revelation: *A Shorter Commentary* (Eerdmans, 2014). According to the publisher:

"G.K. Beale's monumental New International Greek Testament Commentary volume on Revelation has been highly praised since its publication in 1999. This shorter commentary distills the superb grammatical analysis and exegesis from that tome (over 1,300 pages) into a book more accessible and pertinent to preachers, students and general Christian readers."

This goal was achieved and the work has been published to great acclaim, but David realized that the journey was not completed. He was still to realize his dream of making a sound exposition of Revelation accessible to the average Christian.

If the first leg of the journey was to take this from the academic to the pastor, the second leg was to carry it from the pastor to the pew.

Had this process been accomplished in one step, I believe it would not have been as elegant and polished as it now is. Because David's feet are so firmly planted in the scholarship, and he is so familiar with the material, he can relax and freely express himself in everyday language.

Finally, David brings to this volume several decades as a pastor, which is reflected in comments like: "Why do God's people continue to have to suffer as they walk in the way of the cross? Much of Revelation gives the answer to this."

My hope is that this commentary will be used greatly to encourage the church as we "walk in the way of the cross."

Andrew Fountain, M.Div., Ph.D.
Former Principal, Toronto Baptist Seminary
Pastor, New Life Church Toronto
March 2016

AUTHOR'S PREFACE TO
THE REVISED EDITION

I have been working on various projects related to Revelation for nearly fifteen years. In the process, it has become clear to me that a concise explanation of the last book of the Bible understandable to the average person is desperately needed. The world's Christian bookshelves are littered with copies of books which so badly distort Revelation that its true message is hardly recognizable.

God designed Revelation in one sense to be a mystery, just like the parables of Jesus. Confronting this mystery in sincere faith causes genuine believers to seek out its true meaning, while unbelievers who reject it will have their hearts further hardened to God. God gives his Spirit to lead us into understanding of his Word. His mystery is explained by his Spirit. My view is that Revelation can be properly and easily understood in light of its organic connection with the rest of the Bible. My prayer is that the Holy Spirit will show you clearly how this connection works, and what the meaning and message of the book truly are.

I want to express special appreciation to our friends Stuart and Ranjeetha Wakeling of Atlanta for a generous gift which enabled this project to go ahead. Thanks to Matthew G. Tuckey of Newcastle, England, for his invaluable help in proofreading the entire text of the first edition and checking the accuracy of Biblical quotations. Thanks to my friend and colleague Dr. Andrew Fountain for his kind preface and other editorial assistance. I am grateful for the support of churches around the world who encourage my teaching ministry. I cannot overstate my debt to the incomparable work of G.K. Beale, with whom I worked on a previous project, but with the critical proviso that I alone must be held responsible for any deficiencies in the text of this one. Thanks to Joshua Best of David & Brook, Zeeland, Michigan, for his expert production of the book.

Last and by no means least, I am grateful for the support of my children Katie (Josh), Anna (Chris), Michael (Samantha), John, Rachel (Matt), Sarah (Jacob), Julia and James, and the inspiration of our grandchildren Joseph, Eleanor, Tate, Harriet, Ethan and Adelaide. Most of all, thank you to my wife Elaine, who has stood with me in faithfulness to Christ and his church for nearly forty years of marriage.

Soli Deo gloria — glory to God alone.

Stratford, Ontario
June 2020

INTRODUCTION:
DON'T SKIP THIS PART

Revelation is not a handbook to last-days events. It is a pastoral letter written to Christians of every age and generation on how to live lives faithful to God and Christ in the midst of all the challenges a hostile pagan world throws at them. The visions given to John form a prophetic picture of the sovereignty of God working through all the ups and downs of human history. It assures believers that God is Lord over that history, and exhorts them to persevere in obedience in order to inherit an eternal reward that will infinitely compensate for the sufferings they have undergone in this present world due to their faithfulness to him.

Revelation is full of the Old Testament. There are more allusions to the Old Testament in Revelation than in all other books of the New Testament combined. Most scholars estimate there are over 500 such allusions in Revelation's 404 verses, compared with less than 200 in all of Paul's letters. The Reformers established the great principle *scriptura scripturae interpres*, a Latin phrase which means "Scripture interprets itself." Nowhere else in the Bible is this as true as in Revelation. The great mistake of much contemporary interpretation is the tendency of interpret Revelation in light of current news reports rather than the Bible itself.

Yet Revelation is indeed also a prophetic book, but in the proper Biblical sense. For a start, John begins the book by identifying himself as a prophet (1:3). His prophetic ministry is very much in line with the prophets of the Old Testament, for he calls his readers to obedience and warns them of judgment if they fail in this responsibility. We often forget that prophecy in the Bible deals far more with calling people to repentance and obedience in light of God's purposes in history than about the simple prediction of future events.

This dual nature of Revelation — pastoral and prophetic — calls for a radical change in the way in which Christians, especially in the North American context, understand it. Although it does in some places speak of the events immediately preceding the return of Christ, for the most part it addresses each of us precisely in the place where we live now. It calls us to obedience to God's commands and offers us his grace toward that end. It promises us a rich reward if we persevere.

The story line of Revelation retraces that of the Exodus. Christians are portrayed as leaving the bondage of spiritual Egypt or Babylon, crossing the fearful sea where evil resides, and entering the place of God's protection in the wilderness as they fix their eyes on the eventual goal of the eternal promised land. The plagues of Exodus are replicated in the plagues on the various civilizations of human history. In the process, God hardens the hearts of unbelievers while seeking to shock those destined for salvation into repentance. It is impossible to understand Revelation without keeping this story line in place.

A second story line also emerges. This one returns us to the very beginning of human history. Revelation takes us back to the garden of Eden in order to demonstrate that God's goal in that history is to restore the garden but in an even better form, one in which the very presence of evil is forever banished outside its confines. Revelation takes us on a journey from the temple of the garden to the tabernacle of Moses, to the temple of Solomon to the new temple in Christ, and lands us in the eternal temple of God and the Lamb. It takes us from the rivers of Eden to the river of Ezekiel, and from the new river in Christ to the eternal river of the new Jerusalem. It shows us how far along with path we have come through the sacrificial death of the Lamb, while pointing us forward to the altogether greater and more wonderful day when the Lamb's rule will be made manifest to all creation.

This is the fitting, triumphant and glorious note on which Revelation brings the Bible not only to its literary end, but also to its triumphant theological and spiritual climax.

AUTHORSHIP

Revelation is composed of a series of prophetic visions given to John, a Christian leader exiled for his faith on the island of Patmos. John was well known to all the churches of Asia, and his word carried great authority. His use of the Old Testament suggests he was a Jew from Palestine. Many of the themes so prominent in John's Gospel and his letters reappear in Revelation (Jesus as the Word of God, Lamb and shepherd, living water, manna, conquering, obeying the commands of God and others). It is no surprise that from the very earliest times Christians understood Revelation to have been written by the apostle John the son of Zebedee, the beloved disciple. A young man when he first started to follow Jesus, John is now very old, having himself lived the faithful life to which he is calling others.

DATE OF WRITING

The book was written about AD 90. How do we know this? Rome was never referred to as Babylon (as it almost certainly is in Revelation) until after the destruction of the temple and Jerusalem in AD 70. After that, Rome was identified with the Babylonians who did the same thing so many centuries before. The Christians of the seven churches were being pressured to engage in the imperial cult of emperor worship, which was not initiated until the reign of Domitian (81-96). Early Christian leaders believed that it was during Domitian's reign that the book was written. One of these leaders, Irenaeus, was a disciple of Polycarp, who was martyred in AD 156, having been a Christian for 86 years and who knew John personally.

ITS HEAVENLY PERSPECTIVE ON THE VICTORY OF GOD

The heavenly revelation John receives from the throne-room of God and the Lamb, mediated largely through angelic messengers, conveys to him a far different perspective on the world than what he sees with his own eyes. Part of the prophetic nature of Revelation is the way in which God establishes himself as Lord of history and calls people to act on that basis, no matter what any analysis of human history or current events yields. The world is pressuring Christians to compromise, and threatening punishment if they fail to do so. God, on the other hand, promises them if that if they remain faithful, even though they suffer in a human sense, he will keep them spiritually safe. Furthermore, the reward they will receive in the eternal world to come will far outweigh any sufferings they now encounter. The visions John receives show how events in the heavenly realms are interacting with events on earth. The resurrection and the ascension are the points at which the victory of God becomes inevitable. To use a second world war analogy, D-day has occurred, and it is only a matter of time until victory is complete. This message brings strength and comfort to Christians of all ages, not only those experiencing deprivation and persecution, but also those subject to the normal temptations and relatively smaller sacrifices of discipleship common to most in the western world today.

THE FOUR WAYS OF INTERPRETING REVELATION

There are four main ways of interpreting Revelation.

The preterist view. The word "preterist" means "past." According to the preterist view, everything in Revelation happened prior to AD 70, when Jerusalem was destroyed by the Romans. The whole book is a prophetic warning of that event. "Babylon" represents the Jewish people insofar as they have rebelled against God. Unfaithful Israel is about to fall, and Christians must flee from it. This view assumes the book was written well before those events, but against this stands the high probability that the book was not written until many years later. In addition, "Babylon" *never* referred to Israel in ancient Jewish or Christian literature. But after AD 70, it did refer to Rome. In its portrayal of the last battle, Revelation (drawing on Daniel and Ezekiel) refers to the pagan nations of the world gathering against God's faithful people of every race and nationality around the world. It does not speak of Rome attacking faithless first-century Israel. It is difficult to conceive of the cataclysmic battle scenes and cosmic signs referring to a historical event two thousand years ago. It is almost impossible to synchronize this view with the eschatological teachings of Jesus in the Gospels. One final point is worth considering: if this view were true, the book becomes irrelevant for anyone who lived after those first days of the church. Why would God include it in the Bible at all?

The historicist view. According to this view, Revelation divides history into seven sections, each of which is typified by one of the seven churches in chapters 2-3. On this understanding, the seals, trumpets and bowls unfold one after the other in alignment with the seven ages. Revelation describes literal historical events, all of which takes place in the history of the western (European) church. Some of these include the decline of Rome, the rise of the papacy and the Reformation. Again, this view presents us with difficulties. To begin with, there is no internal evidence of any sort that each church represents a period of history. Further, the problem arises how to identify these historical eras. Each historicist interpreter understands them differently, usually taking care to include the historical period in which he himself lived as the last before Christ's return. This gave rise to many different interpretations within this overall view. Finally, this perspective has no relevance for Christians outside the western church, nor would it have had any relevance to those to whom it was originally written. The last century has seen the worldwide expansion of the church at an unprecedented rate, leaving the western church in an increasingly small minority among Christians as a whole. Unsurprisingly, this view has been largely abandoned.

The futurist view. This understanding takes the whole book (apart from the letters of chapters 2-3) to refer to events at the very end of history. Dispensational futurism (promoted in Hal Lindsey's book *The Late Great Plant Earth* and the *Left Behind* series) has become a powerful force, particularly in North American Christianity. Like the historicist view, it interprets the visions literally and chronologically as referring to events of history, but from a different perspective. The key for dispensationalists is the significance of the restoration of national Israel to its ancient land. Though there had always been Jews in Palestine, the establishment of the state of Israel in 1948 gave a powerful impetus to the popularity of this view. This restoration of Israel is understood to take place prior to the events described starting at 4:1. Following this, Christ secretly returns to earth and the church is raptured into heaven. There is a seven-year tribulation on earth described in chapters 6-19, in which the reign of the antichrist begins and the state of Israel is persecuted. As the nations gather together to make war against Jerusalem, Christ returns a second time and defeats them. He then establishes a literal thousand year reign on earth, described in chapter 20. Those entering the millennium are Jews converted during the tribulation, plus a small number of Gentiles. They live long lives, perhaps surviving the entire duration of the millennium. Raptured believers, in immortal bodies, meanwhile, inhabit the new Jerusalem which hovers over earth. Some resurrected believers visit the earth and mingle with those in still-mortal bodies. The temple is rebuilt and the priestly and sacrificial system reinstated as the means of worshiping God. However, unbelievers somehow reappear, and eventually rise in rebellion against Christ. They are gathered together by Satan at the end of the thousand year period. Christ defeats these demonic forces a second time and begins his eternal heavenly reign.

This view is an outgrowth of the dispensationalist theology which teaches that God has two covenant peoples, Jews and Christians. God sent Jesus to establish a literal earthly kingdom. When Jesus was unexpectedly rejected and crucified, God had to revert to Plan B, which was the church. But the church is only a "parenthesis" in God's plan. God must complete his original purpose, and he cannot deal with two covenant peoples at one time. Hence he must take believers out of the world in order to go back to his original intention of installing Christ as earthly king in Jerusalem. Only at the end of time will the two peoples be reunited. Dispensationalism originated in a charismatic vision a young woman called Margaret MacDonald experienced in Scotland in 1830, in which she saw a secret return of Christ. This was taken up by John Nelson Darby, a gifted Bible teacher who was obsessed with the restoration of the state of Israel. Darby then incorporated it as the basis of his theology, as it enabled him to show how God could have two covenant peoples and deal with each separately. Darby developed his ideas in a series of prophetic conferences in England and Canada in the years following. It must be said that such an interpretation of the Bible never previously existed in the entire history of the church. It was a novelty based on a vision.

There are many problems with this view. Here are just some of them:

1. The Bible nowhere teaches a seven-year tribulation. In fact, the word

"tribulation" in the New Testament consistently refers to the entire period of time from Pentecost to Christ's return, which we call the church age (see 1:9, for instance). The idea of a seven-year tribulation is drawn from a twisted interpretation of Dn. 9:24-27, from which no one would draw the idea of a seven-year end-times tribulation *unless* that idea had *previously been read into the text* and assumed as correct. To find out what the text in Daniel means requires careful examination of the Scriptures: (a) Daniel prophesied a period of time specified as "seventy weeks" commencing in a decree to restore and build Jerusalem (Dn. 9:25). (b) Daniel further identified the *beginning* of this time period with the *end* of the seventy year period of judgment of Israel prophesied by Jeremiah (Dn. 9:2; Jer. 25:14). This period of time is identified as a Sabbath rest for the land, and it is ended by the decree of Cyrus to build the house of God in Jerusalem (2 Chron. 36:21-23). This decree went forth in 538 BC. (c) This means that the starting point for the 70 weeks is BC 538. (d) Prophetic numbers in the Bible are always symbolic, and this is no exception. The purpose of the 490 weeks (seventy times seven years) is stated as providing forgiveness (Dn. 9:24). In other words, it is *an escalation of the year of Jubilee* (which was seven times seven years), the year all debts were forgiven. This year of Jubilee is marked by the complete forgiveness of sins in Christ. In other words, it is not a literal 490 years, which would land its fulfillment in BC 48 (making no sense), but is a *symbolic number* referring to the coming time of forgiveness in Christ. The attaining of ultimate forgiveness in the escalated Jubilee (the death and resurrection of Christ) is followed by the destruction of Jerusalem (Dn. 9:26b, 27b), also prophesied by Jesus (Mt. 24:1-2). When the seventieth week comes, the Messiah will die (be "cut off," verse 26a). Then, "the people of the prince who is to come shall destroy the city" (verse 26b). The people are the Romans, and the prince is Titus, commander of the Roman armies at the destruction of Jerusalem in AD 70. Following his death, the Messiah will "make a strong covenant with many" (verse 27a) and will "put an end to sacrifice and offering" (verse 27b). This refers to the new covenant through Christ. The end of sacrifice and offerings could either refer theologically to the end of their function in God's economy, or literally to the end of the sacrificial system that occurred with the destruction of the temple. All this takes up the first half of the final seventieth week. The second half of the week jumps to the end of time and the destruction of the desolator, either the devil or one of his servants (verse 27c). If this seems odd, consider that Peter did exactly the same thing in his interpretation of Joel's prophecy at Pentecost. He moves seamlessly from the outpouring of the Spirit (Ac. 2:17-19) to the events of the end (2:20-21), without any break.

The dispensational interpretation hinges on interpreting the 490 weeks as literal years, but abandoning the clear Biblical connection to the decree of Cyrus and finding another event which might work better. This they find in a the later decree of Artaxerxes, from which a literal 69 weeks times seven yields either AD 32 or 33, though even that is slightly too late to fit the date of Jesus' death. The even bigger problem is that dispensationalists, having defined a week as strictly literal, must throw that idea out the window to fit their assumption that the seventieth week falls at the end of time. *This necessitates a massive (so far two thousand year) gap between the literal 69 weeks and the literal seventieth week.* The seventieth week (a literal seven years) is arbitrarily defined as the "great tribulation" of Rev. 7:14, which comes up against the fact that verse speaks of the vast multitude of saints who have died and entered the presence of the Lord, having endured the trials of the present church age. This suggests the "great tribulation" is to be identified with that age. This is confirmed elsewhere in Revelation and the New Testament. The four other occurrences of the word "tribulation" (Greek *thlipsis*) in Revelation refer to events of the present church age (1:9; 2:9; 2:10; 2:22). Jesus uses the word the same way (Jn. 16:33), as does Luke (Ac. 14:22). Twenty-one out of twenty-three occurrences of the word in Paul refer clearly to present reality (Rom. 5:3; 8:35-36; 2 Tim. 3:12). The New Testament connects the idea of tribulation with the sufferings of this present time. "The great tribulation" is the church age.

2. Revelation nowhere mentions or assumes any restoration of national Israel. In fact, from the very beginning (see on 1:6 and 5:10), it identifies the church (composed of Jews and Gentiles alike) as the new Israel which inherits the promises given under Moses to the old national Israel.

3. Neither does Revelation contain any reference to a supposed "rapture" of the church. Dispensationalists based this teaching on the mention of the "appearing" or "coming" of the Lord in 1 Thess. 4:15. "Coming" there translates the Greek word *parousia*. This word referred to the "coming" of the Emperor or other ruler to visit one of his territories. The citizens of the city would parade out to meet him at his coming, and then they would escort him *back into the city* to take up his reign. This is the opposite to having the Emperor take the citizens away to some other place, deserting his city rather than taking possession of it. Paul is speaking of Christ returning to rule over the new heavens and new earth. A similar meaning occurs in verse 17, where believers will be caught up in the clouds (literally) "for a meeting" (*apantesis*) with the Lord. The word *apantesis* likewise refers to citizens

going out from a city to meet a visiting dignitary whom they will then escort back into the city. The second passage supposedly referring to a rapture is Mt. 24:38-41. Christ's return will be like the days of Noah, when believers entered the ark and the wicked were swept away. On that day, one will be taken and the other will be left. But this text again teaches the *opposite* of the rapture. Believers are not whisked away to Paradise. Rather, *it is the lost* who are taken away to destruction, just like the unbelievers were swept away in the flood. The believers remain. Nowhere does the Bible refer to multiple returns of Christ, and certainly not of any secret return. Rather, Christ's return, like lightning flashing from east to west is visible to all the peoples of the earth (Mt. 24:27, 30). Paul says the same thing when he describes Christ's return in three ways: as "from heaven," "with his mighty angels" and "in flaming fire" (2 Thess. 1:7-8). Christ will appear visibly to the whole world.

4. As the futurist view understands everything in Revelation to be taken literally, it turns the book into something of a science fiction novel, with strange creatures on earth and in heaven. Revelation is interpreted by current events, not the Bible itself, which so clearly provides the symbolic framework which holds it together. The preoccupation with current events leads to the futurist view being continuously revised, as different predicted fulfillments turn out to be incorrect. Futurist commentators have understood a wide variety of individuals (from Hitler to various Popes and political figures in the Middle East such as Saddam Hussein) to be the Antichrist or to be identified as "666." Historical events of every sort have been identified as harbingers of the rapture, from the two World Wars to the Gulf war, various attacks on Israel, the European Union, Saddam's attempt at rebuilding a replica of Babylon, "blood moons" and countless others. Each time, definitive correlations with passages in Revelation are made, but then quietly discarded in the next edition of the book as the predictions prove mistaken. The interpretation of Revelation changes as often as the daily news. Never is there any acknowledgement of mistakes made.

5. Beyond this eschatological farce, which often makes the church a laughing stock with the watching world, the question arises as to why God would include such an important book in the Bible which has relevance to no one but the people living in the very last years before the supposed rapture.

A form of *modified futurism* (also called historic premillenialism) also exists, which rejects the rapture and the role of Israel, but still sees Revelation as referring only to last days events, thus making it of no relevance to Christians of all other ages. This view fails to provide any reason for a millennial rule of Christ, which dispensationalism, with all its fault, does. See further our discussion of millennial views at the beginning of our analysis of chapter 20.

The idealist view. None of the three views described above seem in any way to provide a satisfactory solution to understanding Revelation. We thus turn to the idealist view, which we feel does do justice to the book. It interprets Revelation symbolically, and in the light of the Old Testament references and allusions which form so much of its substance. To interpret the book symbolically does not mean Revelation does not refer to actual events. The key is that in order to determine what events different parts of the book refer to, we must utilize the Old Testament realities behind the visionary symbols. Some of these, such as the lampstands in chapter 1, are identified for us. For most others, we must go back to the Old Testament passages from which they are drawn. The serpent is Satan (Genesis), the locusts are armies hostile to God (Joel), and Babylon is the fallen world system (Isaiah and Jeremiah). To understand the woman of chapter 12, we must go back to Joseph's dream. To understand the earth swallowing the waters and saving the woman, we must go back to Israel's deliverance at the Red Sea. The eagle's wings on which she is carried refer to God's promise to deliver his people in Isa. 40:31. These we explain throughout the book.

The church, composed of people of every nation, is portrayed throughout Revelation as the fulfillment of God's promises to Israel, through the work of Christ taking its place in God's plan. Old Testament prophecies concerning Israel are repeatedly interpreted with reference to the church. The judgments depicted in the seals, bowls and trumpets are cyclical events which recur throughout the church's history. The plagues are symbolic representations of the literal plagues on Egypt, and have the same effect of hardening many unbelievers while shocking others into repentance. The book constitutes an exhortation to Christians to remain faithful to Christ in the sufferings they experience as they refuse to compromise with the world system. All the numbers are symbolic, but receive clear meaning through their Old Testament background and reference. Dispensationalists claim that only their "literal" interpretation upholds the authority of the Bible. In fact, the opposite is true. The idealist view holds that Revelation refers to very real literal events, but explains that such events cannot be identified properly without using a completely Biblical means of interpretation. By interpreting Revelation through current events instead of God's Word, dispensationalists have wreaked havoc with the meaning of the text as God gave it to John.

The millennium depicts the church during its sojourn on earth between Christ's resurrection and his return. Idealist interpreters have sometimes been termed "amillennial," which means literally no millennium, but are better described as believing in an actual, though symbolically understood millennium, which is inaugurated by Christ at his death and resurrection and ultimately fulfilled in his eternal kingdom. The millennium is the time at which God's kingdom enters into history, thus fulfilling Daniel's prophetic vision of the rock hitting the mountain (Dn. 2:35), which Jesus himself interpreted as beginning with his own earthly ministry (Mt. 21:44).

There is only one return of Christ, visible to all, no secret rapture and one end to history. Revelation portrays the church on a journey out of Egypt and proceeding through the wilderness under God's spiritual protection, although subject to earthly attack and harm. It culminates in the church's entry into the promised land of the new Jerusalem. Revelation also portrays the events immediately prior to the Lord's return, but this occupies a relatively small portion of the book. Thus understood, Revelation is powerfully applicable to the lives of Christians of every generation, from first to last.

THE SYMBOLIC NATURE OF REVELATION

Futurist interpreters tend to take Revelation literally. But is this justified? The first verse of the book shows it is not. In verse 1a, John speaks of a revelation "God gave him to show to his servants the things that must soon take place." The verb "show" is the Greek verb *deiknumi*. This verb occurs seven times elsewhere in Revelation (4:1; 17:1; 21:9, 10; 22:1, 6, 8). Each time it is used, it refers to the showing of a pictorial vision, which God then interprets symbolically. This meaning is confirmed by verse 1b, where John continues: "He made it known by sending his angel..." The verb "made known" translates the Greek verb *semaino*, which means to symbolize or signify symbolically. Verse 1b reads literally: "He communicated it [the revelation of v. 1a] symbolically by sending his angel to his servant John." John is alluding in this statement to Dn. 2:28-30, 45, where Daniel interprets the dream of the king concerning the statue. This is the only other passage in the Bible where the same features occur. As in Rev. 1:1a, there is a revelation which God showed to Daniel concerning what will take place. Then, using the same verb *semaino* (in the Greek Old Testament), he says that God has signified or communicated this symbolically. What is signified or communicated symbolically is the meaning of the dream. The interpretation unfolds the symbolic significance of the statue with its four parts composed of various kinds of metals. These parts symbolize four kingdoms which are to come. Thus the dream is to be understood not literally but symbolically. Knowing the meaning of Daniel, John consciously copies the content and carries it over into the interpretation of the revelation he receives. The entire revelation is to be understood (like Daniel's dream) in a symbolic manner, in which the various parts depict realities which are to be understood not literally but in light of their significance elsewhere in the Scriptures.

In the very first verse, therefore, John sets out the principle that the visions to be unfolded in the book have a largely symbolic meaning. The visions may have multiple historical references, and will likely not refer literally to one person or event. The key to their primary meaning will be found in the numerous Old Testament references and allusions which run throughout. The various plagues and judgments, for instance, which form a prominent part of the book, are to be understood in light of their meaning in the Exodus account from which they are largely borrowed. They symbolize the fact of God's judgments on the earth, as these judgments are carried out from time to time in history. The woman of chapter 12 goes back to Genesis 37 and also various texts in Isaiah, and symbolizes the church through the ages. The woman of chapter 17, depicted as a prostitute, is to be understood in light of Isaiah, Jeremiah and Ezekiel's portrayal of historical Babylon, and refers to the wicked and fallen culture of the world and its institutions, which often form a demonic counterfeit to the church, thus explaining why the two women are described in similar but contrasting terms. It is in fact impossible to interpret many of John's visions literally. What are we to make of horses with the heads of lions or locusts with crowns on their heads and the faces of men? What of the creatures full of eyes or the lamb with seven horns and eyes? Yet all these can be accounted for satisfactorily through the principles of interpretation we have suggested.

Understanding Revelation this way leads us to the observation that all the numbers contained in it are likewise to be understood symbolically. Seven, rooted in the creation account, is the number of God and of completion. Thus the "seven spirits" (1:4) actually refer to the totality of the Spirit, or the Holy Spirit. The sets of seven judgments (seals, trumpets, the visions of chapters 12-14 and the bowls) express the completeness of God's judgment. Four is the number of the earth (the four rivers of Gen. 2:10-14). Thus the four winds and the earth's four corners of 7:1 refer to something with worldwide impact. The four sets of seven judgments express God's complete judgment on the earth. Twelve is the number of government expressed through God's people (the twelve tribes and the twelve apostles). One thousand expresses an indefinitely large number or period of time. Thus the millennium refers to the church age as a whole. The 144,000 of chapters 7 and 14 refer to the entire people of God throughout the ages (12 tribes x 12 apostles multiplied by 1000 to express completeness). "Christ" appears seven times, "Jesus" and "Spirit" fourteen times and "Lamb" twenty-eight times. Babylon, by contrast, appears six times, six being the number of fallen humanity (man having been created on the sixth day). The number 666 alludes to the demonic trinity, six repeated three times to reflect its members, the dragon, the beast and the false prophet.

WHY DID GOD CHOOSE TO SPEAK THROUGH SYMBOLS?

The answer to this question is rooted first in Jesus' use of parables, beyond that in the message of the Old Testament prophets and ultimately in the plagues of Exodus. Concerning his use of parables, Jesus said to his disciples: "To you it has been given to know the secrets of the kingdom of heaven, but to them it has not been given" (Mt. 13:11). Concerning unbelievers, he elaborates: "This is why I speak to them in parables, because seeing they do not see, and hearing they do not hear, nor do they understand. Indeed, in their case the prophecy of Isaiah is fulfilled that says, 'You will indeed hear but never understand, and you will indeed see but never perceive'" (Mt. 13:13-14). Prior to Matthew 13, Jesus engaged in teaching, but following his quotation of Isa. 6:9-10, he resorted increasingly to the use of parables. The purpose of the parables was to render the gospel message hard to understand for unbelievers, whose hearts were thus further hardened. But for those whose hearts were right, the parables served to drive them deeper into a desire for understanding. That is why the disciples came to Jesus asking him to explain their meaning. The same pattern is evident in Isaiah. In the opening chapters, Isaiah gives clear denunciations of Israel's sin. After his warning of chapter 6, he begins to resort to prophetic actions which serve to harden the hearts of unbelievers (for instance, 8:1-4; 20:2), while driving believers into a deeper relationship with God through their desire to understand what the prophet was trying to demonstrate through his actions. The same phenomenon is prominent in Ezekiel and Hosea. The hardening of unbelievers' hearts ultimately goes back to the significance of the plagues of Exodus. When Pharaoh rejected the instruction of Moses on the proper worship of God, he suffered the punishment of the plagues, which served only to harden him in deeper unbelief. It is no accident that the plagues of Exodus are the model for the judgments of Revelation.

This becomes very clear through the warning to the churches repeated at the conclusion of each letter: "He who has an ear, let him hear what the Spirit says to the churches." John is quoting both Jesus and Isaiah, fully aware of the context. The symbols and pictures of Revelation serve the same function as the parables of Jesus, the prophetic actions of the prophets and the plagues of Moses. They harden the hearts of unbelievers who scoff or fail to understand, while driving genuine believers further to God in order to understand what he is saying to them. The unbelief of the lost confirms the justice of the divine judgment coming upon them. This in turn explains the apparently strange command to do evil: "Let the evildoer still do evil, and the filthy still be filthy, and the righteous still do right, and the holy still be holy" (22:11). God is not commanding sin, but simply leaving the unbeliever to the consequences of his wrongdoing, which will only increase as his heart further hardens. It is not surprising that unbelievers have no comprehension of the meaning of Revelation. The tragedy is that many believers do not understand. The fact is that Revelation is an easy book to grasp when it is read in light of the Old Testament.

REVELATION AND THE OLD TESTAMENT

There are estimated to be over 500 allusions to the Old Testament in the 404 verses of Revelation — more than in all other books of the New Testament combined. Some portions of the Old Testament are mined many times, the plagues of Exodus and the dreams and visions recorded in Daniel being examples. Normally, there is a clear continuity between Revelation and its Old Testament sources. Judgment through the plagues is thus a theme in both Exodus and Revelation. Old Testament Babylon becomes representative of evil forces opposing

God's people and is described at length in chapters 17-18. Balaam reappears as a false teacher in 2:14, as does Jezebel in 2:20-23. The Genesis tree of life reappears in the new Jerusalem (22:2, 14, 19). The protective sealing of the Israelites, rooted in the Exodus account and appearing also in Ezekiel 9, features in chapter 7. The empowering of the Spirit pictured in Zech. 4:1-6 reappears in 1:12-20. Many more of these allusions will be pointed out in our explanation of the text.

One important theme is how John takes Old Testament references to Israel and sees them as fulfilled in the church. A significant example is the way the idea of a kingdom of priests (Exod. 19:6) is applied to the church in 1:6. The lampstands before the ark now represent the church (1:12-13, 20). Israel's tribulation (Dn. 7:25; 12:7) becomes the tribulation of the church. The leaves of Ezekiel's end-times tree will bring blessing not just to Jews (Ezek. 47:12), but to the faithful of all nations (22:2). The new Jerusalem, populated by the faithful of all nations, transcends the old, physical Jerusalem, which was the preserve of Jews only. This general understanding that Old Testament prophecy is fulfilled in the church (composed of Jews and Gentiles alike) is entirely in line with Paul's understanding of believers in Christ as the sons of Abraham (Romans 4) and the church as the new, spiritual Jerusalem (Gal. 4:21-31). God still has an end-times plan to revive the Jewish people (Romans 11:11-33), but this does not take away from the fact that the new covenant in Christ is with the faithful of every nation, not just the people of Israel. This leads to an important conclusion: *the prophetic focus of Revelation is on the church, not on the Jewish people, and still less on the state of Israel.* Failure to understand this means failure to understand Revelation, and arguably, failure to understand the rest of the New Testament.

The fact that God used the Old Testament as a framework for the series of visions he gave to John should not be surprising. The Old Testament as a whole points to Christ. It shows us who Christ is. Jesus saw himself as the fulfillment of Old Testament prophecy (Jn. 5:45-47). Paul saw the law as fulfilled in Christ (Rom. 8:4). In this aspect, as in many others, Revelation is entirely in line with the rest of the New Testament. To read Revelation through the lens of the latest news reports from the middle east is to miss its point entirely. It needs to be read with the rest of the Bible open in front of us.

OUTLINE OF REVELATION

The various series of judgments portrayed are parallel descriptions of the same events. The pattern is identical within each series. There is a description of judgment followed by a depiction of salvation. The first scene of judgment occurs in 6:12-17 (salvation in 7:9-17). The second scene of judgment is 11:18a (salvation 11:18b). The third is 14:14-20 (salvation 15:2-4). The fourth is 16:17-18:24 (salvation 19:1-10). The fifth is 20:7-15 (salvation 21:1-22:5). Each depiction of a cycle of events ends in a description of the same final judgment and the same eternal salvation. Why, then, are the contents of each series not absolutely identical and sometimes expressed in a slightly different order? Because John is relating what he saw in a series of visions. He is not dictating an exact description of one future historical event. Most of the differences within the various judgments portrayed in the visions are accounted for by the fact that these plagues recur throughout history in varying forms, and are not to be understood as portraying one-off historical events. Put another way, the various sets of visions together build a corporate picture of events to come similar to the way the four Gospels build a corporate picture of the ministry of Jesus. Another significant point to note is that John relates the visions in the order in which he saw them. *The order in which he saw things is not necessarily the order in which those things will happen.* Some of the visions clearly go back in time to before a previous vision. Thus the various sets of judgments are not to be understood as following one after the other from a historical perspective. This logic (expressed in the futurist position) would result in at least five final judgments!

THE CONNECTION BETWEEN THE LETTERS AND THE VISIONS

The letters and the visions are far more closely linked than is often realized. The reason this is the case is because the visions portray *present-day realities in the life of the church and the world,* not just events immediately prior to the Lord's return. Revelation must be understood as relevant to every generation, including that to which it was originally written, and not only to the last generation before the return of Christ. All this underlines the fact that *Revelation is a pastoral letter written to the churches,* even though it includes such rich prophetic elements. It therefore makes sense that the present-day realities of the letters reappear in the visions.

For instance, the believers at Smyrna will endure a brief persecution (2:10), as will those in the vision slain for their faith (6:11). The believers at Philadelphia will receive spiritual protection in the midst of tribulation (3:10) and the names of God and Christ will be written on them (3:12). In the same way, the faithful saints in the vision are sealed and protected against harm (7:3). They likewise have the names of God and Christ written upon them (14:1). Antipas at Pergamum is God's witness (2:15). So are the believers in 6:9 and the two witnesses in 11:3-13. Satan has his throne at Pergamum, where he is accompanied by a false prophet (3:13-14). Satan reappears in the visions as the dragon thrown out of heaven who has established his rulership (throne) on earth and is accompanied by a false prophet (12:9; 13:13-14; 16:13). Jezebel is in the church at Thyatira (2:20-22), but reappears as a model for the Babylonian harlot (17:2-3). In particular, every promise made to faithful believers in the seven churches is fulfilled in the new Jerusalem (the tree of life, freedom from the second death, the new name, and so on).

THE "LATTER DAYS" ARE NOW

Another key to the understanding of Revelation is given by comparing significant texts in Revelation and Daniel. Daniel speaks of things God has "shown him" which will take place in the "latter days" or "after this/in the future" (Dn. 2:28-29, 45). God subsequently reveals to Daniel that these words are to be sealed up until those end times (Dn. 12:9). John quotes Daniel's words in Rev. 1:1, 19, saying that God has also "shown him" what is to take place. But there is a significant alteration. God shows John that the things that were (from Daniel's perspective) to take place in Daniel's "latter days" are now to occur "shortly" or "quickly." God made known to Nebuchadnezzar "what will be in the latter days" (Dn. 2:28). But God made known to John "the things that must soon [= shortly or imminently] take place" (Rev. 1:1). John deliberately uses the words of Daniel to emphasize the fact that *Daniel's future is now present*, and that the events prophesied long ago *are now commencing.*

Daniel spoke of momentous events in the distant future. In the latter days, the fourth earthly kingdom of his vision would be shattered by the rock of the kingdom of God (Dn. 2:44). This coming of the kingdom is connected with the appearance of the "Son of man" who will rule over it (Dn. 7:13-14). In the vision of chapters 4 and 5, John sees these prophesied events as fulfilled in the death and resurrection of Jesus Christ. He is the Son of man prophesied in Daniel 7, and he has been exalted to the right hand of God to receive an eternal kingdom. Jesus himself interprets Daniel's earth-shattering rock as fulfilled in his own ministry (Lk. 20:18). The latter days to Daniel were a future far off and whose secrets were to be sealed until the end time (Dn. 12:9). To John, however, it is something *about to unfold before his eyes.*

The events prophesied by Daniel have begun to occur, set in motion by the death and resurrection of Christ. All that is about to happen — from the events occurring in the seven churches of Asia to the events which will occur as the rest of the church age unfolds — are now being unsealed or revealed, which is what Revelation is all about. The time "after this" is indeed at hand, about to happen quickly, in the same sense that Jesus said the kingdom of heaven was at hand or about to arrive (Mk. 1:15). It is no longer for a distant future, but is right in front of us, about to happen. The visions John is about to unfold represent events which will begin to occur almost immediately, and will continue until Jesus returns. They are indeed for the "latter days," but not the "latter days" in the sense that futurists understand them (the days immediately preceding the return of Christ). *The "latter days" are now.* If this seems strange to us, consider this. In Ac. 2:17-21, Peter declares that at Pentecost the "last days" prophesied by Joel have begun, and he moves immediately and seamlessly in interpreting Joel as announcing both Pentecost (verses 17-19), and (without apparent time delay) the prophesied day of the Lord (the last judgment) in verses 19-21. Thus he collapses all of history after Christ into the category of the last days, and declares we are living in them now. A similar understanding of the last days is found in Hebrews ("In these last days he has spoken to us by his Son," 1:2), James ("You have laid up treasure in the last days," 5:3), and Peter ("[He] was made manifest in the last times," 1 Pet.1:20). John elsewhere interprets it this way himself: "Children, it is the last hour" (1 Jn. 2:18). The Bible understands the latter or last days to be the days commencing with the death and resurrection of Christ, and concluding with his return. This time period — otherwise known as the church age — is the age in which John lived and the age in which we still live, and it is this age which is described in the visions which are about to unfold. For John and for each one of us, it is both present and future, but the meaning once sealed up has now been made clear. God gave this vision to John so that he would be able to understand what was happening around him and respond rightly, so that saints of the tenth century could understand, so that you and I can understand, and so that saints of the future can understand. Grasping this truth is the indispensable basis for a proper understanding of the book of Revelation.

THE MAIN THEMES OF REVELATION

The book has three major messages for believers:

1. The way of the cross is the path to eternal victory. The cross was the foundation of Christ's victory over Satan. Christians are called to follow in Christ's footsteps. The sufferings of believers in this present age assure their victory over the powers of darkness. We suffer hardship now (1:9), but will share later in Christ's kingly rule (1:6). Our spirit will be kept safe in the midst of physical suffering (11:1-7). By contrast, though unbelievers presently carry out evil acts (11:10), these acts serve only to form the basis for their final judgment (11:13, 18). One of the main purposes of Revelation is to exhort believers to remain faithful in the face of adversity in the assurance of final victory. The closing section of the book (22:6-21) repeats this message.

2. God is sovereign over human history. The visionary section of the book is introduced by the vision of the throne room of God and the Lamb in chapters 4 and 5. In these chapters, the word "throne," signifying God's sovereignty, appears seventeen times. This vision demonstrates the authority of God and of the Lamb over all that is about to unfold in the book's remainder. The trials of believers, the apparent victory of the enemy, the eventual destruction of the latter and victory of the church, are all under the sovereign control of God.

3. The history which began in the first garden-temple ends in the garden-temple of the new Jerusalem. The new Jerusalem is the fulfillment of God's plan to establish a garden-like paradise. Adam failed in his commission the extend the boundaries of the original garden. Israel likewise failed in her commission to be a light to the nations. But Christ succeeded where Adam and Israel failed. The boundaries of the kingdom extend throughout the earth in the church age, though only in an imperfect manner. But in the new Jerusalem the garden is perfectly established forever. The serpent, allowed into the first garden, is cast out of the last garden. All God's expressions of covenant with men and women are fulfilled as they worship him in the final, perfect temple.

1

THE BEGINNING

(1:1-20)

PROLOGUE (1:1-3)

John begins with these words: *The revelation of Jesus Christ, which God gave him to show to his servants the things that must soon take place. He made it known by sending his angel to his servant John, who bore witness to the word of God and to the testimony of Jesus Christ, even to all that he saw* (verses 1-2). John describes his vision with three significant words or phrases: it is a *revelation* which God gave him to *show* his servants what *must soon take place* (verse 1). To find out the significance of these phrases we have to go back to Dn. 2:28-30, 45-47. In the Greek translation of these Old Testament verses (the Septuagint), the Greek verb "revealed" appears five times, the verb "show" appears twice, and the phrase "what must come to pass" appears three times. This is the only place in the Old Testament all these words or phrases occur, and it is clear that John is alluding to them here. From the very beginning, John is rooting his vision in the Scriptures, and without an understanding of this it is impossible to interpret correctly what he is saying. The key to understanding the significance of these allusions is that Daniel is speaking of the kingdom of God which will come to pass "in the latter days" (Dn. 2:28). John rewords this as follows: these events will take place "quickly" or "soon." Daniel was interpreting the king's vision of the statue as referring to four kingdoms. The last of the kingdoms would be struck and destroyed by a stone not made by man. This stone would become a mountain which would fill the earth (Dn. 2:35). This would signify the establishment of God's kingdom on earth (Dn. 2:44). The meaning is clear: John is announcing the *arrival* of events Daniel expected to occur *in the last days.* There is no doubt John saw the resurrection of Christ as fulfilling the prophecy of Daniel regarding the inaugurating of the kingdom of God. This indicates to us that what is about to be written concerns *not just the distant future* but what is before us *here and now.* The last days are now. In fact, in the first chapter of Revelation, only one verse (7) alludes to the return of the Lord. This sets the tone for the rest of the book.

John declares: *Blessed is the one who reads aloud the words of this prophecy, and blessed are those who hear, and who keep what is written in it, for the time is near* (verse 3). The message of Revelation, as it unfolds, is not designed to satisfy our curiosity about the calendar of events in the Middle East immediately prior to the return of Christ. It is a pastoral and prophetic exhortation to all those of every generation who read it. Those who obey its message will be *blessed.* The *prophecy* is not a set of predictions but, as in the Old Testament, a divine command from God calling for response. The message of the Old Testament prophets featured calls to repentance and right relationship with God, and was by no means simply about future predictions. Indeed, the fulfillment of future predictions was normally linked to situations where people were getting right with God.

The reason those who hear the prophetic words must heed them is given: *for the time is near.* Here John echoes the words of Jesus in Mk. 1:15: "The time is fulfilled, and the kingdom of God is at hand." In that passage, the verb "to be at hand" has the meaning of "about to arrive" or "is now arriving." The two clauses in Mark are parallel: the time Jesus spoke of is *now fulfilled* and the kingdom *has arrived.* John sees the end-times kingdom of Daniel as having *now arrived* in the person of Jesus Christ. His prophetic words will speak into the heart of the present, not simply the distant future. The prologue sets the tone for the entire book. Hence we can expect from the very start that the words of the entire book will speak to the present experience of every believer. We will find there are some parts that do address situations at the very end of history before the return of Christ, but these comprise only a small portion of the book as a whole.

JOHN GREETS THE CHURCHES (1:4-8)

John now addresses the churches: *John to the seven churches that are in Asia. Grace to you and peace from him who is and who was and who is to come, and from the seven spirits who are before his throne, and from Jesus Christ, the faithful witness, the firstborn of the dead, and the ruler of the kings on earth* (verses 4-5a). His choice of the number seven is deliberate. Seven is a significant number in Revelation. Biblically, it signifies completion, as in the seven days of creation. Hence it becomes linked with God himself. Six, by contrast, is the number of humanity (men and women having been created on the sixth day). In Lev. 4:6, 17 the blood was sprinkled seven times before the Lord. The Jewish festivals lasted seven days, as did the march around Jericho. The seven churches, therefore, represent the church as a completed whole. The prophetic message had significance for these churches in the same way as the letters from Paul and others did for the churches to which they were written. The message has equal significance for us today. We need to see Revelation as addressing our lives in the same way as do Galatians, Ephesians or 1 Peter. John's prophetic message is actually addressed to the entire body of Christ, the church in every age. It is also significant that the conclusion of each of the letters indicates that the letters are addressed to "all the churches." If the truth addressed to each was applicable to the others, why not equally so to us today?

The prophetic message is from God (*him who is and who was and who is to come*) and from Christ (*the faithful witness*). It is also from *the seven spirits who are before his throne.* The reference here is actually to the Holy Spirit, the number "seven" again representing fullness. The seven spirits represent the Spirit in his fullness. The Holy Spirit is needed to bring to believers the *grace* and *peace* John greets them with here. The Holy Spirit is the one who enables and empowers us (Ac. 1:8; Rom. 8:2), and so his work will be needed if believers are to respond obediently to the prophetic words which are about to be revealed. The reason John uses the phrase *seven spirits* instead of "the Holy Spirit" is probably because he is alluding here to Zech. 4:2-9, where seven lamps represent one Spirit who brings grace for the building of the temple. At every stage, John is trying to present his message as the fulfillment of Old Testament revelation. This becomes even clearer when (drawing on Zechariah's picture) Rev. 4:5-6 identifies the seven lamps before the throne with the seven spirits. The role of the Holy Spirit is critical in helping us to become the present-day temple of the church, in which God dwells.

Christ is described here as the *faithful witness, the firstborn of the dead, and the ruler of the kings on earth.* John is alluding to Ps. 89:27, 37, where all of these phrases occur. The Psalm speaks of David, the king who will rule over his enemies and whose seed will sit on his throne forever (verses 19-29). In linking this with the idea of *firstborn of the dead,* John is portraying Jesus as the prophesied seed of David, whose resurrection has resulted in the inauguration on earth of God's eternal kingdom. This kingdom has arrived with Christ's resurrection and ascension and the outpouring of the Holy Spirit at Pentecost. The phrase *kings on earth,* as the related phrase "kings of the earth" elsewhere in Revelation (e.g., 6:15; 17:2; 18:3) refers to those earthly rulers who oppose Christ's rule. That Christ is pictured as already ruling over these kings shows again that the events the visions relate portray events throughout the church age, rather than just those at the very end of history.

John gives praise to Christ: ***To him who loves us and has freed us from our sins by his blood and made us a kingdom, priests to his God and Father, to him be glory and dominion forever and ever. Amen*** (verses 5b-6). This is a direct reference to Exod. 19:6: "You shall be to me a kingdom of priests and a holy nation." Notice how significant is the change of tense. What was prophesied as future in Exodus is now stated as an accomplished fact by John, for the verb ***made*** is in the past tense. This reinforces the thought of verses 1-3 about the present fulfillment of Daniel's kingdom prophecies. ***Kingdom*** can mean "kingship," "royal power," or the exercise of that power. Believers do not merely live within a kingdom, as if the kingdom referred only to a geographical location. They exercise its kingly power, or perhaps more accurately, Christ exercises his kingly power through them. Put another way, the church is the place where or through which the kingdom power of God operates. God has chosen to exercise his kingly rule through his people. There in one phrase is stated both the high calling and the incredible responsibility of Christians. There is no alternative, no "plan B." God has in one sense sovereignly limited himself to operating through us. The church is an imperfect vehicle composed of imperfect people, yet God has chosen to use these people as the means by which his kingdom comes.

The past tense thus expresses the reality that this kingdom rule has begun with the resurrection and ascension of Christ. The kingdom or kingly rule of God is present now on earth. Christians have begun to enter into this role as priests and as kings, even though the fulfillment of the way they perform these roles will only occur in the eternal realm. Christ has made us a kingdom through his sacrificial death: he has ***freed us from our sins by his blood.*** This demonstrates his role as a faithful priest and also "faithful witness" (verse 5). He exercised his role as king through spiritually defeating sin and death on the cross and subsequently being raised from the dead ("firstborn of the dead" and "ruler of kings on earth," verse 5). Christians likewise function as priests and kings by following Christ in their faithful witness to the world and willingness to suffer. Thus they overcome the attacks of the devil, even though they may appear to suffer defeat, as Christ did on the cross. The way in which Christians function as kings will turn out to be ironic, in that it is opposite to the concept of the world. They rule on the model of Christ. Victory occurs through suffering, persecution and faithful perseverance. Christians are called to walk in the way of the cross. Insofar as they rule, they rule as Jesus did, the man who changed history by hanging on a Roman cross.

That John sees Exod. 19:6 as fulfilled in the church is very significant, for this was originally a promise for Israel as a nation. That this promise, which was never fulfilled in physical Israel, is now fulfilled in the church, indicates clearly that the church, as the body of Christ gathered from every nation, Jew first and then Gentile (Rom. 1:16), now *takes the place of* physical Israel as the inheritor of God's promises and as his covenant people. Meanwhile, unbelieving Jews are described no longer as true Jews but as a "synagogue of Satan" (Rev. 2:9). This is a theme we will see revisited frequently in Revelation, and it serves as a framework for understanding Biblical eschatology. The prophetic program of God finds its center not in Israel or events in the Middle East, but in the worldwide church of Jesus Christ. *Change in my understanding*

True

John's words of greeting continue: **Behold he is coming with the clouds, and every eye will see him, even those who pierced him, and all tribes of the earth will wail on account of him. Even so. Amen** (verse 7). This verse contains two Old Testament allusions. The first, **Behold he is coming with the clouds**, is from Dn. 7:13. There, the Son of man is depicted as enthroned over the nations. John sees this verse as fulfilled in Christ coming at the right hand of the Father. These verses appear at first glance to allude to the return (*coming*) of the Lord. However, in verse 1, we saw a clear allusion to Daniel's description of the "coming" of the Son of man to receive an end-times kingdom and authority (Dan. 7:13-14). The revelation given to John shows that this kingdom has in fact been inaugurated at the resurrection, ascension and outpouring of the Spirit. Jesus' final "coming" is only the last and climactic coming preceded by many "comings." He "comes" to the churches continually to encourage them, correct them and admonish them. He comes in this age through his Spirit, and he will come again. In 2:5, 16 and 3:3, John describes his coming *in present judgment* to the churches. While it is certainly true that we will bow in worship and also in sorrow and repentance when we behold Christ at his final return, the same should be true as Christ comes to us now by his Spirit. We grieve over our disobedience and sin, and bow in worship before him, and in joy over the reality of his forgiveness. And so in context, we take this coming with the clouds to refer to all of Christ's comings.

The second Biblical allusion in verse 7 alludes to Zech. 12:10. That text says that in the last days God will cause Israel to ask him for mercy. The result will be that they will look on him whom they have pierced and mourn over him. This is obviously a reference to the cross. But there is an important difference between the two texts.

Zechariah describes *Israel* mourning in repentance, whereas John refers to **all tribes of the earth** doing so, and adds the further phrase **every eye will see him.** What is applied in the Old Testament to physical Israel is now applied to peoples of every nation. The reference is to the repentant mourning of believers. Those who truly mourn Christ's death and what they have done to him are God's people from every tribe on earth. Again, the church appears as the prophetic fulfillment of passages originally referring to national Israel. As Christ comes and comes again throughout history, culminating in his final coming, believers of every nation will mourn and weep as they come in repentance and faith to receive him as Lord and Savior.

The prologue concludes with God's description of Himself: *"I am the Alpha and the Omega," says the Lord God, "who is and who was and who is to come, the Almighty"* (verse 8). Alpha and omega are the first and last letters of the Greek alphabet. The meaning is that he is Lord over all human history. He is the one **who is and who was and who is to come, the Almighty.** He rules over the beginning, the end and everything in between. This is an important thing for John's readers to be reminded of, for many of them, both then and now, are suffering for Christ. One of the consistent messages of Revelation is the assurance Christians have in the fact that, whatever their present circumstances, God is ruling over all. They can take comfort that he is working all things together for their good, a process that will culminate in their final vindication and reward in his eternal kingdom. *Romans 8 : 28–30*

JOHN IS COMMISSIONED WITH THE PROPHETIC REVELATION (1:9-20)

John identifies himself: *I, John, your brother and partner in the tribulation* [*suffering*] *and the kingdom and the patient endurance that are in Jesus, was on the island called Patmos on account of the word of God and the testimony of Jesus* (verse 9). Only one Greek article (*the*) precedes the three words (*tribulation, kingdom* and *patience*). What this means is that all three are closely related to one another. Christians exercise kingdom rulership *only or primarily in* trial, testing and persevering endurance. This paradoxical or ironic form of rule mirrors the manner in which Jesus exercised his authority even from the cross, and Christians are to follow in his path. At the cross, it must have appeared Jesus was a total failure. We look at the cross from the perspective of the resurrection, but what would the disciples or any onlooker have thought when all they saw was a naked man hanging on a Roman cross? Likewise it may often seem to us that we are encountering failure and defeat, yet God wants to remind us that our failure (or weakness, as Paul described it in 2 Cor. 12:9) is often the very means by which the power or victory of God is manifest. John's use of the word "tribulation" to refer to the reality already existing in the first century, and his suggestion that this condition will continue to be characteristic of Christian experience warns us against using the word to refer to a supposed brief period before the Lord's return. Nowhere in Revelation is the word used in that context. The consistent use of the word in the New Testament describes our present Christian experience. Jesus used the word to refer to the whole spectrum of events from the fall of Jerusalem to his return (Mt. 24:4-28). The word is used over twenty times times by Paul to refer to the present experience of Christians; see also on 7:14.

John describes his commissioning: *I was in the Spirit on the Lord's day, and I heard behind me a loud voice like a trumpet, saying, "Write what you see in a book and send it to the seven churches, to Ephesus and to Smyrna and to Pergamum and to Thyatira and to Sardis and to Philadelphia and to Laodicea"* (verses 10-11). The opening phrase I was in the Spirit is an allusion to Ezekiel's commissioning (Ezek. 2:2; 3:12, 14, 24). This is significant, in that John is comparing himself to one of the Old Testament prophets. After this, he heard *a loud voice like a trumpet,* as did Moses in Exod. 16:19-20. The comparison to Moses is strengthened by the command to *write what you see in a book,* just as Moses was told in Exod. 17:14 (or Isaiah in Isa. 30:8 and Jeremiah in Jer. 36:2). John is thus placing himself squarely in the line of the great Old Testament leaders and prophets. Why John was commissioned to send his prophecy to these seven churches in particular we do not know, but there is little doubt that the Biblical significance of the number seven indicates these churches stand for all churches, both then and now.

The vision related in verses 12-20 follows the normal pattern of Old Testament prophetic visions (Isa. 6:1-7; Jer. 1:11-12, 13-14; Ezek. 2:9-3:11; Dan. 8:3-27; 10:2-12:3; 12:5-13; Zech. 4:1-4; 5:1-11; 6:1-8).   First, the vision is related (verses 12-16). Next, the response of the one receiving the vision is recorded (verse 17a). Then finally, the interpretation of the vision is given (verses 17b-20).

Next, John relates his vision of the Son of man: *Then I turned to see the voice that was speaking to me, and on turning I saw seven golden lampstands, and in the midst of the lampstands one like a son of man, clothed with a long robe and with a golden sash around his chest. The hairs on his head were white, like white wool, like snow. His eyes were like a flame of fire, his feet were like burnished bronze, refined in a furnace, and his voice was like the roar of many waters. In his right hand he held seven stars, from his mouth came a sharp two-edged sword, and his face was like the sun shining in full strength* (verses 12-16). The *lampstands* come from Zech. 4:2, where the prophet saw a lampstand with seven lamps on it. In both the tabernacle and the temple the lampstand, with its seven lamps, stood in the presence of God. The seven lamps of Zechariah's vision represent the power of the Spirit (Zech. 4:6), and the lampstand represents Israel. The meaning of the vision is that the Spirit is going to empower Israel to rebuild the temple. John sees seven lampstands. Each lampstand represents one of the seven churches. Together, the lampstands represent the church as a whole throughout the ages. Jesus was probably thinking of the same Old Testament background when he spoke of the church as a lamp to be put on a stand (Matt. 5:15). The risen Christ now addresses the churches he has called into existence. The seven lamps signify the power of the Spirit. The church, as the new Israel, is the prophetic fulfillment of what Zechariah saw with relation to national Israel. The church is likewise to draw its power from the seven lamps, which represent the Holy Spirit (Rev. 1:4; 4:5), as it seeks to build the new temple of God. The use of Exod. 19:6 (in 1:6 above) suggests that the church is composed of priests and kings serving in the end-times temple. At Pentecost, the Holy Spirit brought to earth a beginning manifestation of the eternal temple in heaven. This manifestation can be understood on the lines of what theologians called the "already-not yet." The temple is truly present on earth now, though not in its fulfilled heavenly form, a glimpse of which we see in Revelation 4-5. The significant points are that the temple is present, and that the priests serving in it are no longer physical Israelites, but men and women of every nation belonging to Christ, our great priest and king.

The general background to this vision is in Dn. 7:13-14 and 10:5-6. These are the only places in the Old Testament where the "Son of man" appears. In the Old Testament, the priests tended the lamps and lampstands. Christ, as our eternal heavenly priest, likewise cares for the lampstands, whether by encouragement or by rebuke. Christ's eyes are *like a flame of fire.* This phrase refers to Christ's role as judge (see the similar phrase in 19:12). Christ's feet are *like burnished bronze, refined in a furnace.* His desire is to encourage the church to moral purity (see 3:18 for the same thought). The portrayal of God as the Ancient of Days in Dn. 7:9 is the background to the Son of man's hair and head. This draws a close comparison between Christ and God. The reality of the divinity of Christ is a consistent theme in Revelation. This is reinforced by the fact that the portrayal of the Son of man's voice, *like the roar of many waters*, is taken from Ezekiel's vision of God himself (Ezek. 1:24; 43:2). Christ holds in his hand the *seven stars*. These are identified in verse 20 as the angels of the churches. This shows that Christ's authority extends throughout both earthly and heavenly realms. The *sharp two-edged sword* coming out of Christ's mouth (see also 2:16 and 19:15) is rooted in the prophecies of Isa. 11:4 and 49:2. These speak prophetically of Christ in his role as judge ("He shall strike the earth with the rod of his mouth," Isa. 11:4). His role of judgment extends to the church (2:16) and the world (19:15). His sphere of judgment is not restricted to eternity, but is carried out also in human history.

John responds to the heavenly vision: *When I saw him, I fell at his feet as though dead. But he laid his right hand on me, saying, "Fear not, I am the first and the last, and the living one. I died, and behold I am alive forevermore, and I have the keys of Death and Hades"* (verses 17-18). John's experience is the same as Daniel's (see Dn. 8:15-19 and 10:7-12). Daniel received a vision, fell on his face, and was exhausted, following which he is revived with the help of a heavenly being. John likewise is overcome by fear, and falls on his face. After this, he is strengthened by a heavenly being and receives further revelation, which is the interpretation of the vision of Christ he has just received. The interpretation reveals that Christ, who is speaking to him, has risen from the dead and lives forevermore. This pattern links John closely with Daniel, in the same way 1:10 links him with Ezekiel, Moses, Isaiah and Jeremiah. John is identified in his personal calling and experience with the Old Testament prophets, just as the visions he receives are to be interpreted in light of Old Testament revelation and prophecy.

In Christ's self-description, *I am the first and the last*, he uses the same words God attributes to himself in Isa. 41:4, 44:6 and 48:12, and also in Rev. 1:8. The phrase refers to the complete sovereignty of God over human history. He is Lord over history at its beginning, at its end, and Lord over everything in between. The use of this phrase by the exalted Christ removes any doubt of his divinity. Christ is divine, as much as God the Father is divine. Christ describes himself further as the one who has died and lives forever. This again shows the close identification of Christ with God, as similar words (the One who lives forever) are used of God in Deut. 32:40 and Dn. 12:7. That

Christ has *the keys of Death and Hades* demonstrates his authority over death. Once he was held by death's grip, but now he has been set free from it. Not only that, he also has the power to determine who else will be liberated along with him. This verse assures Christians that, regardless of what sufferings or trials they may now endure, if they persevere they will indeed reign forever with Christ. Revelation assumes that Christians will suffer and even die for their faith, and John's purpose is to prepare them for such realities, while also reassuring them that God is faithful and has prepared an eternal reward far greater in value than any temporary trials they may face in this world.

The prophet is given a charge: *"Write therefore the things that you have seen, those that are and those that are to take place after this"* (verse 19). The commission is threefold. The angel commands John to write down what *you have seen.* This refers to the series of visions John is about to receive. Everything he has seen he is to record. This will eventually compose the entire book as we have it. The series of visions he is to receive deals with the things *that are* and the things *that are to take place after this.* The first phrase emphasizes what is already beginning to happen in John's lifetime as a result of Christ's resurrection, ascension and the outpouring of the Spirit. These events have initiated the latter-day kingdom Daniel prophesied. It is not something to arrive at a later date or when Christ returns, but has now arrived. The second phrase alludes to the fact that the things that are occurring presently are only the initiation of a series of events which will eventually cover the entire church age until Christ returns. These events will be described in the visions about to unfold. Thus the scope of Revelation deals with all the events of world history, commencing with the death and resurrection of Christ, and concluding with his final return.

The chapter concludes as God unfolds a mystery to the prophet: *"As for the mystery of the seven stars that you saw in my right hand, and the seven golden lampstands, the seven stars are the angels of the seven churches, and the seven lampstands are the seven churches"* (verse 20). Use of the word mystery indicates another allusion to Daniel (2:29-30), where the prophet unfolds to the king his divinely-given interpretation of the mystery of the king's vision concerning the coming kingdoms. Dn. 2:29-30 gives us the Biblical foundation for understanding Old Testament prophecy as a "mystery" to be fulfilled in Christ. What Christ reveals here to John represents a full understanding of what Daniel saw in his visions only as a mystery. The mystery, in this vision and the rest of the visions in the book, is about to be explained. The mystery is that Old Testament prophecy is to be fulfilled in an unexpected manner (see on 10:7; 17:5-6; Rom. 11:25; 16:25-27; 1 Cor. 15:51; Eph. 3:4; Col. 1:26-27). *The reality that Christ's sovereign rule over history is exercised even where Christians are suffering.* Christ exercises his authority while standing "in the midst of the lampstands" (verse 13). He walks among the churches even while they are suffering, as chapters 2 and 3 will show. The same mystery is expressed above all in the cross, where the one through whom the world was created was subject to the most shameful death that the world could offer. This mystery is referred to in 1 Cor. 2:7 as the "secret and hidden wisdom of God," by which the Lord of glory was crucified. The progress and nature of the Gospel itself is described as a "mystery" in Rom. 11:25, 16:25 and Eph. 3:3-6. Jesus spoke of the "mysteries ["secrets" ESV, Greek *mysteria*] of the kingdom" (Mt. 13:11). The greatest of these mysteries is the fulfillment of Biblical prophecy (Daniel's "mystery") in a way contrary to what was commonly predicted. In opposition to the Jewish expectation of a conquering Messiah who would drive out the Romans and bring them religious and political freedom, Jesus came as Isaiah's suffering servant, a Messiah whose kingdom was not of this world (Jn. 18:36), and who would be put to death as a common criminal on a Roman cross. This mystery is applied in Rev. 1:20 to the church (the lampstands), as the community of those through the ages following in Christ's footsteps. This sets the stage for the letters to the churches in chapters 2-3.

2

THE LETTERS TO THE SEVEN CHURCHES

(2:1-3:22)

INTRODUCTION

Chapter 1 has revealed that the latter days of Daniel have commenced with the resurrection and ascension of Christ and the outpouring of the Holy Spirit. The visions throughout the book represent events occurring at various points throughout the church age. In some measure at least, they were already occurring when John was writing, for the content of the visions mirrors that of the letters, which were addressed to the present situation of seven churches in Asia Minor. If the seven churches are representative of the universal church, as the numerical symbolism indicates, then the contents of both the letters and the visions are also applicable to the church throughout the ages. The structure of the seven letters is similar. Each begins with a command to write to an angel of the church. Following this, Christ presents himself to the church, and the situation in the church is outlined. Christ gives an encouragement to persevere, or issues a warning to repent. The letters each end with a promise given to those who are obedient to its message. The seven churches fall into three groups. The first and last are in poor spiritual health, the three in the middle are in a mixed situation, and only the second and sixth have proven themselves faithful. While this is not the best picture of spiritual health, it may be widely reflective of the worldwide church at any given point. All of the letters deal with the theme of faithfulness to Christ in the midst of an often-threatening pagan culture.

THE CHURCH AT EPHESUS (2:1-7)

John is commanded to write the first letter: *"To the angel of the church in Ephesus write: 'the words of him who holds the seven stars in his right hand, who walks among the seven golden lampstands'"* (verse 1). In all seven letters, the churches are addressed through an angel who in some sense represents them in heaven. This shows the churches that they have help (in the form of a designated angelic representative) acting on their behalf in heaven. Events in heaven and earth are interconnected. This is also demonstrated by the fact that the worship now proceeding in heaven (chapters 4-5; 7:9-17) is to serve as a model for the church's worship on earth. The interconnection of earthly and heavenly events will become very clear in chapter 12.

As in chapter 1, Daniel gives us the Old Testament background, for there also angels are presented as helping those on earth (Dn. 10:20-21; 12:1). In each letter, Jesus introduces himself with variations of the phrase **the words of him.** This reflects Old Testament language used only of God himself. The similar phrase "These things says the Lord" occurs well over one hundred times in the Old Testament. Christ thus assumes the role of God, and the letters become prophetic messages from God, rather than pastoral epistles only. Christ uses imagery from John's initial vision appropriate to the content of his prophetic message to the church. He comes with the *seven stars* in his hand, and walks among the *seven lampstands.* This illustrates the fact that he is familiar with the life of the churches. The lampstands he called into being beginning with his earthly ministry (Matt. 5:15) are still accompanied by his presence through the Spirit. This is in line with what Jesus promised when he said he would not abandon his people, but would send his Spirit to be with them forever (Jn. 14:16-18).

The letter continues: *'I know your toil and your patient endurance, and how you cannot bear with those who are evil, but have tested those who call themselves apostles and are not, and found them to be false. I know you are enduring patiently and bearing up for my name's sake and have not grown weary'* (verses 2-3). The Ephesian church is praised for testing and rejecting false apostles. They have a discernment which may be rooted in the firm foundations Paul had laid a generation earlier (Ac. 20:28-30). They have suffered patiently and not given up. However, Christ comes with a rebuke: *'But I have this against you, that you have abandoned the love you had at first'* (verse 4). Perhaps they had become inward-looking and lost sight of the mandate to take the love of Christ to the world outside. If we love Christ, we will love the lost. They may also have lost their love for one another. The pursuit of truth must be grounded in the experience of sacrificial love, or a living church will turn into a religious mausoleum. Jesus warned that the love of most would grow cold, but also said that those who persevered would preach the Gospel to all nations (Mt. 24:12-14).

The rebuke continues with a command and a warning: *'Remember therefore from where you have fallen; repent and do the works you did at first. If not, I will come to you and remove your lampstand from its place, unless you repent'* (verse 5). They had experienced amazing things. In the days when the entire province of Asia heard the word of the Lord, Christ's love was expressed powerfully through Paul and through members of the church to the community in which they lived (Ac. 19:10). But if they do not remember and repent, their *lampstand* will be removed. The church which had been used so powerfully to bring light into darkness might be cast into darkness itself. Israel had also been a lampstand (Zech. 4:2, 11), but when the Israelites turned their back on God's commission to be a light to the nations (Isa. 42:6-7; 49:6), their lampstand was removed and they were replaced by the church (Rev. 1:6). In Rev. 11:3-7, 10, the lampstands refer to the church in its capacity as prophetic witness to the world. The church is called to be a witness, in the way Jesus talked of the lamp which was to be put on a lampstand (Mk. 4:21; Lk. 8:16). If they do not thus respond, their church will die — their lampstand will be removed. Jesus himself will come in judgment, and the church at Ephesus will be no more. It is interesting to note that a "coming" of Jesus is referred to here which is definitely not his final return. If Jesus was ready to come in this way to the Ephesian church, he must have come repeatedly throughout history to various churches in similar judgment. This is a sobering reminder that, though the Lord will return in a final sense at the end of history, he comes regularly to visit his church in this present age, both to encourage and to judge (see also our comments on 2:16; 3:3; and 3:20).

But there is still hope for the Ephesians: '*Yet this you have: you hate the works of the Nicolaitans, which I also hate*' (verse 6). The Nicolaitans (see further on 2:12-17), whom the Ephesian church are commended for not tolerating, taught that Christians could participate in the idolatrous culture of Ephesus. The city (see Ac. 19:23-41) was dominated by the cult of the goddess Artemis, goddess of fertility. Her temple had thousands of priests and priestesses. Sexual immorality was an integral part of the temple's function. The city also had temples devoted to the worship of Caesar. To refuse involvement in the pagan religious activities could be dangerous, as it was for Paul, and would likely have cost Christians in many ways, including economic isolation. The church, when it is functioning properly, is always counter-cultural, for which a price, from loss of popularity to loss of income to loss of life, will often be paid.

Christ exhorts the Ephesians with the same words he uses in all seven letters: '*He who has an ear, let him hear what the Spirit says to the churches*' (verse 7a). The phrase is rooted in what Jesus said in the parable of the seeds ("He who has ears, let him hear," Mt. 13:7). Jesus borrowed it from Isaiah (6:9-10), Jeremiah (5:21) and Ezekiel (3:27; 12:2). The phrase was employed in relation to the prophets' use of symbolic actions and parables. The opening words of Revelation indicate that its meaning will be communicated symbolically (see 1:1), so we should not be surprised by this theme. Isaiah's preaching is for the most part clear in the first five chapters (apart from the parable in 5:1-7). Following his powerful encounter with God in chapter 6, he is commissioned to minister in such a way that the ears of those who hear are made dull so that they can no longer hear (6:9-10). Subsequent to this, his teaching features parables and symbolic actions. Ezekiel receives a similar command, in which God tells him to say, "He who will hear, let him hear; and he who will refuse to hear, let him refuse, for they are a rebellious house" (Ezek. 3:27). He is then directed to perform his first symbolic action (4:1). When ordinary teaching failed or was rejected, more extreme methods were required. These prophetic words and actions were designed to sharpen the understanding of true believers, while at the same time drawing others to repentance. The hearts of the rest, whose spiritual deafness prevented them from hearing properly, were hardened. Jesus' use of parables can be seen in a similar light. Prior to Matthew 13, where he quotes Isaiah, his teaching was fairly clear, but after that, he began employing parables instead. The parables were meant to lead believers into deeper understanding, while hardening the hearts of the rest. Those who want to understand will pursue God for that understanding, while the rest will scoff and turn away from what they consider incomprehensible. Such, indeed, is the reaction of many to the symbolism of Revelation. Only those with a heart for God and for truth will go beyond the outward symbols to discover the true meaning in its Biblical context. The theme of prophetic actions and hardening of the heart is ultimate rooted in the plagues of Exodus.

Use of the phrase in the seven letters, therefore, is highly significant. What is about to follow will be like the prophetic actions or Jesus' parables. Revelation features a multitude of strange images – beasts, dragons, harlots, horses, strange creatures, and so on. Use of these often frightening or horrific images is designed to draw believers into a deeper understanding, and also to shock them out of complacency or compromise where these have taken root. Unbelievers, however, will fail to understand the message and sink further into spiritual hardness of heart, though some may be saved. The visions of chapters 4-22 develop the straightforward teaching of chapters 2 and 3, following the same pattern as the prophets and Jesus. This strengthening/hardening function is particularly clear when we look at the trumpet and bowl visions. They are without doubt based on the Exodus plagues, whose dual purpose was to strengthen believers while hardening the hearts of God's enemies.

The letter concludes (as do the other letters) with a promise: *'To the one who conquers, I will grant to eat of the tree of life, which is in the paradise of God'"* (verse 7b). To *conquer* is the condition in each of the seven letters for inheriting the promise of salvation. Believers must obey the exhortation to persevere and remain faithful if they wish to be heirs of the divine promise. In the case of the Ephesians, the threat is the lack of passion to represent Christ to the world around, and possibly lack of love in the church within. The content of the promise is access to the *tree of life.* This refers to the restoration of humanity to its original unfallen state. The tree of life represents the presence of God. Each of the promises to faithful believers at the end of the seven letters (including participation in the tree of life) is fulfilled in the new creation portrayed in chapters 21-22.

THE CHURCH AT SMYRNA (2:8-11)

Christ again introduces himself with an element of the initial vision of chapter 1: *"And to the angel of the church in Smyrna write: 'The words of the first and the last, who died and came to life'* (verse 8). Christ describes himself as *the first and the last.* This is an allusion to the words of God in Isa. 41:4, 44:6 and 48:12, and thus another indication of Christ's divinity. Christ's reassuring words suit the situation of this church, which is facing much hardship: *'I know your tribulation and your poverty (but you are rich) and the slander of those who say that they are Jews and are not, but are a synagogue of Satan'* (verse 9). Some of its members are facing persecution and possible death. But Christ is Lord over all human circumstances and even over death itself. The mention of Jewish opposition suggests that Jews, jealous of the progress Christianity was making, may have informed on the Christians to the Roman authorities. Such instances were known to happen. Citizens in Asia Minor, the province in which all seven churches were located, were expected to participate in some form of emperor worship. Punishment included economic isolation or worse. Jews were exempted from this requirement, but Christians were not. That members of the Jewish community are identified as false Jews and a synagogue of Satan confirms again that the church is seen by Christ as the true Israel.

Members of the church are now warned of coming persecution: *'Do not fear what you are about to suffer. Behold, the devil is about to throw some of you into prison, that you may be tested, and for ten days you will have tribulation. Be faithful unto death, and I will give you the crown of life*'(verses 10-11). We saw above that in Isa. 41:4; 44:6 God described himself as the first and the last. These texts also feature the same command given the Christians at Smyrna: *do not fear* (verse 10). The fact that God addresses the Christians at Smyrna in the same way he addressed the faithful Israelites through Isaiah points again to the fact that Christians are the true Israel. The true gospel is not one of prosperity or ease. Christianity is counter-cultural and commitment to Christ is costly, perhaps even to the price of one's life. Yet in the sovereign purposes of God, even the work of the devil is ultimately under his control, for the ultimate goal of the believers being thrown into prison by the devil is *that you may be tested.* The Greek word translated *(in order) that* expresses the sovereign purpose of God. The devil's strategy was to put Christ to death on the cross, but God turned his nefarious plan around to bring forth salvation for the world. The suffering of the Christians at Smyrna will be turned into their deliverance as their faith is tested and proven genuine: "so that the tested genuineness of your faith — more precious than gold which perishes though it is tested by fire — may be found to result in praise and glory and honor at the revelation of Jesus Christ" (1 Pet. 1:7).

The *tribulation* will not last a literal *ten days.* This is yet another allusion to Daniel, in this case to the ten days Daniel and his friends were also "tested" (Dn. 1:12). Like the Christians at Smyrna, Daniel was tempted to compromise with idolatry, which was likely the main reason he abstained from eating at the king's table, where the food was probably dedicated to idols (see Dn. 1:2; 5:1-4). Food dedicated to the local gods would have been part of the pagan worship in Asia Minor, as well as worship directed toward Caesar who, by the time John was exiled on Patmos around AD 90, was viewed as a god. The significance of Christ's comparing them to Daniel and his friends would have been apparent to these believers. They will undergo a brief but severe period of trial. The Greek word for *tribulation* (*thlipsis*) is one commonly used by Paul to refer to present trials. Times of tribulation mark the church age, and Christians cannot expect to be exempt from such trials. *Tribulation* refers not to a particular time period immediately prior to the return of Christ, but to a regular feature of church life (see on 1:9; 7:14). This is the normal use of the word "tribulation" elsewhere in the New Testament (Rom. 5:3; 12:12; 2 Cor. 1:4; Phil. 4:14; Col. 1:24; 1 Thess. 1:6; Jas. 1:27; see Mt. 24:4-28) The reality of ongoing tribulation is verified by any study of church history. This reminds us of the sad fact that more Christians are being martyred today than ever before. Nevertheless, if they are faithful, these believers will receive *the crown of life.* This is one of the central messages of Revelation, that faithfulness to Christ, though costly in this life, brings an eternal reward far outweighing any earthly suffering. Not only that, another promise is added: *'He who has an ear, let him hear what the Spirit says to the churches. The one who conquers will not be hurt by the second death'* (verse 11). Their overcoming may involve the loss of their earthly life, but it will surely result in their gaining eternal life. Christ alone, the first and the last, holds "the keys of Death and Hades" (1:18) and is alive forevermore.

THE CHURCH AT PERGAMUM (2:12-17)

Christ introduces himself once more with an image from the vision of chapter 1 relevant to the church he is speaking to: *"And to the angel of the church in Pergamum write: 'The words of him who has the sharp two-edged sword'* (verse 12). This image is repeated in verse 16. The Lord brings an encouragement before he delivers a warning. The picture of Christ's sword is not accidental here. It serves as an expression of his authority not only over the church, but also over the kingdom of darkness.

As in Smyrna, Satan is identified as the real enemy of the believers: *'I know where you dwell, where Satan's throne is'* (verse 13a). The first temple in Asia Minor dedicated to emperor worship was constructed in Pergamum. It was a prominent center for this cult. Pergamum was also known for its devotion to Asclepius, the god of healing. This god was represented by a serpent, whose presence lingers in modern medical imagery. This may have reinforced the sense that the city was a center of demonic activity. Various pagan temples were also located on a cone-shaped hill behind the city.

The believers at Pergamum have resisted the demonic power of the cults and the state, to the point that one of their number was martyred: *'Yet you hold fast my name, and you did not deny my faith even in the days of Antipas, my faithful witness, who was killed among you, where Satan dwells'* (verse 13b). Yet, inexplicably, they have tolerated in their midst certain idolatrous practices: *'But I have a few things against you: you have some there who hold the teaching of Balaam, who taught Balak to put a stumbling block before the sons of Israel, so that they might eat food sacrificed to idols and practice sexual immorality. So also you have some who hold the teaching of the Nicolaitans'* (verses 14-15). Balaam enticed Israel into sin through idolatrous and immoral practices (Num. 25:1-3; 31:16). Similar practices were occurring at Pergamum. The situation may well have been similar to the problem of eating meals in pagan temples, which became an issue in the church at Corinth (1 Cor. 10:1-22). The *Nicolaitans* may be related to those connected with Balaam (note the phrase *so also you have some*). It may be of significance that the word "Nicolaitan" means "one who conquers the people," while the word "Balaam" means "one who rules over the people." Some members of the church may have given way to social, religious and economic pressures made worse by the death of at least one of its number. This is suggested by Christ's comment: *so that they might eat food sacrificed to idols and practice sexual immorality.* The phrase *sexual immorality* (Greek *porneia*) is used here and elsewhere in Revelation (e.g., 2:20-23) with both spiritual and physical connotations, the two being inextricably linked. Both spiritual and physical compromise with the idolatrous culture of the city are in mind.

Christ now comes to the church in judgment: *'Therefore repent. If not, I will come to you soon and war against them with the sword of my mouth'* (verse 16). The angel in the Old Testament story threatened Balaam with a sword (Num. 22:23, 31), and by the sword he was killed (Num. 31:8). Christ warns the false teachers they will face a similar judgment, as will those in the church who tolerate them. Toleration of sin is itself a sin, contrary to our culture, which elevates toleration as the greatest virtue. We tolerate the sin of others because ultimately we want others to tolerate our own sin. The Israelites who failed to deal with Balaam's sin were judged (twenty-four thousand died in the plague recorded in Num. 25:9). Paul alludes to this passage when he warns the Corinthians against their own tolerance of idolatry (1 Cor. 10:7-11).

The reward promised for those in Pergamum who are faithful is now given: *'He who has an ear, let him hear what the Spirit says to the churches. To the one who conquers I will give some of the hidden manna, and I will give him a white stone, with a new name written on the stone that no one knows except the one who receives it'"* (verse 17). The hidden (not presently evident) manna is the food to be served at the marriage supper of the Lamb (Rev. 19:9). Food sacrificed to idols is available now -- but at what price? Those who consume it will be shut out from the heavenly banquet. Jesus presented himself as the true heavenly bread or manna, superior to that given through Moses (Jn. 6:32-33). The *white stone* could be bdellium, which manna is compared to in Num. 11:7. In Rev. 3:4, 6:2 and 19:14, "white" represents righteousness. For a fuller description of the *new name*, see the reference to the names of God, Christ and the new Jerusalem in 3:12 to be written on believers. The promise is fulfilled in Rev. 22:4,

"They will see his face, and his name will be on their foreheads." Jesus is the first one to receive a new name (3:12), and all those who now follow him faithfully and without compromise, remaining loyal to his name, will in due course receive that new name also.

The promise of a new name is given to believers in Pergamum and Philadelphia, the two churches in which believers have been faithful to Christ's name (2:13; 3:8). Those who receive Christ's new name in verse 17 are contrasted with those who have received the mark associated with the name of the beast (14:11). Isaiah promised that faithful Israelites would be called by a new name (Isa. 62:2; 65:15). The promise given to these faithful Israelites is now fulfilled not in physical Israel but in the church.

THE CHURCH AT THYATIRA (2:18-29)

As at Pergamum, Christ introduces himself with references to the initial vision in chapter 1 which presents himself as judge: *"And to the angel of the church in Thyatira write: 'The words of the Son of God, who has eyes like a flame of fire, and whose feet are like burnished bronze'* (verse 18). The eyes of fire and feet of bronze are an allusion to the vision of Dan. 10:6. There, Christ appears (just as in Rev. 1:14-15) as an angelic figure with eyes like "flaming torches" and legs like "burnished bronze." He pronounces judgment against the pagan nations. Thyatira's religious life features worship of two gods said to be sons of Zeus. This may explain why Christ presents himself as **the Son of God.**

Christ praises the church for its faithful witness: *'I know your works, your love and faith and service and patient endurance, and that your latter works exceed the first'* (verse 19). Faith and perseverance are used in connection elsewhere in Revelation with persecution. For instance, Antipas the martyr is described as a faithful witness (2:13); the Philadelphians are commended for their faithful perseverance in the face of persecution (3:8-10); and the saints hated by the beast are characterized by endurance and faithfulness (13:7-10; 14:12).

Yet the church at Thyatira, like the church at Pergamum, is tolerating a false teacher: *'But I have this against you, that you tolerate that woman Jezebel, who calls herself a prophetess and is teaching and seducing my servants to practice sexual immorality and to eat food sacrificed to idols*' (verse 20). The fact that our own society places such a high value on the same toleration these churches are condemned for shows these warning words of Christ are of great relevance to us today. Thyatira was a prosperous city with many business organizations which were often linked with idolatrous practices. It would be almost impossible to carry on business without some link with these organizations and their rituals, so Christians were placed in an extremely difficult position. Thyatira's Jezebel (seemingly an individual) must have tried to persuade Christians to compromise and so prosper. Her teaching must have been hard to resist. At Pergamum, Christ held only a "few things" (2:14) against the church. But at Thyatira, the false prophet has led the church astray and into serious sin. This includes *sexual immorality* and idolatry. The first phrase (Greek *porneia*), as elsewhere in Revelation (2:14-15; and see discussion below), refers to all forms of moral, ethical, social and financial compromise with the pagan culture.

In spite of Christ's patience, she has refused to repent: *'I gave her time to repent, but she refuses to repent of her sexual immorality. Behold, I will throw her onto a sickbed, and those who commit adultery with her I will throw into great tribulation, unless they repent of her works, and I will strike her children dead. And all the churches will know that I am he who searches mind and heart, and I will give to each of you according to your works'* (verses 21-23). Whatever attempts there have been at addressing this individual have apparently failed. In 1 Tim. 2:12-14, Paul bases his prohibition against women teaching in the church on the grounds that it was Eve, not Adam, who was deceived (Greek *planao*). Here, the same verb is used in a very strong sense (*seducing*) of this woman teacher leading others astray. As a result, Christ is coming in imminent judgment on this church: *I will strike her children dead.* Those who seek willfully to destroy God's church will face his judgment. Paul says those who build on faulty foundations will escape "but only as through fire" (1 Cor. 3:15). However, those who seek to destroy God's temple will themselves be destroyed (lit: "torn limb from limb;" 1 Cor. 3:17). God's church is his only chosen instrument to bring the Gospel to a needy world, and he will not tolerate attempts to destroy it.

Both the demonic second beast or false prophet (13:14; 19:20) and the prostitute Babylon (18:23) are, like Jezebel, pictured as leading people astray, thus showing again how the letters and visions are closely connected. The portrayal of these horrific figures is meant to shock Christians and prevent them from compromising. Like

Jezebel, the prostitute Babylon will also face judgment. Sexual immorality (Greek *porneia*) is involved in both situations, and is related to profiting from economic activity. The concept of *porneia* in Revelation includes the wider field of moral compromise including compromising one's faith in order to avoid economic hardship. So if Christians engaged in activities related to Roman emperor worship in order to participate fully in the local economy, they would be committing *porneia*. There are lots of ways Christians today can engage in business practices which involve moral compromise — for instance, by paying or receiving money outside the income tax system, by cutting corners on products or services, by becoming business partners with unbelievers selling unreliable or unethical products, and so on.

Some of the commodities traded in Babylon (linen, purple, bronze and slaves) were also linked with Thyatira's commercial life. This signifies that the trials of the later visions concerning Babylon are occurring already in the life of the church at Thyatira. The visions reflect pastoral situations in the life of the churches of every age, including the life of the seven first-century historical churches of Asia Minor. And if we understand the seven churches to be representative of the body of Christ in general, we should not be surprised that the issues present in them appear again and again in subsequent history. We cannot separate the letters and visions, as if the letters dealt with historical realities and the visions deal only with events immediately before the return of Christ. The reality is that both letters and visions are addressed to Christians and churches of every age, and both deal with the same fundamental issues.

If the warnings of the letters are addressed to the church, then the warnings and judgments of the visions also address the church, not just the pagan world. This points to the sad fact that there are always unbelievers in the midst of the church, people who profess faith but do not live it. It may be difficult for us to deal with the idea that Christ judges the church, but the fact remains that, Biblically, Christians do suffer and even die because of disobedience: "That is why many of you are weak and ill, and some have died" (1 Cor. 11:30). Paul delivered a "man to Satan for the destruction of the flesh," so that his spirit might be "saved in the day of the Lord" (1 Cor. 5:5). Of course, we must be very careful to allow God alone to be the judge in such circumstances, and to examine our own hearts before inspecting the sins of others. However, this much is clear: God reveals himself here as the opposite of what he is judging in the Thyatiran church. He will not compromise or tolerate sin – and neither should we.

But not all at Thyatira face God's judgment: *'But to the rest of you in Thyatira, who do not hold this teaching, who have not learned what some call the deep things of Satan, to you I say, I do not lay on you any other burden. Only hold fast what you have until I come'* (verses 24-25). Jezebel may have presented her idolatrous teaching as something "deep" or previously unrevealed. Such teaching is always to be rejected in the light of clear and universally acknowledged Biblical truth. Christians should always be wary of teaching which is supposedly a "new" revelation previously undiscovered by others. Any revelation undiscovered by any faithful believers over the last two thousand years is unlikely to be accurate. The faithful majority in the church is given only one charge: to remain faithful. To be faithful is all that God requires in the end.

Christ's promises are given to those who have conquered in this life: *'The one who conquers and who keeps my words to the end, to him I will give authority over the nations'* (verse 26). The same truth is presented in 12:11: "They have conquered him by the blood of the Lamb and by the word of their testimony, for they loved not their lives even unto death." Paul makes the same point: "What shall separate us from the love of Christ? Shall tribulation, or distress, or persecution, or famine, or nakedness, or danger, or sword? As it is written, 'For your sake we are being killed all day long; we are regarded as sheep to be slaughtered.' No, in all these things we are more than conquerors through him who loved us" (Rom. 8:35-37). Christ is the Lamb slain for our sins (Rev. 5:5-6), and we are called to follow him in the way of the cross. Christians conquer by remaining faithful in their suffering. This suffering includes death but is not restricted to it, for Christians at Smyrna are promised the eternal reward even though only some will suffer imprisonment, let alone death (2:10-11). In verse 26, *the one who conquers* is defined by the parallel phrase *and who keeps my works.* Whether a Christian dies for his faith or simply suffers economic or other injustice, all of this is part of the conquering through faithful endurance we are called to walk in. We are called to be willing to suffer rather than compromise our commitment to Christ and his kingdom, and we will be rewarded accordingly, irrespective of the nature of our trials. Those who are oppressed will gain authority. Those who suffer will rule. Every promise made in the letters to those who have conquered is fulfilled in the eternal kingdom described in chapters 21-22.

To these faithful believers, Christ gives a promise: *'And he will rule them with a rod of iron, as when earthen pots are broken in pieces, even as I myself have received authority from my Father'* (verse 27). This quotation is taken from Ps. 2:8-9, which also refers (2:7) to Christ as God's Son, the same phrase with which Christ has introduced himself to the Thyatiran church in verse 18. Christ received his authority when he ascended to the right hand of God. It was when Christ was seated at God's right hand in the heavenly places (Eph. 1:20) that God "put all things under his feet and gave him as head over all things to the church" (Eph. 1:22). "All authority" is given to the resurrected Christ (Mt. 28:18). Christ's rule has begun on earth, but one day it will be made complete. In that day, Christians will share in a fulfilled sense in that rulership.

They also receive a further promise: *'I will give him the morning star. He who has an ear, let him hear what the Spirit says to the churches'"* (verse 28). In other words, they will receive Christ himself, the "bright morning star" of 22:16. The picture of Christ as both star and scepter (rod), goes back to the prophetic picture of Num. 24:17, 19: "a star shall come out of Jacob, and a scepter shall rise out of Israel... and one from Jacob shall exercise dominion." Christians may suffer now, but one day will share in Christ's lordship over all creation.

THE CHURCH AT SARDIS (3:1-6)

Christ's initial words here are similar to his address to the Ephesians: *"And to the angel of the church in Sardis write: 'The words of him who has the seven spirits of God and the seven stars. I know your works. You have the reputation of being alive, but you are dead'* (verse 1). The two churches have some things in common. Sardis was a city with an illustrious past, but was now in decline. Christ's words of warning indicate the church is in a similar position. It retained a *reputation* (literally "name") of life, while being in truth spiritually dead. Churches can appear healthy on the outside, but many are living off the reservoir of past faithfulness and blessing.

The Christians at Sardis are in this position, and they receive a stern warning: *'Wake up and strengthen what remains and is about to die, for I have not found your works complete in the sight of my God. Remember, then, what you received and heard. Keep it, and repent. If you will not wake up, I will come like a thief, and you will not know at what hour I will come against you'* (verses 2-3). Their faithful works lie in the past. They are now called, as the Ephesians were, to return to their former life of faithfulness. Christ does appear to them, however, holding the **seven stars** (their representative angels). Not only that, he holds the **seven spirits** (or the fullness of the Holy Spirit). There is both heavenly support and supernatural power available for them to experience spiritual renewal. God has more invested in his church and in our lives than we do, and will do anything to bring even disobedient believers back to him. He therefore appeals to them to **repent**. Repentance, meaning literally a change of mind (Greek *metanoia*), refers to a complete turning around of thoughts and behavior, and a consequent moving in the opposite direction. The idea of repentance is also rooted in the Hebrew verb *shuv*, meaning to return. Whatever else repentance involves, it is always, as in the parable of the prodigal son, a return to God. If they do not obey, the future is dark: Christ will **come like a thief.** This "coming" of Christ, as in the threatened judgments on Ephesus (2:5), Pergamum (2:16) and Thyatira (2:22-23), refers not to his final return, but to a historical judgment upon the local church. The judgment may be swift and unexpected. Those who have lost their spiritual edge generally do not recognize or acknowledge the severity of their situation. It is even possible (see below) that some or many members of the church have no true relationship with Christ at all. Of course, Christ also comes throughout history to visit his faithful church with blessing also.

Sadly, only a few of the Christians at Sardis remained faithful: '*Yet you still have a few names in Sardis, people who have not soiled their garments, and they will walk with me in white, for they are worthy*'(verse 4). This phrase about "soiling" refers to some kind of compromise with pagan or idolatrous practices. The word **soiled** also occurs in 14:4, where it refers to those "not defiled with women." In that context, it refers not so much to literal sexual immorality (though that might be involved) as to involvement with pagan or idolatrous activity in the community. The likelihood is that the Christians in Sardis had, for the most part, fallen into a stupor of compromise and of fear of the social and economic consequences of a bold witness for Christ.

But to the remaining faithful believers, three promises are given: '*The one who conquers will be clothed thus in white garments, and I will never blot his name out of the book of life. I will confess his name before my Father and before his angels. He who has an ear, let him hear what the Spirit says to the churches*'" (verses 5-6). In Revelation, **white garments** speak of spiritual purity (3:18; 6:11; 7:13-14; 19:8). The faithful believer is also promised that Christ **will never blot his name out of the book of life.** The "book of life" appears five times in Revelation (13:8; 17:8; 20:12, 15; 21:27). In it are held the names of all believers, recorded before the world's foundation. There are also "books" recording the sins of unbelievers, which provide the basis for their eternal judgment (20:12-13). Similarly, the "book" in Dn. 12:1 records the names of the saved, whereas the "books" in Dn. 7:9-10 appear in the context of judgment. The promise *I will never blot his name out* in no way suggests that the names of the saved might possibly be erased. In fact, it is an assurance of the opposite. The names in the book of life were recorded there before creation (Rev. 13:8; 17:8). They cannot be removed. The names of the lost were never written in the book of life, but only in the books of judgment.

Christ has come to the church at Sardis to determine its true identity: "name" or "names" represent identity in the Bible, and appear four times in this letter. The church, resting on its past laurels, has for some time been in spiritual decline. Many of its members, while professing faith, are not truly saved. As a result, the survival of the church is in jeopardy. No church can truly survive once unbelievers have become the majority. This is a lesson for numerous mainline denominations in our own culture that bear the outward name of Christ, but have long since lost any Christian identity. They are no longer churches in God's sight — merely religious institutions. Calvin was right in his warning, *ecclesia semper reformanda* — the church must be continually reformed. Every generation is responsible for keeping its identity with Christ strong, for once it is lost, that church, movement or denomination may be lost forever. Sadly, history is littered with such examples.

The third promise made to believers in verse 5 is that Christ will confess the faithful believer's name *before my Father and before his angels.* Those who confess Christ's name faithfully, regardless of the cost, will have their names honored by Christ. This reflects Jesus' saying, "Everyone who acknowledges me before men, I also will acknowledge before my Father who is in heaven" (Mt. 10:32). Luke's version of the same account features an acknowledgement before angels (Lk. 12:8). The Gospel accounts deal with the probability of persecution, and the same possibility is present at Sardis. The question is whether those addressed will remain faithful in trial or not.

Christ's desire is for the church to be restored. In 16:15, he addresses believers in words strongly echoing this letter: "Blessed is the one who stays awake, keeping his garments on, that he may not go about naked and be seen exposed!" These words from the bowl visions again show the close connection of letters and visions. The church at

Sardis is already experiencing the trials described in the bowl visions. The powerful imagery of the visions is meant to shock them into realizing the seriousness of the situation they are in. To the extent that we share in the failings of the church at Sardis, the visions are meant to shock us also.

THE CHURCH AT PHILADELPHIA (3:7-13)

Christ's address opens with these words: *"And to the angel of the church in Philadelphia write: 'The words of the holy one, the true one, who has the key of David, who opens and no one will shut, who shuts and no one opens'* (verse 7). In 1:18, where Christ is pictured as holding the keys of Death and Hades. Here he is portrayed as holding the *key of David.* This is an allusion to Isa. 22:22. There Eliakim, who is a type of Christ, holds the same key: "He shall open, and none shall shut; and he shall shut, and none shall open." The picture of Christ in 1:18 holding the keys of salvation and judgment is now elaborated on. These keys are revealed to enable entrance to the eternal kingdom. Eliakim is a type or Old Testament prophetic forerunner of Christ. Whereas once Eliakim ruled over physical Israel, now Christ rules over the church, the true Israel. Christ alone determines who will enter God's kingdom. This has particular significance for the Philadelphians, who were being persecuted by the local Jewish community (verse 9). Contrary to Jewish expectations, it is not national Israel, but the church of every nation, Jews and Gentiles alike, which fulfills Biblical prophecy as the inheritor of God's promises.

Christ addresses these faithful believers: *'I know your works. Behold, I have set before you an open door, which no one is able to shut. I know that you have but little power, and yet you have kept my word and have not denied my name'* (verse 8). The *open door,* as elsewhere in the New Testament, represents the liberty to bear witness to Christ (Ac. 14:27; 1 Cor. 16:9; 2 Cor. 2:12; Col. 4:3). It is true they are a small church. These Christians have not been able to push any doors open, but God has done it for them. How often do we in the western church use human resources to push doors open for God, rather than simply remaining faithful and allowing him to open his doors instead? How often do we undertake programs and ministries he never called us to, but which we had the personnel or financial resources to engage in? How often, in short, are we like Martha making lunches Jesus never ordered, rather than Mary sitting at his feet? They are a small church. However, Christ says to them they have kept his word and not denied him. Their witness is about to bear extraordinary fruit. They are facing opposition, which is not surprising. Christianity is at its healthiest and best when it is counter-cultural.

But God is about to come alongside them in the battle: *'Behold, I will make those of the synagogue of Satan who say they are Jews but are not, but lie -- behold, I will make them come and bow down before your feet and they will learn that I have loved you'* (verse 9). This describes a genuine repentance and turning to God, for to *bow down* is the Biblical word for "worship." It is used ten times in Revelation in a similar context of worshipping God. The allusion here is to Isa. 45:14, 49:23 and 60:14. There the prophet says that in the last days the Gentiles will bow down before Israel and worship the true God. The "Gentiles" of Isaiah (obviously unbelievers) are prophesied to bow before the Jews. Yet here the words of the prophet are fulfilled in reversed fashion, in that physical Israel (ethnic Jews) come to true faith and bow before the church — in other words, become part of the worshipping community of the church. In the Old Testament, it was God who would bring this miraculous event about, but here it is Christ. This is another indication of Christ's divinity and identification with the Father.

Because of their faithfulness in tribulation, Christ will keep the Philadelphians spiritually safe: *'Because you have kept my word about patient endurance, I will keep you from the hour of trial that is coming on the whole world, to try those who dwell on the earth. I am coming soon. Hold fast what you have, so that no one may seize your crown'* (verses 10-11). The phrase *the whole world* should not be taken literally. In Lk. 2:1, the "world" refers only to Palestine, and in Ac. 11:28 to a somewhat wider area. The area designated could be Asia Minor or possibly the Roman Empire as a whole. It is unlikely, as dispensationalism suggests, that it refers to the time immediately preceding the return of the Lord when the church is taken out of the world, for then it would not have the relevance to the historical church at Philadelphia it appears to have. The protection is primarily spiritual, for Revelation does not promise protection from physical suffering. Indeed, such suffering it is to be expected, but believers will be kept safe in the midst of it. Jesus said, "In the world you will have tribulation. But take heart; I have overcome the world" (Jn. 16:33). The church at Philadelphia thus serves as a pattern for faithful churches throughout the church age about to face seasons of tribulation. Tribulation is so often counted a present reality in the New Testament is is hardly surprising that the entire church age is cast as the "great tribulation" (see on 7:14).

The purpose of God's action is to *try those who dwell on the earth.* In Revelation, the phrase "those who dwell on the earth" is frequently used to describe the lost (6:10; 8:13; 11:10; 12:12; 13:8, 12, 14; 14:6; 17:2, 8). While Christians will experience trial, they will be kept spiritually safe in it. The lost, however, will experience bitterness and further hardening against God. They will curse God and refuse to repent (16:9, 11, 21). Christ promises these Christians he is coming to them *soon.* They are to persevere in trial. This coming is not his final return, as it must refer to the fact he will shortly come to help the Philadelphians in their imminent trial. In the same way, Jesus will likewise come throughout the church age to strengthen faithful Christians in distress.

There are four promises here given to the one who conquers: *'The one who conquers, I will make him a pillar in the temple of my God. Never shall he go out of it, and I will write on him the name of my God, and the name of the city of my God, the new Jerusalem, which comes down from my God out of heaven, and my own new name. He who has an ear, let him hear what the Spirit says to the churches'* (verses 12-13). These are really four aspects of the same promise, all being expressions of eternal union with God and fellowship with his presence. The faithful believer will be a pillar in God's temple, and have three divinely-given names written on him. The Philadelphians have entered the kingdom through the unlocking of its doors by Christ (verse 7). Now this promise is given in its fulfilled form: they will enter his presence forever. In this letter, God's temple is placed in opposition to Satan's synagogue. Whatever reality throughout history is represented by the latter — even including religious institutions professing the name of Christ — will always be in opposition to genuine believers who love God and seek his presence. The church on earth must always seek to base its life and existence in the eternal temple and in life in the Spirit, or it will fall into religious legalism, institutionalism and death. The latter reality will be exposed in the visions as an instrument of the devil and his agents.

THE CHURCH AT LAODICEA (3:14-22)

Christ's introductory words to this church are: *"And to the angel of the church in Laodicea write: 'The words of the Amen, the faithful and true witness, the beginning of*

God's creation' (verse 14). Jesus is the *Amen*. In Hebrew, this means *faithful* and *true*. The allusion is to Isa. 65:16: "He who blesses himself in the land shall bless himself by the God of Amen" (translated as "God of truth" in ESV). The blessing of the "God of Amen," Isaiah continues, is the *creation of a new heavens and a new earth* (Isa. 65:17). In 1:5, John described Christ as the faithful witness and firstborn of the dead, and in 1:18 he said of Christ that he was dead and is now alive forevermore. That Christ is **the beginning of God's creation** refers, therefore, *not to the original creation but to the new creation which began with Christ's resurrection.* It is the same truth described by Paul when he spoke of Christ as "the beginning, the firstborn from the dead" (Col. 1:18). Christ identifies himself to the Laodiceans in this way because the truth and faithfulness he embodies is so greatly lacking in them. In addition, they need the power of his new-creation kingdom to bring them out of a state of spiritual death. At least in Sardis a faithful remnant existed, but not so in Laodicea.

The rebuke to the Laodiceans is severe: *'I know your works: you are neither cold nor hot. Would that you were either cold or hot! So, because you are lukewarm, and neither hot nor cold, I will spit you out of my mouth'* (verses 15-16). Thinking of metaphors for spiritual life and death, we might place a positive value on hot and a negative value on cold. This would leave lukewarm as somewhere in between. Yet here lukewarm is identified as the worst situation to be in. Laodicea had two neighboring cities, Hierapolis and Colossae. Hierapolis had hot waters while Colossae had cold water. Both were thought to be of medicinal value. Laodicea had no water at all, however. It had to be piped in via aqueduct, and the result was lukewarm (and dirty) water. Christ compares the spiritual condition of the church to that of the city's water.

The church, by contrast, assessed its condition in relation to its material wealth: *'For you say, "I am rich, I have prospered, and I need nothing, not realizing that you are wretched, pitiable, poor, blind and naked"'* (verse 17). In this, they had precedent in the ungodly Israelites condemned by the prophet: "Ephraim has said, 'Ah, but I am rich; I have found wealth for myself'" (Hos. 12:8). Hosea points out that Israel's prosperity has come through unrighteous means (12:7), accompanied by idolatry and failure to honor God as the source of her wealth (2:5, 8). "Rich" and "wealthy" are associated in Revelation with profit resulting from compromise with the world system (6:15; 13:16; 18:3, 15, 19). This church, like Israel of old, has fallen into a state of collusion with these ungodly forces. The Laodicean Christians (or professing Christians) have allied themselves with idolatry and immorality. Wealth itself is not inherently evil, according to Scripture. It is *the love of wealth* that is condemned (1 Tim. 6:10). Pursuit of wealth as an end in itself will result in spiritual disaster (Mt. 6:24; Ac. 5:1-10). Yet wealth handled to God's glory can be used righteously (Ac. 4:32-37). Wealth gained by godly Christians in business can finance the expansion of the kingdom. A Christian's true prosperity is measured by how much he gives rather than by how much he has. The Christians at Smyrna were spiritually wealthy even though physically poor (Rev. 2:9), whereas the Laodiceans were in the opposite position. They are described as being **wretched, pitiable, poor, blind and naked.** Apart from its bad water, Laodicea was known for three things: its banks, its school of ophthalmology with its famous eye salve, and its textile trade. All three are ironically referred to here. They think they have everything, but in truth they have nothing. The possession of wealth, power and prestige can blind us to the fact we are spiritually bankrupt.

The solution to their problem, however, is at hand: *'I counsel you to buy from me gold refined by fire, so that you may be rich, and white garments so that you may clothe yourself and the shame of your nakedness not be seen, and salve to anoint your eyes, so that you may see'* (verse 18). Gold signifies purity (1 Pet. 3:7), as do white garments (on white as signifying purity see 3:4-5; 6:2; 19:8; and on the shame of nakedness and its relation to idolatry see Ezek. 16:8, 36; 23:29; Nah. 3:5). Blindness signifies lack of spiritual understanding or wisdom. In the vision of chapter 1, Christ was dressed in a golden sash, his hair was white and his eyes were like a flame of fire. The gold, the white garments and the eye salve all point to Christ. He is all they need, but without him they have nothing.

Yet Christ has not given up on them: *'Those whom I love, I reprove and discipline, so be zealous and repent. Behold, I stand at the door and knock. If anyone hears my voice and opens the door, I will come in to him and eat with him, and he with me'* (verses 19-20). The verbs "stand" and "knock" are in the Greek present tense, referring to an ongoing action. Christ faithfully and tenaciously pursues even those whose love has grown cold. The allusion here is to Song Sol. 5:2, "A sound! My beloved is knocking. 'Open to me, my sister, my love...'" Our love may grow lukewarm, but his does not. He calls them to "eat with him," an echo of the deep fellowship of the Lord's Supper.

If they do, whatever they may lose in the scheme of this world will be more than compensated for: *'I will grant him to sit with me on my throne, as I also conquered and sat down with my Father on his throne. He who has an ear, let him hear what the Spirit says to the churches'*" (verse 21). In any wealthy culture such as our own, the predicament of the Laodicean church will reappear. Christ calls us, as he did them, to give up the things we cannot keep in order to gain the things we can never lose.

3

THE VISION OF THE HEAVENLY TEMPLE

(4:1-5:14)

*God is glorified because he is
Creator and Ruler over all (4:1-11)*

*The Lamb is also glorified and has
taken up his rule (5:1-14)*

In the next vision, John sees the throne of God, and Christ enthroned with the Father. The fact that Christ is enthroned and has assumed power in the heavenly realm gives the confident foundation on which suffering believers can conquer the strategies of the enemy. Because Christ has conquered, so also can those who follow him. The contents of this vision, therefore, are closely linked to the introduction and the letters. The introduction speaks of the exalted, victorious Christ, and the letters urge believers to follow him in the way of the cross. The basis of their ability to do so is portrayed in the scenes about to unfold. This reminds us of the integral connection between the letter and the visions.

John's vision is so closely related to Daniel's vision of the Son of man (Dn. 7:9-14) that we must assume he saw fundamentally the same thing. Both men saw a throne with God sitting on it, and fire before him. In both cases, innumerable angels surround the throne. As books were opened, a divine figure comes near the throne and receives an eternal kingdom consisting of people of every nation. Both men are distressed by the vision, but receive wisdom from one of the angelic figures. Finally, in both visions, the saints receive authority to reign under God. Into John's scene are also added details of Ezekiel's first heavenly vision (Ezek. 1:4-28). Both John and Ezekiel saw four living creatures, a sea of crystal and a throne surrounded by fire on which God was seated. Though separated by centuries, all three men were beholding the same heavenly realities.

GOD IS GLORIFIED BECAUSE HE IS CREATOR AND RULER OVER ALL (4:1-11)

The use of the phrase, *After this I looked* (verse 1), simply indicates the order in which John saw the visions. As the book progresses (the same phrase is repeated in 7:1, 9; 15:5; 18:1; and 19:1), it is important to keep in mind that *the order in which the visions are presented* has nothing necessarily to do with the order in which *the events described in the visions occur.* The vision begins: *And behold, a door standing open in heaven! And the first voice, which I had heard speaking to me like a trumpet, said, "Come up here, and I will show you what must take place after this"* (verse 1). The *first voice* is the voice of Christ (a reference to 1:10). The divine voice shows him *what must take place after this.* The phrase *after this* (literally "after these things") alludes to Dn. 2:29, 45, where the same phrase is used to refer to the days when the latter-days kingdom of God is to be established. "After these things" in Daniel has the same meaning as the "latter days" in Dn 2:28. Christ is beginning to show John what must happen in the latter days. This latter-days event has been revealed in the chapter 1 vision as having been inaugurated by the resurrection and ascension of Christ and the consequent establishment of God's kingdom. *What must take place after this* does not refer to events of the distant future, but to the events occurring between the first and second coming of Christ, including the events unfolding at the very time John was writing.

It is extremely important to note that 4:1 introduces not only the description of the heavenly temple in 4:1-5:14, but also the rest of the visions in the book (4:2-22:5), all of which are included in the phrase *what must take place after this.* This means that *all the visions about to unfold deal with the events of the church age* commencing with Christ's resurrection and ascension and the outpouring of the Spirit. Through these events, the new-creation kingdom of God has been inaugurated on earth. As we proceed, we will note that some visions may have multiple fulfillments in history. That the "latter days" have already begun is corroborated by the rest of the New Testament, which consistently asserts that the period of the "latter days" or "last days" was set in motion by the work of Christ (Ac. 2:17-21; 1 Tim. 4:1; 1 Pet. 1:20; Heb. 1:2; Jas. 5:3; 1 Jn. 2:1; Jude verse 18).

John is ushered into the heavenly court: *At once I was in the Spirit, and behold, a throne stood in heaven, with one seated on the throne. And he who sat there had the appearance of jasper and carnelian, and around the throne was a rainbow that had the appearance of an emerald* (verses 2-3). This places John in the company of Old Testament prophets like Isaiah (6:1-7) and Micaiah (1 Kgs. 22:19-22), as well as Ezekiel and Daniel, who saw similar visions of God's throne room. In chapters 4 and 5, there are seventeen mentions of God's throne, which represents God's authority. The purpose is to emphasis the authority and sovereignty of God over all human history. John's readers, facing suffering, persecution and the pressure to compromise, need to be assured of this in order to persevere and remain faithful. The three precious stones of verse 3 (*jasper and carnelian... and... emerald*) represent God's glory, as they do in the fuller list in chapter 21, especially jasper in 21:11, which is the only stone mentioned there in explicit connection with the glory of God. They point back to the precious stones of the garden (Gen. 2:12), at the same time as they point forward to the restoration of the garden in the new Jerusalem. The *rainbow* that is *around the throne* reminds the readers of God's covenant promises to his people, as in the days of Noah.

The vision continues: *Around the throne were twenty-four thrones, and seated on the thrones were twenty-four elders, clothed in white garments, with golden crowns on their heads* (verse 4). In the Old Testament, there were twenty-four groups of Davidic priests (1 Chron. 24:3-19), twenty-four Levitical gatekeepers (1 Chron. 16:17-19), and an identical number of Levitical worship leaders. All these were connected with the worship that took place at the earthly tabernacle. The heavenly elders may well be heavenly representatives of the earthly church as it worships. This reminds us of the supernatural and powerfully significant nature of the worship of the church. In 21:12-14, in the description of the eternal temple of the new Jerusalem, the twelve tribes and the twelve apostles are mentioned together. This suggests the twenty-four elders represent the faithful people of God throughout the ages. Their identification as heavenly beings is corroborated by 7:9-17, where they are distinguished from the crowd of the redeemed saints. In 5:8, they present the prayers of the saints. Like the angels who represent the seven churches and Daniel's angels who represent nations, the elders attend the heavenly court to provide supernatural support to the earthly church as it worships. The reality being conveyed is that the church is represented in heaven by powerful heavenly beings having their own *thrones* and *golden crowns.*

John sees further heavenly signs: *From the throne came flashes of lightning, and rumblings and peals of thunder, and before the throne were burning seven torches of fire, which are the seven spirits of God, and before the throne there was as it were a sea of glass, like crystal* (verses 5-6a). Moses saw similar heavenly sights and sounds (Exod. 19:16). This is not surprising in light of the fact that the plagues about to unfold are modeled on the plagues of Exodus. In 8:5, 11:19 and 16:18, these phenomena are associated with the judgment of God. The *seven torches of fire, which are the seven spirits of God* (verse 5) alludes to the seven lamps Zechariah saw in his temple vision (Zech. 4:2-3, 10). The *seven spirits,* as in 1:4, refer to the Holy Spirit. The lamps are also associated with the Spirit in Zechariah (Zech. 4:6). *Before the throne* he saw a *sea of glass, like crystal.* In 15:2, "those who had conquered the beast" stand beside this sea, singing "the song of Moses." This suggests that the sea of glass represents the ultimate calming by God of the evil activity represented by the Red Sea. The

Red Sea stood in the way of the children of Israel gaining their freedom, and in Christ its removal has been decisively inaugurated. This action will be completely fulfilled in the eternal kingdom. In the meantime, the sea is pictured as the home of the beast (Rev. 13:1), thus representing the still-present reality of evil in this fallen world. By contrast, in the new Jerusalem, the sea is "no more" (Rev. 21:2), and a new river "bright as crystal" flows from God's throne. God has now stilled these demonic waters and established his throne over them.

The vision continues: *And around the throne, on each side of the throne, are four living creatures, full of eyes in front and behind: the first living creature like a lion, the second living creature like an ox, the third living creature with the face of a man, and the fourth living creature like an eagle in flight. And the four living creatures, each of them with six wings, are full of eyes all around and within, and day and night they never cease to say, "Holy, holy, holy, is the Lord God Almighty, who was and is and is to come"* (verses 6b-8). Around the throne, John sees *four living creatures.* They are *full of eyes in front and behind.* The four have different faces, but each has six wings. Ezekiel saw four-faced creatures with many eyes but only four wings called cherubim (Ezek. 1:1-28; 10:1-22). Isaiah saw creatures with six wings called seraphim (Isa. 6:1-7). Both sets of beings are pictured as attending the throne of God, as are these creatures in Revelation. Similar heavenly realities are being revealed to John as to these Old Testament prophets. The cherubim, seraphim and the creatures here would seem to represent a similar, high order of angelic beings. The four faces are symbolic representations of the diverse parts of creation, showing God's lordship over all of it. The many eyes of the living beings show that they represent God, his sovereignty on earth and his faithfulness to his people, for "the eyes of the Lord run to and fro throughout the earth, to give strong support to those whose heart is blameless toward him" (2 Chron. 16:9). The four living creatures have two functions. Like Isaiah's seraphim (Isa. 6:3), they offer praise and worship to God, saying *Holy, holy, holy is the Lord God Almighty.* They also administer God's judgment against humanity (Rev. 6:1-8, 15:7). God's title here, *the One who was and is and is to come,* expresses his sovereignty over all human history.

John sees more: *And whenever the living creatures give glory and honor and thanks to him who is seated on the throne, who lives forever and ever, the twenty-four elders fall down before him who is seated on the throne and worship him who lives forever and ever. They cast their crowns before the throne, saying, "Worthy are you, our Lord and God, to receive glory and honor and power, for you created all things, and by your will they existed and were created"* (verses 9-11). As often as the *living creatures give glory and honor and thanks to God,* the elders join with them in worship. Both groups worship *him who lives forever and ever* (verses 9-10). The same term in relation to God appears in Daniel in passages which describe rebellious earthly kings who are humbled before him (Dn. 4:30; 11:36). This description of God yet again underlines his sovereignty over all human history, including those forces who oppose him and seek to destroy or harass his people. Suffering Christians can find in this truth comfort and encouragement not to give up in the battle. This is confirmed by the statement in verse 9 that he is *seated on the throne.* The power of God manifested in the heavenly temple will also operate on earth, an assurance intended to bring comfort to Christians presently suffering trials, and to encourage them to remain faithful in the midst of them.

The description of the elders' praise concludes in verse 11: God is worthy *to receive glory and honor and power.* Two reasons are given as to why God is worthy: he *created all things* and he sustains all things: *by your will they existed* [lit: "were"]. The first phrase is in the Greek aorist tense, which refers to a definite act in the past, in this case God's creation of the world. The second phrase, where the verb "were" is in the imperfect tense, refers to the *ongoing action* of God to this very day in sustaining and preserving the the world he created. In spite of sometimes distressing and painful trials, where we may question God's power or commitment to us, the fact is that he is still ruling the universe. He has not retired or died! Even in the midst of trials, Christians should follow the example of the heavenly beings, so that our worship of God on earth is modeled on their worship of God in heaven. Regardless of what is happening around us or to us, the central truth is that God is worthy to be worshiped and glorified.

THE LAMB IS ALSO GLORIFIED AND HAS TAKEN UP HIS RULE (5:1-14)

John's vision of God on the throne continues: *Then I saw in the right hand of him who was seated on the throne a scroll written within and on the back, sealed with seven seals. And I saw a strong angel proclaiming with a loud voice, "Who is worthy to open the scroll and break its seals?"* (verses 1-2). John sees in his right hand *a scroll written within and on the back, sealed with seven seals.* This is an allusion to Ezek. 2:9-10, where the prophet also sees a scroll in God's hand with writing on the front and back. That scroll, as the following chapters in Ezekiel reveal, represents the judgment of God on humankind. Daniel also saw books of judgment in the presence of God (Dn. 7:10), shortly after which the Son of man appeared to take his kingdom (Dn. 7:13-14). Daniel was ordered by the angel to "seal the book" recording these divine judgments until "the time of the end" (Dn. 12:4, 9). Daniel's time of the end (see on 1:1) has been inaugurated by the resurrection of Christ. This mean we should also expect exactly what is about to happen in chapter 5: that Daniel's book has been unsealed by Christ.

A *mighty angel* comes forth, asking, *Who is worthy to open the scroll and break its seals?* Daniel's book, seen in a vision five hundred years earlier, is about to be unsealed. Daniel is the only place in the Old Testament where we find this idea of books being sealed and unsealed. The book represents God's plan of salvation and of judgment, and the angel's question concerns the identity of the One worthy to administer this plan. Bible scholars have debated whether the book represents a scroll or a codex. If you visit the British Library in London, you can see the oldest existing complete copy of the New Testament, called the Codex Sinaiticus. It is clearly identifiable to the onlooker as a book, rather than a scroll. In a codex, each seal could enclose a section of the book, and the contents were revealed segment by segment as the seals were broken. The codex was used much more commonly in John's day than the scroll, and so this is likely what he saw. This explains the visions which follow — the seals, trumpets and bowls, and so on. Each is revealed as the book goes along. But if it were a scroll, a summary of the contents was often written on the outside of the scroll by means of various seals, which represented witnesses to the contents. When a particular seal was broken, a part of the contents was revealed (as in each of the subsequent visions). A final possibility is that John saw a Roman will. These were sealed by seven witnesses, the contents sometimes summarized on the outside. When the one whose will it was had died, the will could be unsealed and the inheritance disbursed. This fits the context in chapter 5 of the death of Christ as initiating the release of the promise of God's salvation.

This promise of salvation for humankind involves its restoration to Paradise, where we will eat of the tree of life (2:12). But as the right to dwell in Paradise was forfeited by a man (Adam), so it must be regained by a man (Christ). The mighty angel of verse 2 is looking for the identity of this man. At first, things look bleak: *And no one in heaven or on earth or under the earth was able to open the scroll or look into it, and I began to weep loudly because no one was worthy to open the scroll or to look into it* (verses 3-4). But he receives instruction to stop weeping: *And one of the elders said to me, "Weep no more; behold, the Lion of the tribe of Judah, the Root of David, has conquered, so that he can open the scroll and its seven seals"* (verse 5). The two titles of Christ come, respectively, from Gen. 49:8-12 and Isa. 11:1-10. Both speak of a conquering Messiah who will come to judge his foes. The letters have exhorted Christians to remain faithful by conquering. They are now given the reason why they can be confident in their ability to fulfill this mission: it is based on the fact Christ himself has conquered. His victory becomes our victory, through the presence and power of his Spirit within us.

The vision continues: *And between the throne and the four living creatures and among the elders I saw a Lamb standing, as though it had been slain* [lit: "as slain"], *with seven horns and with seven eyes, which are the seven spirits of God sent out into all the earth* (verse 6). This alludes to Isa. 53:7, where the lamb led to slaughter is a prophetic picture of the coming Messiah. The phrase "as slain" represents a Greek perfect participle, which refers to a continuing reality: the Lamb not only *was slain* but *continues to exist as slain,* and those who follow him must walk the same way. The seven eyes of the Lamb are identified with the *seven spirits of God*, representing (as in 1:4 and 4:5) the Holy Spirit. Zechariah sees a stone with *seven eyes* (the eyes of God) on it set before Joshua the high priest. The stone is then related to removing the iniquity of the land (Zech. 3:9), following which the prophet sees seven lamps connected with the moving of God's Spirit. The Lamb also has *seven horns* (representing the fullness of his divine power). In the Old Testament, horns are a symbol for power or might (Deut. 33:17; Ps. 89:17). In Dn. 7:21, the horn that comes out of the fourth beast oppresses the saints until the Ancient of Days comes and brings divine judgment. The fourth beast (Dn. 7:23) is identified with the fourth kingdom of Dn. 2:40-44, which is overcome by the arrival of God's kingdom. The seven horns of the Lamb represent the fullness of his power. The slain Lamb is pictured as reversing the victory of the evil horn of Daniel through his death on the cross. The Lamb, resurrected and ascended, now stands before the throne of God, from which he exercises God's power. The Lion has overcome by becoming a Lamb. God's victory is won in an ironic and unexpected manner. The conquering Messiah the Jewish people expected fulfilled his mission on a Roman cross. This is a consistent theme in Revelation: in chapters 4-22, Jesus is referred to as Lamb twenty-seven times.

Even as in Daniel's vision, the Son of man came before God in order to receive authority to rule (Dn. 7:13-14), so now John sees the Lamb approaching the throne: *And he went and took the scroll from the right hand of him who was seated on the throne. And when he had taken the scroll, the four living creatures and the twenty-four elders fell down before the Lamb, each holding a harp, and golden bowls full of incense, which are the prayers of the saints* (verses 7-8). The heavenly beings begin to worship the Lamb even as they worshiped God, thus showing the Lamb's divinity. They then present *the prayers of the saints* which, as 6:10 reveals, call for the judgment of God upon evildoers and his deliverance of the righteous. This is a powerful reminder to Christians, especially those going through times of tribulation, that their prayers have supernatural effect and are supported by a heavenly ministry.

The heavenly beings begin to sing: *And they sang a new song, saying, "Worthy are you to take the scroll and to open its seals, for you were slain, and by your blood you ransomed people for God from every tribe and language and people and nation, and you have made them a kingdom and priests to our God, and they shall reign on the earth"* (verses 9-10). The new song of the heavenly host comes from a variety of Old Testament passages (Ps. 33:3; 40:3; 96:1; 98:1; Isa. 42:9-10). It is a song of triumph in God's victory over his enemies. The content of the song expresses the fact that the Lamb is worthy of praise because of his sacrificial death. Those ransomed from every nation have been made *a kingdom and priests to our God, and they shall reign on the earth* (verse 10). This is the prophetic fulfillment of the promise made to Moses concerning Israel (Exod. 19:6), but now fulfilled in the church composed of people from every nation (Rev. 1:6). The significance of this promise is underlined by its mention in the initial vision of chapter 1, and by the fact it is repeated here. The kingdom of God has been initiated by the work of Christ, and this results in the redeemed taking up their reign on earth. The best Greek text of verse 10 suggests that *reign* is in the present tense, and this conforms to the idea of the kingdom arriving in Christ, which is the truth established in the initial vision. There, the arrival of kingdom was seen as about to take place imminently, or even as already beginning (1:1). This is reinforced by the theme of God making his people a present kingdom and priesthood (1:6 and the present verse). Christ is the beginning of the new creation (3:14), the new order or kingdom which has begun. The prophesied latter-day kingdom of Daniel has arrived in Christ. The way in which Christians reign is not like that of any worldly ruler. They reign, as did Christ, by carrying the cross and following the way of the slain Lamb. Yet they can be assured of final vindication, as the rest of the book makes clear.

John sees a great heavenly host: *Then I looked, and I heard around the throne and the living creatures and the elders the voice of many angels, numbering myriads of myriads and thousands of thousands, saying with a loud voice, "Worthy is the Lamb who was slain, to receive power and wealth and wisdom and might and honor and glory and blessing!"* (verses 11-12). Daniel likewise saw the great throng of heavenly beings (Dn. 7:10) in the vision to which the passage so often alludes. The fact that the Lamb is worthy *to receive power and wealth and wisdom and might and honor and glory and blessing* echoes David's prayer at the dedication of the temple materials (1 Chron. 29:11), and is appropriate as it is the eternal temple being portrayed here. The vision comes to its conclusion: *And I heard every creature in heaven and on earth and under the earth and in the sea, and all that is in them, saying, "To him who sits on the throne and to the Lamb be blessing and honor and glory and might forever and ever!" And the four living creatures said, "Amen!" and the elders fell down and worshiped* (verses 13-14). Christ is to be glorified even as God is. This continues the theme of Christ's divinity, which is a major feature of Revelation. The vision ends in verse 14 with this magnificent picture of the worship of God by all his created beings. The saved of all ages worshiping God are seen from the perspective of eternity. They are joined in their praise by the heavenly beings who represent and support them.

The vision of the heavenly temple contained in chapters 4-5 makes repeated reference to Daniel's vision of the Son of man who appears before the Ancient of Days to receive a kingdom and its authority. This prophetic vision is fulfilled in the death of the Lamb, which authorizes him to approach the throne of God and receive the authority of the eternal kingdom prophesied in Daniel. The focus on chapter 4 is the giving of glory to God as Creator, while the focus of chapter 5 is the giving of glory to the Lamb as Redeemer. The redemptive work of Christ will result in all creation giving glory to God. The vision as a whole expresses the sovereignty of God and of Christ over all history and creation. As such, this vision serves as a foundation for the description of how this sovereignty is worked out in history through the judgments of God and his care for his church, which are the subject of the rest of the book.

4

THE SEVEN SEALS

(6:1-8:5)

The first six seals (6:1-17)

The sealing of believers (7:1-8)

*The great multitude of saints
in heaven praise God (7:9-17)*

The seventh seal (8:1-5)

THE FIRST SIX SEALS (6:1-17)

The vision of chapter 5 showed that Christ has received authority from the Father, thus fulfilling Daniel's prophetic vision of the Son of man approaching the Ancient of Days. The seals are the first of a series of three parallel sets of visions (the other two being the trumpets and bowls). All three depict judgments of God during the church age. These judgments have a dual purpose: to refine believers by testing their faith, and to harden the hearts of unbelievers who refuse to repent in spite of the evidence of God's disapproval of their sin. The letters to the churches (chapters 2-3) have shown that this process of judgment has already begun, and believers are already being exhorted to remain faithful in the face of persecution and temptations to compromise their faith. The basis of this exhortation is the assurance that God is sovereign over all that is happening. The fact that Christ has taken his seat in heavenly authority has precipitated the opening of the seven seals. The seal judgments as well as the others thus commenced in the first century and continue until Christ returns. This demonstrates that God is ruling over all subsequent events of history. This in turn is intended to bring comfort to suffering believers throughout the world during the church age.

The seals are in fact opened by Christ himself: *Now I watched when the Lamb opened one of the seven seals* (verse 1a). Now only has Christ's death initiated the seal judgments, Christ himself is executing them. The judgments of the first four seals consist of war, famine, death and plague. This fulfills the prophecy of Ezekiel concerning four judgments of sword, famine, wild beasts and plague (Ezek. 14:14-21). The purpose of Ezekiel's trials was to punish the unbelieving majority while purifying the righteous remnant. This prophecy, pertaining to the faithful and unfaithful in Israel, is now universalized to include believers and unbelievers among all nations. Jesus likewise prophesied war, famine and persecution (Mt. 24:6-28). Jesus warned believers to endure during these difficult times, which would affect them as well as unbelievers. Both Ezekiel and Jesus presented these judgments as occurring alongside each other. This suggests the trials should not be seen as isolated incidents which take place one after the other, but rather are generally characteristic of the entire period in which they occur. The time from Christ's resurrection until his return will thus be marked by recurring periods of such varied judgments. Suffering presents an opportunity for Christians to find their strength in God, even while the hearts of those around them are being further hardened.

After the breaking of the first seal, John hears a voice: *And I heard one of the four living creatures say with a voice like thunder, "Come!" And I looked, and behold, a white horse! And its rider had a bow, and a crown was given to him, and he came out conquering, and to conquer* (verses 1b-2). *Thunder* (as in 4:5) signifies judgment. Christ appears in 19:6 riding on a white horse, and some have thought he is the rider here. However, the vision is based on Zechariah's picture of four horses sent by God as emissaries of punishment (Zech. 6:1-8). Likewise, the first four judgments of the trumpet and bowl visions present calamities parallel to those in Zechariah's vision. The horses and their riders are demonic in nature, bringing war, plague and death, of which God is never the ultimate author. Hence, it is unlikely the rider is Christ. However, the rider does operate under divine authority: he is sent out as a result of Christ opening the seal. Furthermore, the statement is made that his crown *was given to* him. The phrase *was given* is a form of speech called the "divine passive," and signifies God as the author of the action (see also 6:11; 7:2; 9:1). This offers further comfort to believers that, in spite of appearances, God is still in charge. God has bound the devil (see on 20:2; also Lk. 11:22), with the result that the enemy operates after the resurrection and ascension only within the boundaries God has set. Satan presents himself as an imitator of Christ (see chapters 12-13). With this in mind, it is likely that the first rider represents the deceptive activity of Satan as he seeks to conquer the saints, even as he did at Corinth, by masquerading as an angel of light (2 Cor. 11:14).

The second horseman is now called forth: *When he opened the second seal, I heard the second living creature say, "Come!" And out came another horse, bright red. Its rider was permitted to take peace from the earth, so that people should slay one another, and he was given a great sword* (verses 3-4). Jesus said, "Do not think that I have come to bring peace to the earth. I have not come to bring peace, but a sword" (Mt. 10:34). These verses point to the persecution of believers, as use of the word "slay" elsewhere in Revelation alludes to the death of Christ or of those who believe in him (5:6, 9, 12; 6:9; 13:8; 18:24). The fact that the beast was "slain" (13:3) is actually a mockery or false imitation of Christ's death. The reference may be to the believers pictured as slain in verses 9-11. Of course, the havoc will also touch the lives of unbelievers, even as Jesus prophesied in Mk. 13:17-20, where the sufferings of all the peoples would be cut short for the sake of the elect.

The third rider brings famine: *When he opened the third seal, I heard the third living creature say, "Come!" And I looked, a behold, a black horse! And its rider had a pair of scales in his hand. And I heard what seemed to be a voice in the midst of the four living creatures, saying, "A quart of wheat for a denarius, and three quarts of barley for a denarius, and do not harm the oil and wine!"* (verses 5-6). In the Roman world, food rationed in times of famine was weighed out by means of scales, so the scales here stand for a time of famine. A denarius was a day's wage, and in the time of famine this would buy *a quart of wheat* or *three quarts of barley*. These prices were eight to sixteen times the normal price. However, the rider is told not *to harm the oil and wine.* The idea is that the necessities of life will become so costly no one will have money to buy the extras, so there is no need to destroy them. In times of famine or natural disasters, Christians may be affected more than others. Their failure to compromise with the values of the pagan society around them may cause aid to be denied to them. Sadly, we sometimes see this today in nations where Christians are a persecuted or disliked minority.

The fourth and last rider to be released: *When he opened the fourth seal, I heard the voice of the fourth living creature say, "Come!" And I looked, and behold, a pale horse! And its rider's name was Death, and Hades followed him. And they were given authority over a fourth of the earth, to kill with sword and with famine and with pestilence and by wild beasts of the earth* (verses 7-8). According to 20:13-14, Death and Hades designate the place where the unsaved dead are kept prior to the day of judgment. They are thus linked with the realm of Satan. In 1:18, Christ declares he has the keys of Death and Hades, and this verse once again affirms God's control over all Satanic forces. Their evil activities ultimately are turned for good by God.

Various Old Testament texts declare God's judgment on idolatry in a four-fold form (Lev. 26:18-28; Deut. 32:24-26; Jer. 15:1-4; Ezek. 14:12-23). In particular, the Ezekiel passage is significant because, with its similarity of content, it is the closest direct prophetic forerunner to this vision. "Four" in the Bible is the number of the earth (Gen. 2:10-14; Rev. 19:8). The four living creatures are angelic representatives of the physical creation in their praise and worship of God. The four judgments pictured in the horses and their riders represent God's judgment on the whole earth throughout the entire period of the church age. Hardships caused by natural, economic or military forces are used by God to harden the hearts of unbelievers and express a provisional form of judgment. Those whose hearts are open will be awakened by these judgments to turn their hearts to Christ. Those who are already believers are given an opportunity to bear witness and demonstrate their faithfulness, in the assurance that God will use the trials to draw them closer to himself and thus foreshadow their eventual eternal reward. The fact that the first four judgments affect only *a fourth of the earth* indicates that they do not affect every person, every region or every nation, but are occurring on a regular basis at various points throughout the world, whether on a smaller or a larger scale.

This raises the question as to how God could be pictured as sending or allowing judgments which affect his own people. The Biblical answer is that, though God is the author only of good, he uses even trials to work good in his faithful people. He used even the cross to bring about our salvation. James reminds us to "count it all joy" when we encounter "trials of various kinds," since the testing of our faith in trials produces a good result in that we are "perfect and complete, lacking nothing" (Jas. 1:2-4). Likewise, Peter says that though "we are grieved by various trials," these trials cause our faith to be refined and will result in "praise and glory and honor at the revelation of Jesus Christ" (1 Pet. 1:6-7). The vision of chapter 5, in which the Lamb receives authority from the Father, is rooted in Daniel's vision of the Son of man coming into the presence of the Ancient of Days and receiving authority. The four evil beasts (representing the totality of the earth's evil kingdoms) are indeed destroyed in Daniel's vision. However, the fulfillment of this vision occurs in a step-by-step manner. Although Christ has won the victory over evil, this victory will not be consummated until his return. In the meantime, the power of evil remains on the earth, yet its authority is limited and its days numbered. For those who love God, he indeed works all things together for good, even the "sufferings of this present time" (Rom. 8:18, 28).

The first four seals present the judgments of God on the earth throughout the history of the church age. The fifth seal (verses 9-11) pictures deceased saints in the presence of the Lord: *When he opened the fifth seal, I saw under the altar the souls of those who had been slain for the word of God and for the witness they had borne* (verse 9). That they have been *slain* (verse 9) shows they were victims of the second horseman who unleashed slaying on the earth. In verse 11, they are also pictured as "killed," which links them with the fourth horseman who brought death. Chapters 2 and 3 have shown that those who are conquerors include all who remain faithful to Christ, up to and including those who, like Antipas (2:13), were actually martyred. It is likely that the vision of deceased saints here includes all who have suffered up to and including death, and so "slain" and "killed" should probably be taken in a figurative sense. Every believer in some sense "loses" his life for Christ's sake (Mk. 8:35). Paul speaks of various forms of suffering, from tribulation to the sword, all of which he brings under the general heading of being "killed" and "slaughtered" (Rom. 8:35-39). This vision, therefore, likely describes all faithful deceased saints. They are pictured as being *under the altar.* This refers to the place of God's protection after their earthly sufferings are over. The altar is the place of God's presence ("the golden altar before the throne," 8:3; "the golden altar before God," 9:13). The altar of the physical tabernacle or temple was the place of earthly sacrifice. In that place, there was a real but limited sense of God's presence (Exod. 40:34-35; 2 Chron. 7:1-3). The heavenly altar represents the place of Christ's sacrifice. That sacrifice released the forgiveness of our sins and enabled our adoption as sons and daughters of God. As a result, even in this life we are able to enter into God's presence and experience his spiritual protection. But these saints have entered into that presence and protection in an ultimate manner.

John hears the voices of these saints: *They cried out with a loud voice, "O Sovereign Lord, holy and true, how long before you will judge and avenge our blood on those who dwell on the earth?"* (verse 10). The same cry is uttered by an angel in Zech. 1:12. The angel's appeal is answered by God's sending forth the four horsemen in judgment (Zech. 6:1-8, the passage prophetically fulfilled by John's vision here). This is also the cry of the Psalmist for God's justice (Ps. 6:3; 74:10). It occurs in Ps. 79:5, which is significant because the cry of the saints here is rooted in Ps. 79:10: "Let the avenging of the outpoured blood of your servants be known among the nations before our eyes." This is not primarily a cry for revenge, but for the manifestation of God's own justice and the revelation of the fact that he is just. Believers understand this. God's justice is shown by his judgment of sin in the person of his own Son (Rom. 3:25-26). The sins he had previously passed over have now been judged in Christ's own death, in order that God be shown to be completely *holy and true.* But the manifestation of God's justice and the vindication of his character will be fully revealed and made known only when Christ returns. At that time, *those who dwell on the earth* will be judged. This phrase is an expression which in Revelation stands for all unbelievers (8:13; 11:10; 13:12; 13:14; 17:2). The nature of this judgment will be unfolded as the book progresses.

The ultimate answer to these prayers for the avenging of blood is not given until 19:2, yet here there is a preliminary response: *Then they were each given a white robe and told to rest a little longer, until the number of their fellow servants and their brothers should be complete, who were to be killed as they themselves had been* (verse 11). How do we understand the phrase *a little longer?* We are already living in the "latter days," according to chapter 1, and these days will extend until the Lord's return. But we need to look at things in terms of God's attitude toward time. Will the Lord return imminently? Peter answered this question for us: "With the Lord one day is as a thousand years, and a thousand years as one day" (2 Pet. 3:8). Deceased saints in eternity experience time from God's perspective. Those saints, as well as Christians still suffering on earth, can be assured of ultimate victory and an eternal reward which will far outweigh the difficulties of this present time: "For this light momentary affliction is preparing for us an eternal weight of glory beyond all comparison, as we look not to the things that are seen but to the things that are unseen" (2 Cor. 4:17-18).

The sixth seal (verses 12-17) presents a further development of God's answer to the prayer of the saints in verses 9-11. The time of the sixth seal is the last judgment: *When he opened the sixth seal, I looked, and behold, there was a great earthquake, and the sun became black as sackcloth, the full moon became like blood, and the stars of the sky fell to the earth as the fig tree sheds its winter fruit when shaken by a gale. The sky vanished like a scroll that is being rolled up, and every mountain and island was removed from its place* (verses 12-14). The *earthquake* of verse 12 is also pictured in 16:18, where it is undeniably a reference to the last judgment. The statement *every mountain and island was removed from its place* in verse 14 is likewise described in the judgment scene of 16:20, and similar language is again used in the portrayal of the last judgment in 20:11. Old Testament texts speak of the last judgment in almost identical ways. For instance, verse 12 says *the sun became black as sackcloth, the full moon became like blood.* This clearly alludes to the description of the final judgment in Joel 2:31: "The sun shall be turned to darkness, and the moon to blood, before the great and awesome day of the Lord comes." Verses 13-14 state that *the sky vanished like a scroll that is being rolled up* and it will be as when *the fig tree sheds its winter fruit.* By comparison, Isa. 34:4 says that in God's final day of vengeance, the sky will "roll up like a scroll" and it will be like "leaves falling from a fig tree."

At the last judgment, vengeance will come upon all people: *Then the kings of the earth and the great ones and the generals and the rich and the powerful, and everyone, slave and free, hid themselves in the caves and among the rocks of the mountains, calling to the mountains and rocks, "Fall on us and hide us from the face of him who is seated on the throne, and from the wrath of the Lamb, for the great day of their wrath has come, and who can stand?"* (verses 15-17). The judgment commences with *the kings of the earth and the great ones,* just as in the depiction of the last judgment in Isa. 34:12, where the nobles are particularly mentioned. Those trying to escape God's wrath will be forced to hide *in the caves and among the rocks.* The reference is to Isaiah's further portrayal of the last judgment, where men must flee to "caverns of the rocks" to hide from God's terror (Isa. 2:18-21). According to Isaiah, this judgment comes on account of idolatry (Isa. 2:20). The idolatry is focussed on "idols of silver and gold" — the very things which are to be removed in the destruction of the existing creation. The "earth-dwellers" of Revelation are at home in this world, with its material wealth, injustice, false religion and moral pollution, some or all of which they have made their god. This idolatry is expressed later in Revelation in worship of the beast by the same group of people — kings, mighty men, and all men, free and slave (19:18-19). In verses 12-14, six classes of things are to be destroyed and six classes of men to be judged. The number of this judgment is six, the number of fallen man. Idolatry is man's worship of created things and of himself, and he will be judged for it by their destruction and by his own.

The idolators call *to the mountains and rocks,* asking these to hide them from the wrath of God and the Lamb. This is based in the cry of the idolaters in Hos. 10:8: "And they shall say to the mountains, 'Cover us,' and to the hills, 'fall on us.'" Jesus quoted the same passage in Lk. 23:30, alluding to the coming days of terror and judgment. The picture here is of Adam and Eve hiding in the garden. God has determined that history will end the same way it began. The only difference is this time there will be deliverance for the believer. The passage ends with the reason for the flight of the lost: *For the great day of their wrath has come, and who can stand?* The words come from Joel 2:11: "For the day of the Lord is great and very awesome; who can endure it?" The fact that this is a reference to the last judgment is confirmed by the phrases "great day" in 16:14 and "great supper" in 19:17-18, both of which passages without doubt refer to the last day. The judgment of verses 12-17 comes from both God and the Lamb. This highlights the fact Christ exercises the authority of God himself, and thus is yet another way in which Revelation points to his divinity.

THE SEALING OF BELIEVERS (7:1-8)

The chapter opens with a new vision: *After this I saw four angels standing at the four corners of the earth, holding back the four winds of the earth, that no wind might blow on earth or sea or against any tree* (verse 1). The phrase *after this* (as in 4:1; 7:9; 15:5; 18:1; and 19:1) refers to the *order in which John saw the visions*, not the *order in which the events portrayed in the visions occurred*. This vision, which John experienced subsequent to the previous one, *nevertheless comes before it chronologically*. The previous vision portrayed events throughout the church age culminating in the last judgment. This vision, however, refers to the protective sealing of believers, commencing with the beginning of the church age at Christ's resurrection. The purpose of the sealing is that these believers will not be harmed when they go through the trials unleashed by the seals of chapter 6. The *four winds* indicates that events involving the earth as a whole are being spoken of. This is indicated by the similar phrase in Jer. 49:36; Dn. 8:8; 11:4; Mt. 24:31; Mk. 13:27. Zech. 6:1-8 identifies the four winds with the four horses, which in turn are to be identified as the four horses and horsemen of Rev. 6:1-8. Judgments involving the whole earth are being spoken of. The four winds or four horsemen are being temporarily held back until the believers are sealed.

The vision continues: *Then I saw another angel ascending from the rising of the sun, with the seal of the living God, and he called with a loud voice to the four angels who had been given power to harm earth and sea, saying, "Do not harm the earth or the sea or the trees, until we have sealed the servants of our God on their foreheads"* (verses 2-3). Before harm is done to the earth or those who dwell in it, God's servants must be sealed. The vision is rooted in Ezekiel's vision, in which God commands an angel to put a mark on the foreheads of those faithful to him before striking Jerusalem in judgment (Ezek. 9:4-6). Ezekiel's vision in turn is based on the mark of blood on the door of the Israelites protecting them from harm during the first Passover (Exod. 12:7, 13, 22-28), and ultimately to the protective mark on Cain (Gen. 4:15). The vision pictures the church standing at the beginning of a new Exodus, being led into a period of trial and testing, yet one in which it will be protected from spiritual harm by the hand of God. This picture gains added meaning as the trumpet and bowl visions unfold, both series being last-days mirror images of the plagues on Egypt. The demonic powers portrayed in the vision of chapter 6 are not allowed to harm God's servants. This protection is not absolute, for we have seen that believers are subject to trial and suffering in this present age, and some have died for their faith. The protection, therefore, must be primarily spiritual in nature. Some measure of physical protection may be involved, however, for in 9:4, the demonic forces are commanded not to harm those with God's seal on their forehead. Likewise the children of Israel suffered some of the plagues of Egypt, but were protected from others.

The number of the sealed is given: *And I heard the number of the sealed, 144,000, sealed from every tribe of the sons of Israel: 12,000 from the tribe of Judah were sealed, 12,000 from the tribe of Reuben, 12,000 from the tribe of Gad, 12,000 form the tribe of Asher, 12,000 from the tribe of Naphtali, 12,000 from the tribe of Manasseh, 12,000 from the tribe of Simeon, 12,000 from the tribe of Levi, 12,000 from the tribe of Issachar, 12,000 from the tribe of Zebulun, 12,000 from the tribe of Joseph, 12,000 from the tribe of Benjamin were sealed* (verses 4-8). The same group with the same number is mentioned in 14:1 as standing on the heavenly Mount Zion with the Lamb, with the name of God and of the Lamb written on their foreheads. *The seal and the name, therefore, must be identical.* The seal is identified with God's ownership in 2 Tim. 2:19: "But God's firm foundation stands, bearing this seal: 'The Lord knows who are his.'" By contrast, the earth-dwellers have on their foreheads the mark of the beast, which is likewise his name (13:17; 14:9-11), signifying their ownership by the beast. The seal on the saved and the mark on the lost are thus both *symbols of ownership, not literal marks.* The picture may go back to the plate of pure gold placed on Aaron's forehead like the "engraving of a signet" (or "seal") in Exod. 28:36. The seal showed that he belonged to God. Many of the twelve stones of Aaron's breastpiece (Exod. 28:17-21) reappear in Rev. 21:19-20 in the description of the new Jerusalem. The seal is what guarantees believers access to the heavenly city. The nature of this sealing is primarily spiritual. They also will suffer in the trials that come on the earth, in addition to the persecutions they may endure on account of their faithfulness to Christ. However, while these trials harden and embitter the earth-dwellers (9:20-21), they serve only to purify the faith of believers. The sealing keeps them safe from giving way to the pressure to compromise or deny Christ. In light of 2 Cor. 1:22, Eph. 1:13 and 4:30, the seal is to be identified with the Holy Spirit, though this is not clear from the text of Revelation itself.

The question now arises -- who are the 144,000? Premillennialism suggests they are a literal group of Israelites of this exact number living during a tribulation which occurs immediately before the return of Christ. There are several problems with this view. *First*, every number in Revelation is symbolic rather than literal. This is clearly the case here. The number twelve represents the people of God, and is squared. The squaring includes the faithful saints of both old and new covenants. The resulting number, 144, is then multiplied by a factor of one thousand, which represents a large indefinite number, as in 2 Pet. 3:8. One thousand in the 2 Peter text alludes to the entire church age. 144,000 thus represents the indefinitely-large number of God's faithful people throughout history. The same idea is conveyed in 21:13-14, where the twelve tribes and twelve apostles together form the foundations of the new Jerusalem. This is a significant point, because the name of the "new Jerusalem" is to be written on the *Gentile* believers in the church at Philadelphia (3:12). If this is the case, it clearly identifies them, as well all other Gentile Christians, as part of the 144,000. As Jewish Christians are the foundational root of the tree (Rom. 11:17), they also are included. *Second*, the question must be asked why God's protection would extend only to Jews, rather than to his new covenant people of every race and nation?   *Third*, the word "tribulation" (Greek *thlipsis*) consistently refers in the New Testament to the *whole of the present church age*, during which God's people face opposition and suffering. For instance, 21 of 23 uses of "tribulation" in Paul refer to the present age (for further references, see on verse 14 below).

Our solution to the identity of the 144,000 is confirmed by looking at the wider context of Revelation. In 5:9, it is said that Christ "ransomed people for God from every tribe and language and people and nation." The same group of 144,000 are said in chapter 14 to have been "redeemed from the earth" and "redeemed from mankind" (14:3-4). That is, they have been redeemed or ransomed from the nations of the earth. This identifies the 144,000 with *believers of every nation*. Immediately after the sealing, John sees "a great multitude.... from every nation, from all tribes and peoples and languages" (7:9), similar to the description in chapter 14. We argue below this is the same group as portrayed in verses 1-8. The natural interpretation is that he is speaking here and in chapter 14 of the same group of people. This group cannot possibly be a literal number consisting of Jews only.

All Satan's followers bear his mark or name, and all the Lamb's follower's bear the Lamb's mark or name. If this is in fact true, then it must be the case that all of God's people of every tribe and nation and every stage of history must be considered as sealed, and thus are to be included in the symbolic number of the 144,000. Judah is mentioned first in the list of tribes. This is in line with the fact that Christ has been identified in 5:5 as the Lion of the tribe of Judah. Often in the Old Testament (Ezek. 34:23; 37:24-26; Ps. 16:8-11; and see Ac. 2:25-28), it is prophesied that the Messiah will be a descendant of David (and thus of Judah). The significance of this is that Christians of all races and nations are included in the number of the descendants of Judah, and are thus identified as the true Israel. This confirms the identification of the church of all nations as the new Israel made in 1:6 and again in 5:10, where the statement of Exod. 19:6 about Israel as a kingdom of priests is applied now to the church.

THE GREAT MULTITUDE OF SAINTS IN HEAVEN PRAISE GOD (7:9-17)

A new vision commences: *After this I looked, and behold, a great multitude that no one could number, from every nation, from all tribes and peoples and languages, standing before the throne and before the Lamb, clothed in white robes, with palm branches in their hands* (verse 9). The phrase after this refers to the order in which John saw the visions, not the order in which the events described in the visions occur. In this case, *the same reality is presented as in the previous vision, but from a different perspective.* In the vision of verses 1-8, John sees the church represented by *numerical symbolism.* But in verses 9-17, he sees the *actual number: a great multitude.* In 5:5, the Lamb is presented as the "Root of David." This corresponds to the first vision of the church portrayed symbolically in the form of the twelve tribes of Israel. But in 5:10, it states that the Lamb has ransomed believers "from every tribe and language and people and nation." This in turn corresponds to the *great multitude* that John sees here. The two groups are identical. They are the prophetic fulfillment of Daniel's vision in which the Son of man receives dominion over the "saints of the Most High," who are said to come from "all peoples, nations and languages" (Dn. 7:14, 22, 27).

Whereas 7:1-8 pictures the saints as sealed and thus protected spiritually from the judgments unfolding in chapter 6, 7:9-17 pictures glorified saints in heaven rejoicing before the throne of God. The same group of saints (God's people of every nation throughout the ages) is seen first as protected by God on earth, and second as rejoicing with God in heaven. The *great multitude that no one could number* is the fulfillment of the promises to Abraham in Gen. 17:5: "I have made you the father of a multitude of nations," and to Jacob: "I will... make your offspring as the sand of the sea, which cannot be numbered for multitude" (Gen. 32:12). Paul confirms explicitly in Rom. 4:13-25 that Abraham's fatherhood is by no means limited to believing Jews, but includes those of all nations. This vision again presents Christians of all nations as the true Israel.

This is made even more striking by the statement that the multitude had *palm branches in their hands.* This alludes to the Feast of Tabernacles, during which the Israelites used palm branches to construct the booths they lived in during the festival (Lev. 23:40-43). The feast was instituted to remind the Israelites of God's faithful provision for them in the wilderness. Christians are presented in Revelation (see 12:6) as living in the wilderness between their exit from spiritual Egypt (at the cross) and their entrance into the Promised Land (at the return of Christ). That is why John sees the plagues which originally came on Egypt falling now as a judgment on present-day unbelievers. Christians are thus presented as the true Israel, which further confirms the fact that the believers of every nation of verses 9-17 are identical to the picture of the twelve tribes in verses 1-8. Now these saints are celebrating the heavenly fulfillment of the Feast of Tabernacles.

The praise ascends to God: *And crying out with a loud voice, "Salvation belongs to our God who sits on the throne, and to the Lamb!" And all the angels were standing around the throne and around the elders and the four living creatures, and they fell on their faces before the throne and worshiped God, saying, "Amen! Blessing and glory and wisdom and thanksgiving and honor and power and might be to our God forever and ever! Amen"* (verses 10-12). The entire heavenly host joins with the redeemed saints in singing God's praise. This reminds us that worship of God is the primary activity of heaven. If we do not devote ourselves to his worship and praise on earth (Rom. 12:1), how are we to be prepared for what we will do in heaven? We also need to ask the question how our worship of God on earth reflects these heavenly scenes of glorified praise.

The saints are ***clothed in white robes***, which signify their spiritual purity (see verses 13-14). They have truly been conquerors, as the Christians of the seven churches were exhorted to be, refusing to compromise with the world-system regardless of personal cost or sacrifice. The entire host attributes salvation to God alone and gives him the glory he is due. This reminds us to be diligent in giving God glory in every aspect of our lives. Rom. 12:1 reminds us that worship, properly understood, is the presentation of our lives as a sacrifice living, holy and acceptable to God.

This group is now identified: ***Then one of the elders addressed me, saying, "Who are these, clothed in white robes, and from where have they come?" I said to him, "Sir, you know." And he said to me, "These are the ones coming out of the great tribulation. They have washed their robes and made them white in the blood of the Lamb"*** (verses 13-14). The definite article ("the") in the phrase ***the great tribulation*** adds emphasis. It means *that* great tribulation which the Bible speaks about. So this is not just any tribulation, but one specifically alluded to in the Scriptures. The phrase "the great tribulation" is drawn from the prophecy of Dn. 12:1: "And there shall be a time of trouble, such as never has been since there was a nation till that time." Jesus alludes to the same verse in Mt. 24:21: "For then there will be great tribulation, such as has not been from the beginning of the world until now, no, and never will be." The common dispensationalist view is that this tribulation occurs only at the end of the age immediately prior to the return of Christ (prior to which the church will be "raptured" from the world). This view is incorrect. The tribulation is referred to in 1:9, 2:9-10 and 2:22 as a *present reality, affecting both believers and unbelievers.* Several reasons can be given for this: (1) Revelation consistently interprets the prophecies of Daniel as finding fulfillment from the time of the resurrection and ascension. (2) The context of Matthew 24 shows Jesus was referring to a time long before his return (compare Mt. 24:21 with Mt. 24:23-27). (3) Jesus elsewhere views tribulation as a present reality for believers (Jn. 16:33), so when he speaks of tribulation in Mt. 21:20, 29, we can assume he is referring to something characteristic of what believers are to expect between his resurrection and his return. (4) At least 21 out of 23 uses of "tribulation" (Greek *thlipsis*) in Paul are clear references to the present life and experience of Christians (Rom. 5:3; 12:12; 2 Cor. 1:4, 8; 6:4; Eph. 3:13; Col. 1:24; 1 Thess. 1:6; 3:3; 2 Thess. 1:4, etc.). (5) The same is true in Heb. 10:33 and Jas. 1:27. So the New Testament use of "tribulation" seems to exclude the possibility that a particular event immediately prior to Christ's return is referred to here. Instead, the "great tribulation" is to be identified with the church age, the age in which Christians journey through a dangerous wilderness subject to attack, yet protected spiritually by God.

These saints *have washed their robes and made them white in the blood of the Lamb.* The only place where the saints in general are pictured as being made white (= in white clothes) is in Dn. 11:35 and 12:10, and this passage draws from that vision. The saints are those of every tribe and nation who have followed the Lamb *throughout the course of the church age.* All those of *every* generation with their names written in the Lamb's book of life are clothed in white garments (3:5) -- not just saints of an extremely-short period before the Lord's return. The Laodiceans of the first century were exhorted to buy white garments (3:18). The saints are pictured in this vision as coming out of their sojourn on earth during the church age and into their eternal reward, in the same sense that they are said to have come out of the great tribulation. Thus the church age and the great tribulation are one and the same thing. In 22:14, the washing of robes is the precondition *for anyone of any period of history* to enter the new Jerusalem. According to 1:1, Daniel's "last days" have begun with the arrival of God's kingdom in Jesus. Ever since then, the saints have endured tribulation, refused to compromise and been refined, with the end result that they are now portrayed (from an eternal perspective) in verses 9-17 as having obtained their eternal reward.

The explanation of the heavenly elder continues: *"Therefore they are before the throne of God, and serve him day and night in his temple; and he who sits on the throne will shelter them with his presence"* (verse 15). These believers have become a new priesthood. According to 1:6 and 5:10, Christians of all races and nations are the prophetic fulfillment of the promise originally given to Israel that they would become a kingdom of priests and a holy nation (Exod. 19:6). The portrayal of Christians in verses 15-17 as priests serving God in the heavenly temple develops this idea even further. Believers in Christ, Jew and Gentile alike, take the place of national Israel as the inheritor of God's promises. This vision also fulfills the vision of Ezekiel that God would set his "sanctuary in their midst forever" and that his "dwelling place" would be with them (Ezek. 37:26-28). This dwelling of God with his people will cause the nations to "know that I am the Lord who sanctifies Israel, when my sanctuary is in their midst forever" (Ezek. 37:28). Startlingly but very clearly, the latter-days Israel is now revealed as the church of every nation. In the same way, the latter-days kingship of David (Ezek. 37:24) is fulfilled in the reign of his descendent, the "Lion of the tribe of Judah" (Rev. 5:5). The sanctuary is placed not in a restored physical Jerusalem, contrary to the claims of dispensationalism, but is situated in his heavenly temple and in the new Jerusalem, in which believers of all nations will dwell (see chapters 21-22).

The words of the elder conclude. The same idea regarding Israel and the church appears in verses 16-17: *"They shall hunger no more, neither thirst anymore; the sun shall not strike them, nor any scorching heat. For the Lamb in the midst of the throne will be their shepherd, and he will guide them to springs of living water, and God will wipe away every tear from their eyes."* The previous verse shows how promises given to Israel through Ezekiel are fulfilled in the church. Now a further promise given to Israel through Isaiah is also fulfilled in the lives of Christian believers: "They shall not hunger or thirst, neither scorching wind nor sun shall strike them, for he who has pity on them will lead them, and by springs of water will guide them" (Isa. 49:10). Yet this makes sense of God's words to Isaiah in the same passage: "It is too light a thing that you should be my servant to raise up the tribes of Jacob and to bring back the preserved of Israel; I will make you as a light for the nations, that my salvation may reach to the ends of the earth" (Isa. 49:6). This promise is at least spiritually fulfilled in the present age, for the offer of the "water of life without price" is extended to all in Rev. 22:17. The further promise of Isaiah 25:8 is also alluded to: "He will swallow up death forever; and the Lord God will wipe away tears from all faces..." This promise receives its consummated fulfillment in the eternal city.

This picture of the entire body of the saints in God's presence in verses 9-17 is written to give saints suffering on earth assurance of the great reward coming to them on account of their faithfulness and refusal to compromise with the world system. It is applicable to all faithful Christians, in that all those who truly follow Christ will pay a price in some form or another. This may range from mild forms of social isolation to death itself. A very similar portrait of the saints in glory is found in 21:3-4, 6 and 22:3. The saints have received the rewards promised to the earthly saints in the seven churches. The latter passages describe how the saints have received the rewards promised to them on earth: they have now been given the white robes (3:4-5), the security of a place in the eternal temple (3:12), and food that will cause them never again to hunger (2:7, 17).

THE SEVENTH SEAL (8:1-5)

The last seal is accompanied by silence: *When the Lamb opened the seventh seal, there was silence in heaven for about half an hour* (verse 1). According to the futurist view, the seventh seal has no content, but simply leads into the following trumpet and bowl judgments which occur subsequently in time. This view, however, is mistaken. The content of the seal is divine judgment. The Old Testament gives the background. Hab. 2:20 states: "But the Lord is in his holy temple; let all the earth keep silence before him." The next verses, commencing at Hab. 3:3, describe the judgment of God: "God came from Teman…. before him went pestilence, and plague [a significant word in Revelation] followed at his heels" (Hab. 3:3-5). Similar to this is Zech. 2:13: "Be silent, all flesh, before the Lord, for he has roused himself from his holy dwelling." The verses immediately before this discuss the coming judgment on Babylon and the restoration of Jerusalem (as pictured in Revelation 17-22). Finally, Zeph. 1:7 states: "Be silent before the Lord God! For the day of the Lord is near…" Only a few verses later the prophet announces: "The great day of the Lord is near… A day of wrath is that day… I will bring distress on mankind… In the fire of his jealousy, all the earth shall be consumed; for a full and sudden end he will make of all the inhabitants of the earth" (Zeph. 1:14-18). The seventh seal thus completes the thought of the final judgment begun in the sixth seal. There is no need to give further detail, as this will be abundantly provided in the parallel accounts of the same event in 11:18; 14:14-20; 16:17-21; 18:9-24; 19:19-21; 20:11-15.

The duration of the silence is *about half an hour.* "Hour" in Revelation frequently refers to the sudden nature of God's judgment (3:3; 11:13; 14:7; 18:10). "Half" occurs in conjunction with mentions of judgment in Dn. 7:25; 9:27 and 12:7. This further demonstrates that all the numbers in Revelation are symbolic rather than literal. The phrase simply represents the fact that the judgment will be sudden and unanticipated. This confirms Jesus' warning: "The Son of Man is coming at an hour you do not expect" (Mt. 24:44).

John sees further detail: *Then I saw the seven angels who stand before God, and seven trumpets were given to them. And another angel came and stood at the altar with a golden censer, and he was given much incense to offer with the prayers of all the saints on the golden altar before the throne, and the smoke of the incense, with the prayers of the saints, rose before God from the hand of the angel* (verses 2-4). The seven trumpets introduce the next series of judgments, but before he can proceed further with this vision, he sees an angel with incense offering prayer. Incense is often associated with God's hearing prayer in the Old Testament. In Lev. 16:12-13, the priests are depicted as offering incense. In 7:15-17, Christians have been portrayed as priests and as the fulfillment of the Levitical priesthood. Here, it is not animal sacrifices but their prayers which are offered with incense before God. The altar is the same altar described in 6:9. The incense given by God to the angel represents the prayers of the deceased saints standing under that altar (6:10). The response they received in 6:11 was to wait until "the number of their fellow servants and their brothers should be complete." The fact of the incense going up indicates that their petitions have now been received by God. This is further confirmation that the sixth and seventh seals depict the final judgment. *Once this is understood, the entire futurist view of Revelation collapses.* The reason for this is that the futurist view sees the various sets of judgments as expressing separate and subsequent series of events, all these being restricted to a very short period of time before the Lord's return. We have argued, however, that the events referred to in all three sets of judgments (seals, trumpets and bowls), as well as the seven visions of conflict in chapter 12-14, are a *general description of the trials of believers and the judgment of unbelievers during the entire church age.* Each set of judgments concludes with a depiction of the last judgment at the return of Christ. This proves they are parallel descriptions of the same events, much like the four Gospels are parallel descriptions of the ministry of Christ. According to chapter 20, as we will see, this same church age is described figuratively as a long period of time (a millennium), at the conclusion of which comes yet another parallel description of the last judgment at Christ's return.

The vision draws to a conclusion: *Then the angel took the censer and filled it with fire from the altar and threw it on the earth, and there were peals of thunder, rumblings, flashes of lightning, and an earthquake* (verse 5). These words, marking the end of the seal judgments, are almost identical to the descriptions of the last judgment in 11:19 (the end of the trumpet judgments) and 16:8 (the end of the bowl judgments). The same angel, with "authority over fire," reappears in the description of the last judgment in 14:18-19. Clearly, all four passages describe the same event. The association of judgment with thunder and lightning is rooted in the description of Mount Sinai in Exod. 19:16-19. That judgment was also accompanied by trumpet blasts.

These events were prophesied by Ezekiel in a very similar passage. In Ezekiel 9, judgment begins with God's people being marked on the forehead by an angel to guarantee their safety. According to Ezekiel's prophecy, the unbelieving and rebellious city of Jerusalem will fall under God's judgment, but those sealed will be saved. Although there was an initial historical fulfillment in the final destruction of Jerusalem by the Babylonians, John sees this prophetic word as ultimately fulfilled in the sealing of Christians on their foreheads (7:3). Unbelievers will fall under judgment throughout the church age, but Christians will be spiritually protected, even though in other ways they may suffer (see further on 11:1-2). The unbelieving world will fall under total judgment at the end of history, and Christians will be completely delivered. As Ezekiel's judgment progresses, an angel is commanded: "Fill your hands with burning coals from between the cherubim, and scatter them over the city" (Ezek. 10:2). The final element of Ezekiel's vision is fulfilled here as the angel throws the *fire from the altar* on the earth.

After the interlude of chapter 7, describing the saints in glory, these verses take up where 6:17 left off, and conclude the scene of the final judgment. While the judgments on unbelievers throughout the church age are a preliminary answer to the prayers of the saints in 6:10, these verses represent the final and completed answer. Christians throughout the ages can take comfort that, whatever their measure of suffering has been on account of their testimony to Christ, an eternal reward far more precious and lasting than that suffering awaits them. They will receive this reward initially on their death and translation into God's presence (7:9-17), and ultimately at Christ's return as they enter the new creation portrayed in chapters 21-22.

5

THE SEVEN TRUMPETS

(8:6-11:19)

Revelation portrays four sets of seven judgments brought by God on an unbelieving world during the church age. The trumpets are the second of these sets (seals, trumpets, visions of conflict and bowls). All four describe the same series of events, but from slightly different perspectives. In the same way, the four Gospels all describe the same set of events, but from different perspectives. The trumpet judgments, like the bowl judgments, are based on the plagues of Exodus. The trumpet judgments place particular emphasis on the fact that the plagues are brought by God to harden the hearts of unbelievers and seal their doom, even as was the case with Pharaoh and the Egyptians. The first trumpet features hail, fire and blood and is modeled on the plague of hail and fire (Exod. 9:22-25). The second and third trumpets feature the poisoning of the sea and the waters and are modeled on the plague on the Nile (Exod. 7:20-25). The fourth trumpet brings darkness, just as did the Egyptian plague (Exod. 10:21-23). The fifth trumpet involves locusts, like the original plague (Exod. 10:12-15). The purpose of the plagues was not so much to cause the Egyptians to repent as to demonstrate their hardness of heart and the rightness of God's judgment against them, and to release that judgment. According to Exod. 4:21, the plagues were sent to harden Pharaoh's heart with the result that he would *refuse* to let the people go. This in turn would release the judgment of God against Pharaoh and his nation (Exod. 7:3-4). Most importantly, however, the plagues were sent simply so that God himself would be glorified over all the gods of Egypt (Exod. 7:5; 8:10). The same pattern plays out in the trumpet judgments. The Exodus plagues turn out to be prophetic forerunners of these judgments. Although some may repent, the ultimate purpose of the judgments is the hardening of the hearts of unbelievers and the bringing to pass of God's judgment. The ultimate goal of the judgments, however, is to glorify God and demonstrate his authority over the nations of the world.

But why did John see trumpets? How do they play into this overall scenario? At Mount Sinai, shortly after the Israelites left Egypt, a "very loud trumpet blast," along with thunder and lightning, marked the presence of God on the mountain. The sound of the trumpet "grew louder and louder" as God came down and called Moses up to meet with him. God's first words to Moses were: "I am the Lord your God who brought you out of the land of Egypt, out of the house of slavery" (Exod. 20:2). The sound of the trumpet signaled the ultimate judgment of God on Egypt expressed through the deliverance of his people. The second passage of significance, of course, is the story of Jericho. The trumpets blown by the priests on seven successive days are not about warning, but judgment. The physical ark was present at Jericho (Josh. 6:11-13), and now the heavenly ark is revealed in the eternal temple at the blowing of the seventh trumpet (11:19). The first six trumpets of Jericho are preparatory to the final trumpet, even as the disasters of the first six trumpet judgments lead up to the final judgment of the seventh trumpet (11:15-19). The destruction of Jericho is a prophetic forerunner of the destruction of the wicked earthly city "symbolically called Sodom and Egypt" (11:8). Like the sixth and seventh seals, the sixth and seventh trumpets deal with events surrounding the return of Christ, his final victory and the last judgment. This shows they are parallel accounts of the same set of events. The overall significance of the trumpets is that they highlight the fact that Revelation portrays the journey of the church out of Egypt (Babylon), into the protected place in the wilderness (the church age), and eventually into the promised land (the new Jerusalem).

THE FIRST FOUR TRUMPETS (8:6-12)

The trumpet judgments begin: *Now the seven angels who had the seven trumpets prepared to blow them.* This new vision has been introduced in verse 2 with the words "Then I saw." It was temporarily interrupted by the conclusion of the seals vision (verses 3-5). Although John saw this vision after that of the seal judgments, the events related in it occur at the same time as those related in the seals. *The first angel blew his trumpet, and there followed hail and fire, mixed with blood, and these were thrown upon the earth. And a third of the earth was burned up, and a third of the trees were burned up, and all green grass was burned up* (verse 7). The fire is not literal, but figurative. This is the case elsewhere in Revelation. For instance, the "seven spirits of God" (the Holy Spirit) are described in 4:5 as "seven torches of fire." The angel of 10:1 had "legs like pillars of fire," and Jesus' eyes are described as "like a flame of fire" (1:14; 2:18; 19:12). At the outset of the book, John spoke of visions communicated by symbolic means (see 1:1). The fire symbolizes God's judgment. It has its origins before God's throne (4:5), even as the trumpets have their origin "before God" (8:2). The first trumpet deals with the destruction of agriculture (the judgments come on earth, trees and grass). As with the Exodus plague of hail and fire, on which it is based, it affects only a portion of the food supply (Exod. 9:26, 32). It is similar to the third seal judgment, which brings a partial famine (6:6). Ezekiel prophesied a judgment of famine on disobedient Israel (Ezek. 4:16), and the judgment would be symbolized by fire (Ezek. 5:1-4). If this also lies behind John's vision, then disobedient Israel is pictured here as a prophetic forerunner of the last-days evil world system later to be identified as spiritual Babylon (chapters 17-18).

The second angel blew his trumpet, and something like a great mountain, burning with fire, was thrown into the sea, and a third of the sea became blood. A third of the living creatures in the sea died, and a third of the ships were destroyed (verses 8-9). The Old Testament often uses mountains as a symbolic representation of nations being judged by God (Isa. 41:15; Ezekiel 35; Zech. 4:7). In Revelation, mountains also speak of kingdoms, good or bad (14:1; 17:9; 21:10). This vision is likely rooted in Jeremiah's portrayal of Babylon as a "destroying mountain" which itself will be destroyed by fire (Jer. 51:25) and sink into the waters (51:64). *The third of the sea* alludes to the plague on the Nile (Exod. 7:20-21). The judgment pictures the destruction of maritime commerce, and thus of international trade. This is fleshed out explicitly in the depiction of the judgment of Babylon in 18:11-19.

The third angel blew his trumpet, and a great star fell from heaven, blazing like a torch, and it fell on the rivers and on the springs of water. The name of the star is Wormwood. A third of the rivers became wormwood, and many people died from the water, because it had been made bitter (verses 10-11). Fire symbolizes God's judgment, in this case focussed on the international maritime economic system. This would bring economic ruin and famine. Stars refer elsewhere in Revelation to angelic beings representing people or nations, and such a being of an evil nature could be involved here. This is supported by the fact that in Isa. 14:12-15, Babylon seems to be represented by an angelic being cast down from heaven. *Wormwood* refers to Jeremiah's prophecy that God would judge disobedient people by giving them wormwood (translated "bitter food" in ESV) and poisoned water (Jer. 9:15; 23:15). There and elsewhere in the Old Testament (Deut. 29:17-18; Prov. 5:4; Am. 5:6-7), wormwood (a bitter herb which pollutes water) is used in a figurative sense to refer to the harsh results of God's judgment.

The fourth angel blew his trumpet, and a third of the sun was struck, and a third of the moon, and a third of the stars, so that a third of their light might be darkened, and a third of the day might be kept from shining, and likewise a third of the night (verse 12). The Exodus plague of darkness is the background here (Exod. 10:21-29). The darkness is not literal. Joel 2:1-10 speaks similarly of the sun and moon growing dark as a *figurative description* of God's judgment on Israel. The last judgment is pictured in Revelation in similar but more drastic terms (6:12-13). Particularly significant for an understanding of this trumpet judgment is Zeph. 1:15-16, where the prophet describes God's judgment on Israel as "darkness and gloom," and "as a day of trumpet blast." The judgments Zephaniah was referring to were not eschatological, but came to pass in the course of Israel's history, and obviously did not involve a literal darkness. Darkness describes the life of any nation or society which rejects the ways of God. Sin is its own punishment, and ungodly ways serve only to deepen the darkness in which people live.

That the events described in the first four trumpets occur throughout the church age is indicated by two things. First, like the seals, they are precipitated by the resurrection and ascension of Christ to his heavenly throne. From the moment Christ ascends and begins to rule, the judgments commence. Second, they are all clearly differentiated from the final judgment. They do not strike all the earth's people, but various nations at various times. The trumpets are modeled on the plagues of Exodus and are described in 9:20 as "plagues." According to 22:18, "plagues" describe divine judgments which may strike at any point during the church age. Moses prophesied that the Old Testament plagues would come upon a disobedient Israel (Deut. 28:27). Amos declared the fulfillment of this word: "I sent upon you a pestilence after the manner of Egypt... yet you did not return to me" (Am. 4:10). Micah (7:8-17) took it further, prophesying that in the latter days (which Revelation understands as beginning with Christ), the nations of the world would experience the judgments that came upon Egypt. At the same time, in the midst of suffering and battle, God would protect his people: "He will bring me out to the light; I shall look upon his vindication" (Mic. 7:9). This prophetic word of Micah is fulfilled in these plagues. Through the sufferings, deprivation and death continually occurring in history, unbelievers are confronted with the reminder that the world and their lives remain in the hands of God and that their idolatrous trust in things other than God has been gravely and fatally misplaced.

INTRODUCTION TO THE LAST THREE TRUMPETS (8:13)

The last three trumpets are introduced by a phrase indicating a new vision: *Then I looked, and I heard an eagle crying with a loud voice as it flew directly overhead, "Woe, woe, woe to those who dwell on the earth, at the blasts of the other trumpets that the three angels are about to blow!"* (verse 13). That the eagle flies *directly overhead* is a foreboding of disaster. Creatures flying "directly overhead" in Revelation anticipate the coming of judgment (14:6; 19:17). Eagles often signal coming destruction in the Old Testament (Deut. 28:49; Jer. 4:13; 48:40; Lam. 4:19; Ezek. 17:3; Hos. 8:1). The fifth and sixth trumpets differ from the first four in that they have a universal impact, strike directly at unbelievers (rather than just their environment) and have the explicit involvement of demons. Beginning at 8:13, the spiritual nature of this judgment becomes very clear.

THE FIFTH TRUMPET (9:1-12)

The last three trumpets are introduced by announcement of a further vision: *And the fifth angel blew his trumpet, and I saw a star fallen from heaven to earth, and he was given the key to the shaft of the bottomless pit* (verse 1). The star is similar to that in 8:10, likely an evil angel representing people on earth and sharing in their judgment. It is significant that Jesus uses very similar words to describe Satan's fall from heaven: "I saw Satan fall like lightning from heaven" (Lk. 10:18). This angel may well be the "angel of the bottomless pit" mentioned in 9:11. This fallen angel is *given the key to the shaft of the bottomless pit.* The phrase *is given* is a "divine passive," indicating the key is given by Christ, who holds the keys to Death and Hades (1:18). Satan has no power to unleash his fury on earth unless given permission by Christ to do so. Beginning at this verse, we see ever more clearly the sovereignty held by God and Christ over the forces of evil, and that God is working through all events of history, even those in which believers suffer. This is meant to give comfort to believers as they refuse to compromise with the culture around them and choose instead to remain faithful to Christ.

The narrative continues: *He opened the shaft of the bottomless pit, and from the shaft rose smoke like the smoke of a great furnace, and the sun and the air were darkened with the smoke from the shaft* (verse 2). This is the ultimate fulfillment of the prophecy of Joel 2:10, 31; 3:15 regarding God's judgment, at first visited on historical Israel but now in the last days coming on the nations of the world. **Smoke,** here as elsewhere in Revelation (14:11; 18:9, 18; 19:3) indicates divine judgment. The smoke and the resulting darkness refer to the spiritual deception of unbelievers. Darkness in the New Testament symbolizes the spiritual blindness which causes people to reject God and Christ (Lk. 11:36; Jn. 1:5; 3:19-21; 8:12; 11:10; 12:35-36; Rom. 13:12; 2 Cor. 4:4; 1 Pet. 2:9; 1 Jn. 1:5). As a result of Christ's resurrection, the devil and his agents are beginning to be judged, and along with this comes judgment on those on earth who have followed them. Their deception by the enemy is a form of divine judgment. Sin is its own punishment.

The locusts come upon the earth: *Then from the smoke came locusts on the earth, and they were given power like the power of scorpions of the earth. They were told not to harm the grass of the earth or any green plant or any tree, but only those people who do not have the seal of God on their foreheads* (verses 3-4). They are *given power* by God. This is another occurrence of the "divine passive." God is understood as the one enabling the action. As in the Exodus plague, it is God who sends the locusts (Exod. 10:12). But there is a difference here. The locusts in Exodus harmed the vegetation, but here they are instructed not to *harm the grass* but only the unsealed people. The seal, mentioned first in 7:4, signifies God's ownership of the saints. Their immunity from this trial indicates at the least the spiritual protection under which they live, in spite of other worldly trials they may endure. The darkening of the sun and air probably indicates an intensification of the plague of darkness in the fourth trumpet judgment (8:12). Such judgments bring fear, torment and confusion to unbelievers. There is an analogy to those Exodus plagues which harmed the Egyptians but not the Israelites (Exod. 8:22-24; 9:4-7, 26; 10:21-23).

The limits of the powers God has granted the locusts are now given: *They were allowed to torment them for five months, but not to kill them, and their torment was like the torment of a scorpion when it stings someone. And in those days people will seek death and will not find it. They will long to die, but death will flee from them* (verses 5-6). The five-month period is probably symbolic, like other numbers in Revelation, though some have suggested it may allude to the life-cycle of locusts. The torment is spiritual and psychological: *people will seek death and not find it.* Elsewhere in

Revelation "torment" has this kind of connotation. It is not the same as physical suffering (11:10; 14:10-11; 18:7, 10, 15; 20:10). Believers are not subject to this kind of suffering, for they have found their security in Christ. Moses prophesied that in the latter days, Israel would face the plagues of Egypt once again. The disobedient people of every nation take the place of disobedient Israel in this prophetic fulfillment, in the same way the church of every nation takes the place of obedient Israel. In Deut. 4:30, Moses warns the Israelites of the trials that would come upon them in the "latter days." In Deut. 28:27, 60-61, he identifies these as latter-day sicknesses and plagues of Egypt. These plagues would include locusts (28:38, 42), as well as "madness" and "confusion of mind" (28:28), "darkness" (28:29), a "trembling heart" and a "languishing soul" (28:65). The Egyptians lived in terror as they realized Yahweh was the only true God and his power was limitless. So now will unbelievers tremble as they begin to understand that their idolatrous worship of things other than the true God are bringing the judgment of that God upon them. Meanwhile, Christians will remain secure in the knowledge that God is sovereignly protecting them in all things (Rom. 8:28-39).

Next comes a detailed description of the locusts: *In appearance the locusts were like horses prepared for battle: on their heads were what looked like crowns of gold; their faces were like human faces, their hair like women's hair, and their teeth like lions' teeth; they had breastplates like breastplates of iron, and the noise of their wings was like the noise of many chariots with horses rushing into battle. They have tails and stings like scorpions, and their power to hurt people for five months is in their tails* (verses 7-10). The description contains repeated uses of the word "like," as John tries to relate the vision as clearly as he can. He sees something very similar to what Joel saw, and borrows from Joel's language to express it. Joel saw a plague of locusts attacking Israel, the onslaught being initiated, as here, by the blowing of a trumpet (Joel 2:1-11). God uses the locusts to judge disobedient Israel. Only a remnant will be saved (Joel 2:31-32). For Joel, the locusts represented enemy armies. In John's vision, the locusts harm the people, not the vegetation (as in Egypt), bringing a spiritual famine more than a physical one. John draws a picture of an enemy army. The locusts are given human characteristics of a ferocious nature. Their teeth are *like lions' teeth*. This comes from Joel 1:6: "A nation has come up against my land... its teeth are lions' teeth." The *noise of their wings was like the noise of many chariots with horses rushing into battle.* This comes from the description of the locust army in Joel 2:4-5: "Their appearance is like the appearance of horses... as with the rumbling of chariots, they leap... like a powerful army drawn up for battle." The statement that *they have tails and stings like scorpions* is drawn from Jeremiah. He speaks of an enemy army of horses who devour the land in judgment and compares them to serpents and adders that bite (Jer. 8:16-17). The judgment spoken of by Jeremiah comes on idolators (Jer. 8:2), just as does John's judgment (as will become clear in verse 20). Later, Jeremiah speaks of an enemy army God has raised up to judge Babylon, in which the horses are "like bristling locusts" (Jer. 51:27). Significantly, the judgment of Jeremiah 51 is also initiated by trumpets: "Blow the trumpet among the nations" (Jer. 51:27). Futurist interpreters see here a reference to war helicopters or strange creatures like those in a science fiction novel. But the imagery should be understood instead through its Old Testament background, allowing Scripture to interpret itself. The locusts represent the judgment of God on the sin of disobedient people. Joel's locust army is a literal, historical army God used to judge Israel. John's army is spiritual and demonic in nature, bringing judgment on unbelievers through confusion and despair. In neither case are either actual locust-type creatures (or war helicopters!) referred to.

These demonic forces *have as king over them the angel of the bottomless pit. His name in Hebrew is Abaddon, and in Greek he is called Apollyon* (verse 11). In the Old Testament, Abaddon is linked with Sheol, the place of the dead (Job 26:6; 28:22; Ps. 88:11; Prov. 15:11). The identification of this demonic angel as "king" over the others may indicate it is Satan himself. Apollyon in Greek means "Destroyer." Satan's kingdom is built on fear and destruction. He uses people for his wicked ends and then destroys them. History is littered with examples. By contrast, God's purposes for his people are always constructive or edifying. Even when he is refining those faithful to him, he is bringing good purposes out of it for them (Rom. 5:3-5; 8:28; 1 Pet. 1:6-9).

The fifth trumpet concludes with the statement, *The first woe has passed; behold, two woes are still to come* (verse 12). This does not mean that these events have already taken place. Rather, it is the vision which has concluded. The contents of the phrase "still to come" is literally "after these things," which refers to the latter days, but can also describe the order in which visions come one after another (see 4:1). Two more visions of woe are now to be described. In fact, the first five trumpet judgments refer to events occurring throughout the church age, and hence the events of the fifth trumpet would by no means have been exhausted at the time John received the vision.

THE SIXTH TRUMPET (9:13-21)

Then the sixth angel blew his trumpet, and I heard a voice from the four horns of the golden altar before God, saying to the sixth angel who had the trumpet, "Release the four angels who are bound at the great river Euphrates" (verses 13-14). Mention of the altar reminds us of the saints' cry for justice which came from "under the altar" (6:9). "Horns" refer to strength in the Bible (Ps. 22:21; 75:10; Dn. 7:2; Mic. 4:13), which signals that the reality of God's power is pictured here. The angelic voice orders the release of the *four angels who are bound at the great river Euphrates.* These are demonic angels, confined against their will in the same way as the demonic forces imprisoned in the bottomless pit pictured in 9:1-3. The "four winds of the earth" which are temporarily held back in 7:1 are the same evil beings as the four angels here who have been bound but are now released. Their mission will affect the whole earth. From the four rivers of Gen. 2:10-14 to the four corners of the earth in Rev. 7:1, the number four expresses the idea of the whole earth. The Euphrates is not the *literal* place where these angels are bound. The real meaning of "Euphrates" is found in the Old Testament. The regions around the Euphrates (Isa. 7:20; 8:7-8; Jer. 46:10) are identified as those areas from which enemy armies come. The background to this vision comes especially from Jeremiah. He also speaks of the army riding on horses and wearing armor (46:4 = Rev. 9:16-17), coming from the Euphrates (46:10 = Rev. 9:14), "like a serpent" (46:22 = Rev. 9:19), and "more numerous than locusts" (46:22-23, reminding us of Rev. 9:3). The Euphrates reappears in the sixth bowl vision (16:12), thus suggesting that the events of that vision and the sixth trumpet vision are the same. Originally, the Euphrates was home to both the Babylonian and Assyrian empires, which conquered Israel and Judea respectively. Both were agents of God's judgment on his people's unfaithfulness. Those empires are long gone, never to arise again in a literal sense (Jer. 51:26). In John's vision, the Euphrates is Biblical code for the spiritual (not literal or geographical) place from which the attack of Satanic forces comes.

The four angels, previously bound by God, are now released (also by God) on their deadly mission: *So the four angels, who had been prepared for the hour, the day, the month, and the year, were released to kill a third of mankind. The number of mounted troops was twice ten thousand times ten thousand; I heard their number* (verses 15-16). Even though Satan is involved, God is always sovereignly ruling over history. The size of the demonic army could literally be calculated as two hundred million, but is symbolic, as with other numbers in Revelation. The word *murias* ("ten thousand") is used in Greek to refer to an innumerable multitude, and the plural is used in the Greek translation of the Old Testament in the same way (Gen. 24:60; Lev. 26:8; Deut. 32:30; 2 Chron. 25:11-12; Mic. 6:7; and especially Dn. 7:10). It is used symbolically here to refer to an indefinitely large number.

The horses are described: *And this is how I saw the horses in my vision and those who rode them: they wore breastplates the color of fire and of sapphire and of sulfur, and the heads of the horses were like lions' heads, and fire and smoke and sulfur came out of their mouths* (verse 17). This emphasizes their destructive power, reinforced by the mention of *fire and smoke and sulfur.* This recalls the destruction of Sodom and Gomorrah, the only place in the Old Testament where fire, smoke and sulfur occur together (Gen. 19:24, 28). Smoke is linked in 9:2-3 with the confusion or darkness that symbolizes satanic deception. This deception is part of the divine judgment. Fire and sulfur (or brimstone) are used in Revelation to describe the final judgment of the wicked (14:10; 21:8) and of the dragon, beast and false prophet (19:20; 20:10). The account of the destruction continues: *By these three plagues a third of mankind was killed, by the fire and smoke and sulfur coming out of their mouths. For the power of the horses is in their mouths and in their tails, for their tails are like serpents with heads, and by means of them they wound* (verses 18-19). The demonic angels of verse 15, commissioned to kill a third of mankind, carry out their mission through these evil horses. The unbelievers pictured here are already spiritually dead, but now they are physically killed. The fact that *the power of the horses is in their mouths* reinforces the idea of deception introduced by the smoke. Deception is a threat even within the churches, as 2:6, 14-15 and 20-21 show. The horses are not literal, but figuratively represent deceptive forces of the enemy. The horses' tails are *like serpents with heads, and by means of them they wound.* Futurist writers attempt to identify these creatures with weapons of modern warfare depicting a battle in the middle east, but the Biblical references clearly point to a figurative understanding. The creatures represent demonic forces of deception. The serpent-like tails simply reinforce the link of the horses to Satan himself, who is known in Revelation as the "serpent" (12:9, 14-15; 20:2). Jesus describes demons as "serpents and scorpions" (Lk. 10:19). The fact that the sting of the serpent comes first in the form of deception points us back to the fact that Jesus calls the Pharisees serpents *because they were blind guides leading others astray* (Mt. 23:16, 33). Prov. 23:32-35 speaks of wine as a serpent whose sting leads to delusion. This deception is a prelude to the last judgment. It is probable that, like the fifth trumpet (9:4), this judgment does not affect those who are sealed (faithful believers). Unlike the fifth trumpet, however, the sixth trumpet involves mass death, and thus points to a time just before the final judgment.

These plagues, alas, have little redemptive effect: *The rest of mankind, who were not killed by these plagues, did not repent of the works of their hands nor give up worshiping demons and idols of gold and silver and bronze and stone and wood, which cannot see or hear or walk, nor did they repent of their murders or their sorceries or their sexual immorality or their thefts* (verses 20-21). These judgments are modeled on the plagues of Egypt. Like those plagues, they demonstrate the utter reality and sovereignty of God. However, also like those plagues, they serve only to harden unbelievers in their deception and rebellion. The basic sin here is that of idolatry – refusal to worship the one true God. Idolatry, however, inevitably leads on to a whole sorry list of other transgressions (verse 21). The root cause of this sinful behavior is that the idolator becomes as blind and foolish as the idol he worships: "Their idols are silver and gold.... they have mouths but do not speak; eyes but do not see. They have ears but do not hear... Those who make them become like them" (Ps. 115:4-8). The same truth is expressed by Paul's observation that refusal to worship the Creator leads to worship of the creation instead: "They exchanged the truth of God for a lie and worshiped and served the creature rather than the Creator" (Rom. 1:25). This in turns leads on to all manner of sin (Rom. 1:26-32). When we turn away from the living God and begin to worship anything other than him, Satan himself is revealed as the real power behind the idolatry. The enemy leads those deceived by his wiles into all manner of conduct which is abhorrent to God. We should be reminded that we do not have to set up pagan statues in our homes to qualify as idolaters. The pursuit of anything other than God himself is idolatrous, no matter how it manifests itself.

VISION GIVEN BETWEEN THE SIXTH AND SEVENTH TRUMPETS (10:1-11:13)

At the end of the sixth trumpet, John receives a new vision: *Then I saw another mighty angel coming down from heaven* (verse 1a). The vision about to unfold reminds us again that Revelation does not unfold a catalog of events listed in chronological order, but rather consists of a series of visions given to John which may or may not have a chronological sequence. At 10:1, John's vision of the trumpets is interrupted. This interruption continues until the vision of the trumpets resumes in 11:14. In this new vision, John is recommissioned to prophesy. The prophecy he is given concerns the relationship between believers and unbelievers during the church age, culminating in the final judgment. At that point, he resumes and concludes the relating of the trumpet vision, in which that judgment is set forth. This vision thus explains the *theological basis for the judgment on the wicked in the first six trumpets*. At the same time, it shows that these plagues are God's answer to the prayers of the saints for vindication (6:9-11; 8:3-5). The vision is divided into two parts. The first part (10:1-13) features the recommissioning of John by Christ as a prophet. The second part (11:1-13) concerns spiritual warfare during the church age.

JOHN RECOMMISSIONED AS A PROPHET
(10:1-13)

The *mighty angel* is likely the "strong angel" of 5:2, both of whom cry out with a "loud voice" (verse 3, as in 5:2). The angel is *wrapped in a cloud, with a rainbow over his head, and his face was like the sun, and his legs like pillars of fire* (verse 1b). The angel is so closely linked to Christ that he may be like the angel of the Lord in the Old Testament, a manifestation of God or Christ himself. Why do we say this? He is *wrapped in a cloud.* Elsewhere in Revelation, only Jesus is associated with clouds (1:7; 14:14). In the Old Testament, clouds are linked to God alone. Furthermore, the angel has a *rainbow over his head*, just like the appearance of God in Ezek. 1:26-28. The rainbow is around the throne of God in Rev. 4:3. His face is *like the sun,* just like that of Christ in Rev. 1:16, and his feet *like pillars of fire*, similar to those of Christ in 1:15. God appeared in the wilderness both in the pillar of fire and in the cloud (Exod. 13:20-22; 14:24; Num. 14:14). The point of this vision is to reassure God's people that he is with them in this present age in which God's people live in the wilderness (12:6), awaiting Christ's return. In verse 3, the angel's voice is "like a lion roaring," linking him with Christ, the "Lion of the tribe of Judah" (5:5).

The description of the angel is resumed: *He had a little scroll open in his hand* (verse 2a). In the vision of the heavenly temple, God gave a scroll to the Lamb, who alone could open it (5:1-5). Now the angel (probably Christ himself) gives the scroll to

John (as verse 10 will show). The fact that the book is given to John shows how John follows in Christ's footsteps, but the fact it is *little* differentiates between the great book opened by Christ himself (5:8-9) and the little one held in the hands of his followers. The meaning of both scrolls must be closely related. Both deal with the unfolding of world history following the resurrection of Christ and culminating in his return. On the basis of his death and resurrection, Christ took the great scroll and began to implement what was written in it concerning himself. This was the establishment of God's kingdom as prophesied by Daniel, and now fulfilled in the "last days" initiated by Christ's resurrection and ascension to the right hand of God. The contents of that scroll are set forth in chapters 6-22, culminating in the vision of the new Jerusalem. However, the vision of chapter 5 also revealed that this victory would occur in a mysterious and unexpected fashion, modeled on the suffering of the Lamb. Christ inherited the promises of God through suffering, and the vision of chapters 10 and 11 will show how his people follow the Lamb along that same path. The little scroll, therefore, represents the way in which Christians follow Christ in the path of suffering and resurrection, declaring the power of his cross in this fallen world.

The description continues: *And he set his right foot on the sea, and his left foot on the land, and called out with a loud voice, like a lion roaring. When he called out, the seven thunders sounded. And when the seven thunders had sounded, I was about to write, but I heard a voice from heaven saying, "Seal up what the seven thunders have said, and do not write it down"* (verses 2b-4). The living creature of 6:1 had "a voice like thunder," like the voice of the great heavenly multitude in 19:6. The seven thunders are thus some form of heavenly beings. John hears what the thunders say but is told to *seal [it] up* and *not write it down.* In many Old Testament passages, thunder refers to judgment (Exod. 9:23-34; 1 Sam. 7:10; Ps. 29:3). This is the case with the "voice like thunder" of 6:1, which initiates the seal judgments. What the seven thunders spoke probably relates to divine judgment. Why they are not revealed we do not know, though it may be because the seal, trumpet and bowl judgments are sufficient to indicate the plan of God during the church age. The vision about to unfold deals not so much with the nature of the judgments unbelievers will undergo throughout the church age, but rather the *reason* for those punishments. They suffer (as chapter 11 will unfold) because they reject the message of the two witnesses and persecute them.

And the angel whom I saw standing on the sea and on the land raised his right hand to heaven and swore by him who lives forever and ever, who created heaven and what is in it, the earth and what is in it, and the sea and what is in it, that there would be no more delay, but that in the days of trumpet call to be sounded by the seventh angel, the mystery of God would be fulfilled, just as he announced to his servants the prophets (verses 5-7). This angel is described similarly to the angel of Dn. 12:7. That angel also "was above the waters;" he also "raised his right hand and his left hand toward heaven;" and he also "swore by him who lives forever." This alerts us to the fact that the subject matter of the messages of the two angels will be similar. Daniel's angel prophesies concerning the last days, specifically referring to the "time, times and half a time" (Dn. 12:7). John identifies this period with the three and a half years or forty-two months of 11:2. Daniel's angel orders the vision to be sealed until that time. This is the vision now unfolded to John (see 1:1). To show further the continuity of God's self-revelation in Scripture, the words of Daniel's angel in turn mirror the prophetic words of God to Moses in Deut. 32:40. There also, God speaks of a coming vengeance that is "sealed up" (Deut. 32:34). But now, there is to be *no more delay.* The "little while longer" (6:11) the praying saints of 6:10 had to wait will draw to a close *in the days of the trumpet call to be sounded by the seventh angel.* This last trumpet call announces the end of history, the Lord's return and the establishment of his everlasting kingdom (11:15). According to Dn. 12:7, after the three and a half years (the "time, times and half a time"), the "shattering of the power of the holy people" will end. John announces that at the time of the seventh trumpet, the *mystery of God* will be *fulfilled, just as he announced to his servants the prophets.* Note the close similarity to Rom. 16:25-26, where the "mystery that was kept secret for long ages" has "now been disclosed and through the prophetic writings has been made known to all nations." Where the word "mystery" occurs in the New Testament, it frequently describes the way in which Old Testament prophecy has been fulfilled in ways not expected by the Jewish people (in addition to Rom. 11:25 see also Mt. 13:11; Mk. 4:11; Lk. 8:10; 2 Thess. 2:7; Eph. 3:3-4, 9).

This mystery is that of the cross. How could God save his people through putting his Son to the death of a common criminal? The mystery continues with the question the saints ask through the ages, "Why do God's people continue to have to suffer as they walk in the way of the cross?" Much of Revelation gives the answer to this, as it unfolds the warning judgments of God through history sent against unbelievers, his strengthening and purifying of his people in the midst of their suffering and persecution, and his eventual rewarding of those faithful saints in his eternal kingdom, along with his final condemnation of the wicked. At that final point, the mystery — the triumph of God through suffering and the cross — which began to be revealed at the resurrection, will be fully explained. The mystery involves the fact that believers, while suffering physical defeat, are inheriting spiritual victory. Their suffering itself constitutes part of the evidence which will convict the wicked on the day of judgment. Although this will only be fully apparent from the perspective of eternity, God gives strength and comfort through his Spirit to us now to encourage us that he does indeed work all things, even the hard things, together for our greater and eternal good (Rom. 8:28). Meanwhile unbelievers, apparently triumphant over the church, are storing up for themselves the judgment of God which is provisionally unleashed in the first six trumpets, but only fully expressed in the seventh. The little scroll or book shows that believers are following in the footsteps of the One who holds the large book, the One who suffered apparent defeat on the cross only to rise again in triumph on the third day. And, as 11:1-13 will show, the present defeat of the faithful church is the very means by which that church will rise triumphant in the judgment while looking upon the destruction of her enemies. But only those to whom God reveals this mystery can understand it. Daniel could not comprehend it. The Jews certainly did not understand it, for while hearing they did not understand. Otherwise, Paul says, "they would not have crucified the Lord of glory" (1 Cor. 2:8). But to the disciples was revealed "the mystery of the kingdom of God" (Mk. 4:10-11). And now the angel begins to reveal it to John, to the seven churches, and to each of us through the ages who read this prophetic message of comfort and assurance.

The vision resumes: *Then the voice that I had heard from heaven spoke to me again, saying, "Go, take the scroll that is open in the hand of the angel who is standing on the sea and on the land." So I went to the angel and told him to give me the little scroll. And he said to me, "Take and eat it; it will make your stomach bitter, but in your mouth it will be sweet as honey"* (verses 8-9). John is told to *take the scroll* from the angel (Christ), in the same way Christ took the scroll from the Father in 5:7. The original scroll contained God's judgments on the world. John, representing the church, in taking the similar scroll, participates in the authority of Jesus in judging the world. Jesus told his disciples they would sit on twelve thrones of judgment (Mt. 19:28). John is told to eat the scroll; *it will make your stomach bitter, but in your mouth it will be sweet as honey.*

These verses are based on Ezekiel's commissioning, in which he also is told to eat a scroll which is sweet in his mouth (Ezek. 2:8-3:3), but later evokes a bitter response (3:14). That John, like Ezekiel, eats the scroll signifies his complete commitment to its contents. The scroll is sweet because it contains God's words, which are sweeter than honey (Ps. 19:10). The bitterness describes the rejection of the divine message by a disobedient people, whether the Israel of Ezekiel's day or the "peoples and nations and languages and kings" (verse 11) of the church age, who already in John's day were rejecting God's words and sealing their doom. Jeremiah had a similar experience of eating God's words and in bitterness seeing them rejected (Jer. 15:15-18). The word *bitter* appears in Revelation only here and in the bitter waters of the third trumpet plague (8:11). This shows that the bitterness, symbolizing the rejection of the gospel and God's judgment on unbelievers, extends throughout the church age, during which the third trumpet judgment takes place. It also shows that this judgment had already begun in the days of John himself.

Having eaten the scroll, John is recommissioned: *And I took the little scroll from the hand of the angel and ate it. It was sweet as honey in my mouth, but when I had eaten it my stomach was made bitter. And I was told, "You must again prophesy about many peoples and nations and languages and kings"* (verses 10-11). The previous commissionings occurred in 1:10-20 and 4:1-2. The first commissioning resulted in the visions of chapters 2-3. The second commissioning resulted in the visions of chapters 4-9. This third commissioning leads on into the vision of chapter 11. As chapters 12 and following elaborate the vision of chapter 11, it is possible that this commissioning may extend to the rest of the book. The verb *prophesy* does not refer merely to predicting events of the future. Prophecy reveals God's will for the present. It is to be "heard" and "kept" (1:3; 22:7, 9). In this sense, John is a prophet in continuity with the Old Testament prophets, who called their hearers to repentance and obedience to the will of God. To understand Revelation as a series of predictions about a future the vast majority of its readers will never experience is to empty it of its true prophetic content, and make it irrelevant to all but the very last generation of believers before Christ's return.

SPIRITUAL WARFARE DURING THE CHURCH AGE (11:1-13)

The second part of the vision between the sixth and seventh trumpets now unfolds. The first part (chapter 10) focusses on John's recommissioning as a prophet. The second part (chapter 11) gives the content of the prophetic message. The message involves the judgment of those who persecute the church. The vision portrays explicitly what the trumpets only imply: the fierce conflict during the church age between God and the church, on the one hand, and the beast and the forces of evil, on the other. As such, it serves as a transition to the second half of the book, where these themes will be further developed.

THE MEASURING OF THE TEMPLE (11:1-2A)

John measures the temple: *Then I was given a measuring rod like a staff, and I was told, "Rise and measure the temple of God and the altar and those who worship there, but do not measure the court outside the temple; leave that out, for it is given over to the nations, and they will trample the holy city for forty-two months"* (verses 1-2). The futurist view sees this as referring to a rebuilt temple in the days immediately prior to the return of Christ, and the worshipers are a remnant of believing Jews. Those in the outer court are unbelieving Jews and will not be protected. Gentiles will attack Jerusalem during a literal forty-two month period and persecute the remnant. This text must be understood in the same way as the rest of Revelation -- figuratively rather than literally. The measuring of verse 1 is identical with the sealing of 7:3-4. It refers to the spiritual security God gives to his people in spite of whatever physical suffering they may endure in the world. The sealing in turn is linked with the mark placed on the foreheads of the faithful in Ezek. 9:4-6, which itself goes back to the mark of the blood which protected the Israelites in Exodus 12. This is confirmed by Zech. 1:16 and Jer. 31:38-40, where God measures the new Jerusalem in order to protect everything inside it. The prophetic measuring also fulfills the prophecy of Ezekiel 40-48, where the angel measures the latter-day temple or city of God, and declares that God is present within its bounds (Ezekiel 40-42). Similar Greek words for "measuring" are used approximately sixty times in the Greek Old Testament translation of Ezekiel. The same measuring rod reappears in Rev. 21:15-17, where it signifies the security of the new Jerusalem. This temple is to be occupied by Jewish and

Gentile Christians. All Christians are part of God's temple in this present age (Eph. 2:11-22). Likewise, Revelation teaches that all Christians will be pillars in God's eternal temple (3:12). The apostles represent the church of every nation present in the new Jerusalem (21:12-14).

In Ezekiel and in Revelation 21, the measuring denotes the presence of God in the community of faith in the eternal temple. In Revelation 11, it refers to the same presence of God indwelling and protecting those who compose God's temple on earth in the church age. The "temple of God" in the New Testament (outside of those places where the literal Jerusalem temple is in view) always refers to the church, either corporately (1 Cor. 3:16-17; 2 Cor. 6:16; Eph. 2:21) or represented by its members (1 Cor. 6:19). In Revelation, it refers to the eternal dwelling place of God, whether thought of as a present heavenly reality or as a future fulfillment in which all believers of every nation will participate (3:12; 7:15; 14:15, 17; 15:5-8; 16:1, 17; 21:22). The picture here refers to Christians as both the temple and as priests worshiping in it. This sounds odd, but the same picture is found in 1 Pet. 2:5 (see also Rev. 1:6 and 5:10). Ezekiel's prophecy concerning the last-days temple finds provisional fulfillment in the temple Jesus created on earth, and final fulfillment in the new Jerusalem. Nowhere in Revelation does the word "temple" (Greek *naos*) refer to a literal temple building. It refers either to the present heavenly temple, or to the future temple of the new Jerusalem. In 11:1-2, the people of God on earth are seen as part of the spiritual, heavenly temple into which deceased believers enter literally. Christ referred to his body as a new temple (Jn. 2:19-22), which is fulfilled in the new Jerusalem where the Lamb is the temple (Rev. 21:22).

The altar represents the place of sacrifice, and is identified in 6:9-10 with the sufferings faithful Christians faced on earth. If the temple represents the church in its spiritually-protected relationship with Christ, then the outer court, which is to be "trampled," represents the church in its interaction with the hostile pagan cultures in which it lives. The outer court is identified with the holy city in verse 2, and the holy city is the "beloved city" of 20:9 which is attacked by the end-time forces of evil. Both outer and inner courts belong to God, and the security of both will be fully established in the new Jerusalem. The outer court, however, is not to be measured. This implies it does not fall under the protection of God in the same way as the inner part of the temple. The phrase *leave that out* is literally "cast that out." This is the same Greek verb which refers to the rejection and persecution of God's people in this present age (see Mt. 21:39; Mk. 12:8; Lk. 4:29; 20:15; Jn. 9:34-35; Ac. 7:58). Christians must be prepared to endure suffering for the sake of Christ. This may be subtle (being socially excluded by others, for instance) or more severe. But we can be assured that our reward, whether through the presence of the Spirit now or our life in eternity late, is always incomparably greater.

THE FORTY-TWO MONTHS (11:2B)

What, then is the meaning of the *forty-two months*? If everything else in the vision is symbolic, so also must the time period be. The immediate reference is to Daniel (7:25; 12:7, 11-12), who prophesied a period of tribulation which would last for a "time, times and half a time" (=three and a half years or forty-two months) or 1,335 days (the same). For Daniel, this time was in the distant future, but for John it has begun (see 1:1), and will proceed throughout the church age until the return of Christ. Ultimately, the significance of the number probably lies in the forty-two encampments of the children of Israel in the wilderness (Num. 33:5-49), and the forty-two months of Elijah's judgment on Israel (Lk. 4:25; Jas. 5:17). Additionally, some scholars reckon that the children of Israel spent forty-two years in the desert, including a two-year period prior to their refusal to enter the Promised Land. The time references to the ministries of Moses and Elijah are reinforced by their identification as the two witnesses in the next verses (4-13). The trumpet plagues (in the midst of which this vision occurs) take us back to God's judgments on Egypt by which his people were released into the wilderness. In 11:6-8, 12:6 and 12:14, the community of faith are pictured as battling against Egypt, or as being protected in the wilderness. Here God is using both the situation of the Israelites and of Elijah as typological or prophetic illustrations pointing toward the events of the last days. The forty-two months is thus a Biblical way of linking together Moses, Elijah and the church. Verse 8 suggests that the trampling was initiated by Christ's death in Jerusalem ("where their Lord was crucified") and will continue until the end of the three and a half year period at the time of the last judgment (see on verses 13-19).

THE TWO WITNESSES (11:3-6)

The measuring of verse 1 involves the spiritual protection of God's people. The purpose of this measuring or process of protection is now explained: *"And I will grant authority to my two witnesses, and they will prophesy for 1,260 days, clothed in sackcloth." These are the two olive trees and the two lampstands that stand before the Lord of the earth. And if anyone would harm them, fire pours form their mouth and consumes their foes. If anyone would harm them, this is how he is doomed to be killed. They have the power to shut the sky, that no rain may fall during the days of their prophesying, and they have power over the waters to turns them into blood and to strike the earth with every kind of plague, as often as they desire* (verses 3-6). God's plan is designed to protect the witness of the church throughout the church age. His people will undergo suffering, but he will strengthen them so that they remain faithful as his witnesses. In these verses are depicted two prophetic figures, identified as *my two witnesses* who will *prophesy for 1,260 days, clothed in sackcloth.* They are further portrayed as *the two olive trees and the two lampstands that stand before the Lord of the earth.*

These witnesses are not individuals, but are to be identified with the church as it bears witness from the days of John until the Lord's return.

This interpretation is based on a number of considerations. (1) They are called *lampstands*, which 1:12-25 clearly identifies as the church(es). (2) Olive trees and lampstands both allude to the Holy Spirit, who is poured out upon all God's people (not just two), who will then prophesy (Joel 2:28-32; Ac. 2:17-21). (3) According to verse 7, the beast will "make war" on them. This alludes directly to Dan. 7:21, where a nation is attacked, not isolated individuals. (4) According to verses 9-13, the whole world will witness the (apparent) defeat of the witnesses. This is only understandable as a portrayal of something happening to the worldwide church (contrary to the unlikely view of futurists that it involves an isolated event viewed on television!). (5) The witnesses prophesy for three and a half years, the same time that the holy city (clearly the church) is trampled underfoot (verse 2), the "woman" of 12:6 (also clearly representing the church) is oppressed, and those dwelling in heaven (the deceased saints awaiting the resurrection of 13:6) are blasphemed.

olive trees
Zechariah's vision
Zech. 4:6 by my Spirit

The fact that there are two witnesses is significant. The words for "witness" (verse 3) and "testimony" (verse 7) are legal terms in Greek. The presence of two witnesses was the Old Testament requirement for determining a legal offense (Num. 35:30; Deut. 17:16). That is why Jesus sent out disciples in groups of two as legal witnesses to the gospel message (Matt. 18:16; Lk. 10:1-24; Jn. 8:17). Paul followed the same procedure (2 Cor. 13:1; 1 Tim. 5:19). Two angels, not one or three, bore witness to the resurrection (Luke 24:3) and to Christ's return (Ac. 1:10-11). The witnesses are *clothed in sackcloth*. This identifies them with John the Baptist and his prophetic forerunner Elijah (Mk. 1:6; 2 Kgs. 1:8). They mourn over the coming legal judgment on the world and its people.

The witnesses stand *before the Lord*, in the same way the actual lampstands stood in the tabernacle and temple. This signifies that they are spiritually protected, even though exposed to attack in their earthly existence. The witnesses are part of the new temple in Christ. The portrayal of the olive trees comes from Zechariah's vision of two olive trees standing before the lampstand in the temple (Zech. 4:12-14). Zechariah's olive-tree witnesses also "stand by the Lord of the whole earth" (4:14). In his vision, Zechariah saw a king and a priest (Zerubbabel and Joshua) re-estab-lishing a literal temple. In the prophetic fulfillment, John sees a corporate witness (the church), which he has already identified as kings and priests (1:6; 5:10; also 20:6) helping to establishing a spiritual and eternal temple. Zechariah saw an angel measuring Jerusalem with the goal of building God's house in it (Zech. 1:16-17; 2:1-5). Measuring is thus a symbolic way of referring to God's protection. John is given a measuring rod by an angel, signifying the protection by God of his spiritual temple, the church.

The powers given to the witnesses in verses 5-6 demonstrates the result of God's measuring in verse 1. They are protected by him against spiritual harm so that they can faithfully carry out their prophetic witness. The fire that *pours from their mouth and consumes their foes* signifies the pronouncing of God's judgment on the world's sins. This alludes to the prophetic commissioning of Jeremiah: "I am making my words in your mouth a fire, and this people wood, and the fire shall consume them" (Jer. 5:14). Christ's judgment is pictured figuratively as a sword coming out of his mouth (1:16; 2:12, 16; 19:15). In verse 6, the witnesses are revealed as the fulfill-ment of the Old Testament expectation that Moses and Elijah would return in the latter days to restore Israel: *They have the power to shut the sky, that no rain may fall during the days of their prophesying, and they have power over the waters to turn them into blood and to strike the earth with every kind of plague, as often as they desire.* In Mk. 9:4-7, Moses and Elijah, as the two witnesses legally needed, appear on the mountain in order to testify that Jesus is the Son of God. Moses and Elijah represent the law and the prophets, and the comparison to them here indicates that the church is the fulfillment of the latter-days restoration of Israel prophesied throughout the Old Testament. The specific references in verse 6 are to Elijah's power to withhold rain from the earth (1 Kings 11) and Moses' ability to turn water into blood (Exod. 7:17-25). Use of the word *plague* also takes us back to the ministry of Moses. The three and a half year period of the witnesses' ministry corresponds to the same time period of Elijah's ministry of judgment by drought (Lk. 4:25; Jas. 5:17), and to the forty-two encampments of Israel under Moses in the desert. The judgments are not literal. As with the seal and trumpet visions (also referred to as "plagues," 9:20), they are symbolic of all judgments God brings against unbelievers to remind them of their rebellion and their eventual doom.

The opening verses of this chapter have been full of symbolism. John has been told to measure the temple, but exclude the outer court. There are olive trees, and lampstands and fire coming from mouths. The judgment symbolized by the fire and blood speak of any means by which God reminds unbelievers of his authority over the natural creation. Particularly significant for the understanding of this passage is the incident in which the disciples suggest to Jesus that they follow Elijah's example by calling down fire on the disobedient villages of the Samaritans (Lk. 9:51-56). Jesus rejected their request, but shortly afterward sent out thirty-six groups of two (legal) witnesses to declare both the grace and the judgment of God. In this same way, the two witnesses in John's vision declare the judgment of God not by calling down literal fire, but by declaring the Gospel and the consequences of disobeying it. The nature of the plagues they bring are closely related to the trumpet plagues, which in turn are rooted in the plagues of Exodus. In both cases, the judgments are described as "plagues" (verse 6 and 9:20). They are directed against "those who dwell on the earth" (8:13 and 11:10). They are initiated by those who are given power to pronounce God's judgment (9:13 and 11:6). Both involve famine (8:7 and 11:6), death (9:15 and 11:5) and harm of various kinds (9:10 and 11:5). Fire comes from the mouths of those with the power to kill (9:17-18 and 11:5). Water turns into blood (8:8 and 11:6). There are supernatural phenomena involving the sky or heavens (8:10 and 11:6). Finally, the result of all this is that unbelievers are "tormented" (9:5-6 and 11:10). Both sections conclude with some unbelievers being killed (9:20 and 11:13). We have already seen that the trumpet and seal judgments represent two sets of visions describing the same general events. This section, placed between the sixth and seventh trumpets, retells the story of both trumpet and seal judgments from yet another perspective. The particular emphasis of the vision is on what happens *to the church* during the period commencing with the resurrection and ending with the Lord's return.

THE FINAL BATTLE AND THE LAST JUDGMENT (11:7-13)

The vision moves to the very end of history: *And when they have finished their testimony, the beast that rises from the bottomless pit will make war on them and conquer them and kill them, and their dead bodies will lie in the street of the great city that symbolically is called Sodom and Egypt, where their Lord was crucified. For three and a half days some from the peoples and tribes and languages and nations will gaze at their dead bodies and refuse to let them be placed in a tomb, and those who dwell on the earth will rejoice over them and make merry and exchange presents, because these two prophets had been a torment to those who dwell on the earth* (verses 7-10). The church finishes its witness (**testimony**) to Christ at the end of history, immediately before the Lord's return. In 6:11, during the seals vision, John is shown that a time will come when the full number of the saints to be killed is completed, and this verse describes that day. At the time of the completion of their witness, the faithful believers will be killed. Jesus spoke of a time when the church would appear to be defeated, when Christians would be "put to death" and "hated by all nations." This would be a time, he said, when "many will fall away and betray one another and hate one another." At that time, "lawlessness will be increased" and "the love of many will grow cold. But the one who endures to the end will be saved" (Mt. 24:9-13). The words that Christ speaks to John here, **the beast.... will make war on them and conquer them and kill them** are the same as the angel spoke to Daniel. Daniel was told that the horn that arises from the fourth beast "made war with the saints and prevailed over them" (Dn. 7:21). The parallelism of these verses to Matthew 24 and Daniel 7 shows that the two witnesses are symbolic representatives *of the people of God as a whole*, for it is the people of God who are referred to in both other texts, *not certain individuals.* The same event is described again in Rev. 20:8-10, where the beast makes final war against "the camp of the saints and the beloved city."

The fact that **the beast... arises from the bottomless pit** does not mean that the beast has no function or power until the very end of the church age. What it means is that, by God's permission, his deceptive activity is allowed to manifest openly and with little constraint at that time. But this apparent release is meant only to expose the power of evil for what it is, and prepare it for its ultimate judgment. The same event is described in 17:8, where the beast rises "from the bottomless pit" and goes "to destruction." The final warfare of the beast against the saints at the very end of the church age will result in the beast's final destruction. The same event is described for a third time in 20:7 ("when the thousand years are ended, Satan will be released from his prison"). This final warfare against the church will make it seem as though the church is defeated: **their dead bodies will lie in the street of the great city that symbolically is called Sodom and Egypt, where their Lord was crucified.** In the Old Testament, lack of burial constituted a gross indignity (Ps. 79:1-5; Isa. 14:19-20). At the end of the age, the influence of the church will seem to have been suppressed, marginalized or even eradicated owing to the severity of the persecution. The **great city**, which in chapter 17 is portrayed as end-times Babylon, is here compared to Sodom, Egypt and even the Jerusalem which crucified Christ. This city is to be understood **symbolically**, as these multiple references indicate. Babylon and Egypt were the places of captivity, and Sodom and Jerusalem symbolize man's rebellion and evil. The city is not in any one location, but represents the activity of an evil power in the hearts of rebellious people across the world. That the event occurs on a worldwide basis is shown again in verse 9, where it is said that it will be witnessed by **peoples and tribes and languages and nations** (this does not, as dispensationalism supposes, refer to an event taking place in Jerusalem broadcast across the world on television). This will occur for a period of **three and a half days**. This phrase identifies a much shorter period than the three and a half years (verse 3; also 12:14 and 13:5) of the witnesses' testimony. The church will proclaim the gospel throughout the church age, but at its very end will face a short period of intense persecution and apparent defeat. The parallel to Christ's ministry is obvious. The three and a half years corresponds roughly to the powerful ministry of Christ on earth, whereas the three and a half days corresponds to the time he spent in the tomb. The church follows in the footsteps of her Lord. This latter apparent defeat will be a source of rejoicing for *those who dwell on the earth. Those who dwell on the earth* is a phrase used throughout Revelation to refer to unbelievers whose judgment comes on account of their persecution of the saints and on account of their idolatry (3:10; 6:10; 8:13; 13:8, 12, 14; 14:6-9; 17:2, 8).

But as these devastating events are occurring, something even more surprising takes place: *But after three and a half days a breath of life from God entered them, and they stood up on their feet, and great fear fell on those who saw them* (verse 11). These words are taken from Ezek. 37:5, 10. This is the ultimate fulfillment of Ezekiel's vision of the dry bones. Ezekiel's picture of the spiritual resurrection of Israel (God's breath breathed back into his defeated people) is fulfilled initially in the outpouring of the Spirit on the church, but here is described its consummated fulfillment. Whether this refers to the final resurrection of the saved or to a final glorious triumph of the church coinciding with Christ's return is not clear, though there is not a great difference between the two. This resurrection is the vindication of the witnesses and their testimony. As a result, *great fear fell on those who saw them.* This is not a holy fear marking repentance, but rather the reversal of their previous attitude of rejoicing. Similar fear fell upon the Egyptians at the deliverance of the children of Israel at the Red Sea (Exod. 15:16; Ps. 105:38). The parallel is not an accident, for the plagues performed through Moses have been mentioned in verse 6, and form the background to the trumpet judgments as a whole.

The triumph of the church continues to unfold: *They they heard a loud voice from heaven saying to them, "Come up here!" And they went up to heaven in a cloud, and their enemies watched them* (verse 12). This verse cannot be interpreted as a "rapture," which is followed by a further period of tribulation and a thousand-year millennium. The reason is that this event immediately precedes the sounding of the seventh trumpet, the last judgment and the beginning of God's eternal reign (verse 15). There is no room, as in the futurist view, for a tribulation or millennium to follow. The vision simply reveals that God's last act before consummating the destruction of the world and bringing the return of his Son is the taking up of the church into eternity. Biblically, the *cloud* refers to the presence of God with his people (Exod. 13:21-22; Num. 14:14; Deut. 1:33; Ps. 78:1; Isa. 4:5; Ezek. 1:4; Dn. 7:13; Mt. 17:5; 24:30; Mk. 9:7; Lk. 9:34-35, Ac. 1:9). The fact that the church goes up to heaven in a cloud signifies that its witness has been vindicated, even as the witness of Christ was vindicated by his resurrection (Ac. 1:9-11). It also signifies the church has entered into the fullness of God's presence. This will be obvious to the "earth-dwellers": *their enemies watched them* as it happened. This probably refers to the context of the final judgment, at which their doom will be unfolded. The taking up of believers into heaven, the end of history and the last judgment are all part of the same event.   •

At the same time as the church is vindicated, judgment falls upon the lost: *And at that hour there was a great earthquake, and a tenth of the city fell. Seven thousand people were killed in the earthquake, and the rest were terrified and gave glory to the God of heaven* (verse 13). The *great earthquake* also appears in 6:12 and 16:18, both of which describe the last judgment. The earthquake initiates that judgment, which is completed by the blowing of the seventh trumpet in verse 15. The wording comes from Ezek. 38:19, where a "great earthquake" destroys Gog. In verses 11-12, the church fulfills the resurrection vision of Ezekiel 37, and in verse 13 the generation of unbelievers living immediately prior to Christ's return fulfills the judgment vision of Ezekiel 38. The fact that *a tenth of the city fell* and *seven thousand people were killed* points to an initial judgment on a substantial number of unbelievers. As with all numbers in Revelation, these are figurative in nature. The rest *were terrified and gave glory to the God of heaven.* This could mean a mass repentance (they gave glory to God). However, *terrified* (Greek *emphobos*) is used in the Bible to refer to human fear, not the fear of God. The ministry of the witnesses (the church) is modeled on the ministry of Christ. His resurrection was accompanied by an earthquake and an angel speaking, and was witnessed by unbelievers who "trembled and became like dead men" (Matt. 28:4). Here also there is an earthquake, an angelic voice speaking from heaven (verse 12) and unbelieving witnesses who are terrified. The phrase *gave glory* may go back to Nebuchadnezzar's giving glory to God (Dan. 2:46-47; 4:36), as Nebuchadnezzar represents Babylon, the forerunner of the end-times Babylon of verse 13. At the same time as Nebuchadnezzar gave praise to God, he carried on worshipping idols (Dn. 3:1). There is no indication elsewhere in Revelation, and particularly in the parallel visions of seals, bowls and trumpets, of a last-minute mass conversion of the lost.

THE SEVENTH TRUMPET (11:14-19)

The blowing of the sixth trumpet was described in 9:13-21. This is followed by the vision of 10:1-11:13, which describes the events of the period from the resurrection to the Lord's return, but featuring the witness of the church and the attack against it, rather than the plagues depicted by the trumpets. Now John returns to the trumpet vision. The sounding of the seventh trumpet represents the end of history, as is clear from the angelic pronouncement of 10:7, that "in the days of the trumpet call to be sounded by the seventh angel, the mystery of God would be fulfilled." According to 8:13, the last three trumpets represent the three woes, and thus the seventh trumpet is the final woe: *The second woe has passed; behold, the third woe is soon to come. Then the seventh angel blew his trumpet, and there were loud voices in heaven, saying, "The kingdom of the world has become the kingdom of our Lord and of his Christ, and he shall reign forever and ever"* (verses 14-15). The eternal and consummated reign of God over creation commences, with Christ ruling beside him. This is the fulfillment of Daniel's vision of the Son of man receiving a "kingdom.... that shall not be destroyed" (Dn. 7:14). God has established total sovereignty over all creation, and the devil is completely vanquished.

The heavenly worship continues: *And the twenty-four elders who sit on their thrones before God fell on their faces and worshiped God, saying, "We give thanks to you, Lord God Almighty, who is and who was, for you have taken your great power and begun to reign. The nations raged, but your wrath came, and the time for the dead to be judged, and for rewarding your servants, the prophets and saints, and those who fear your name, both small and great, and for destroying the destroyers of the earth"* (verses 16-18). As in 4:4, the elders are angelic representatives of both Old Testament and New Testament saints (twelve tribes plus twelve apostles). Three times prior to this, God has been addressed as the One who was, who is and who is to come (1:4, 8; 4:8). Now he is still addressed as the One *who is and who was.* Instead of being addressed as the One who "is to come," however, he is pictured here as the one who has *taken [his] great power and begun to reign.* This describes the fact that, with the sounding of the seventh trumpet, God's everlasting kingdom has been established. Immediately prior to this *the nations raged*, but this rage was of no effect. Instead, the last judgment is inaugurated: *the wrath of God... and the time for the dead to be judged.* Every other use of *wrath* (Greek *orge*) in Revelation refers to the final judgment (6:16, 17; 14:10-11; 16:19; 19:15). This is the same judgment of the dead described in 20:12-13. The only difference is that this verse gives the reason for the judgment. Following the Old Testament principle of an eye for an eye, it is time *for destroying the destroyers of the earth.* The punishment fits the crime (see also 14:8-10; 16:6; 17:14; 18:6, 7-8 for the same reality). The background to this verse is Jer. 51:25: "Behold, I am against you, O destroying mountain... which destroys the whole earth." In Jeremiah's vision, the mountain is *earthly Babylon*. Verse 13 spoke of the fall of a great city, which in 17:18 is revealed as *spiritual Babylon*. In 19:2, in a passage depicting the last judgment closely parallel to this text, God judges spiritual Babylon (all the unbelieving peoples of the earth) for her destructive work and avenges on her the blood of his servants.

This passage and its parallels shows once again how the visions of Revelation describe *the same set of events from different perspectives*, rather than presenting a chronological listing of events, where we would have to understand what is portrayed in 11:18 as occurring before anything described in the rest of the book, and after everything described beforehand.

The portrayal of the seventh trumpet closes in verse 19: ***Then God's temple in heaven was opened, and the ark of his covenant was seen within his temple. There were flashes of lightning, rumblings, peals of thunder, an earthquake, and heavy hail.*** In Revelation, these phenomena are always indicators of the final judgment (4:5; 8:5; 16:18). The seven trumpets recall the seven trumpets of Jericho (Joshua 6). The heavenly ***ark of his covenant*** is revealed, even as the earthly ark, following the trumpeters, led the procession around the besieged city. Following both sets of trumpets comes an earthquake and the victory of God's people. The trumpet plagues are modeled on the plagues of Exodus. They conclude on a note of triumph. Even as the children of Israel entered the earthly Promised Land at Jericho, so now the saints of every nation enter the heavenly Promised Land.

6

VISIONS OF CONFLICT

(12:1-15:4)

*The first vision: Battle in earth and heaven
(12:1-18)*

*The second vision: The devil uses the spiritual
power behind evil human governments to
attack the church and deceive the lost (13:1-10)*

*The third vision: The state uses its religious
allies to persecute the church and deceive
the lost (13:11-18)*

*The fourth vision: The Lamb and the
144,000 on Mount Zion (14:1-5)*

*The fifth vision: Judgment of the wicked
and reward of the faithful (14:6-13)*

*The sixth vision: The final judgment
(14:14-20)*

*The seventh vision: The saints glorify God
for his victory (15:1-4)*

This section falls in between the depiction of the trumpet and the bowl judgments. Like the other sections, it can be divided into seven parts, each of which consists of a different vision introduced by phrases like "I saw" and "Behold." These seven visions describe the same panorama of history, from the earthly ministry of Christ to his final return, as do the other three sets of seven judgments (seals, trumpets and bowls). Chapters 1-11 have set forth a picture of conflict between the church and the world in the context of the suffering of believers and the judgment of unbelievers. Chapters 12-22 develop these themes in greater depth. Chapter 12 introduces the devil as the author of evil. In 6:8, we are told of a figure called "Death," and in 9:11 of a king called "Destroyer," ruler of the bottomless pit. Then in 11:7, we read of a beast rising from that bottomless pit who will make war on the saints. Whatever the nature of these shadowy figures, we are now told clearly of the one who stands behind them all. The devil uses his agents, the beast, the false prophet and Babylon to further his nefarious purposes. In chapters 12-20, John is given visions revealing the rise of four figures (the dragon, the beast, the false prophet and Babylon) and then detailing their fall, in exact reverse order (Babylon, the false prophet, the beast and finally, the dragon). This highlights the role of the devil as the source of all rebellion against God and as the chief persecutor of his people. Chapter 12 introduces the visions of the latter half of Revelation, and is a pivotal section of the book.

THE FIRST VISION: BATTLE IN EARTH AND HEAVEN (12:1-18)

THE WOMAN, THE DRAGON AND THE MALE CHILD (12:1-6)

The vision commences: *And a great sign appeared in heaven: a woman clothed with the sun, with the moon under her feet, and on her head a crown of twelve stars* (verse 1). The sun, moon and twelve stars are a reference to Joseph's vision in Gen. 37:9 (the twelfth star of Revelation representing Joseph himself). The twelve stars thus represent the twelve tribes of Israel. But the woman also depicts the restored Israel of the end-times which, as we have seen, is repeatedly identified in Revelation as the church. Isaiah portrays the Israel to be restored in the last days as a woman (Isa. 52:2; 54:1-6; 61:10; 62:1-5). He sees spiritual Israel as a bride with a crown on her head. He prophesies that restored Israel will be as a bride wearing a crown (Isa. 62:5). In Revelation, crowns represent the share of the saints in the kingship of Christ (2:10; 3:11; 4:4, 10; 14:14), and their reward for the persecution they have suffered. The brightness of the woman's appearance (*clothed with the sun*) reflects the same brightness in the face of Christ (1:16). Her glory is the reflected glory of Christ. That the woman represents both the old and new covenant communities becomes even clearer in verses 11-17, where her seed or offspring is not only Christ, but also the entire community of Christ's followers.

John's vision of the woman continues: *She was pregnant and was crying out in birth pains and the agony of giving birth* (verse 2). The vision is rooted in Gen. 3:14-16. After Eve's pain in childbirth, her seed is prophesied to bruise the head of the serpent. The woman gives birth to the One who will restore what was lost in the Garden. The woman here represents the faithful remnant of Israel. This is borne out by three prophetic words from Isaiah which form the background to this vision. According to Isa. 7:10-14, a sign will be seen as "high as heaven," the virgin will be with child, and will bear a son. In John's vision, a sign appears in heaven (verse 3), a woman is *pregnant*, and she gives birth to a son (verse 5). A similar picture occurs in Isa. 26:16-19. Israel is "pregnant," "cries out in her pangs," and is "near to giving birth." Although she fails in her endeavor, a day of restoration (pictured as a resurrection) will come. In that day, the Lord will punish the "fleeing serpent" and "slay the dragon that is in the sea." A third picture comes in Isa. 52:1-11. Sarah gives birth in order that eventually, through the faithful remnant, God's truth will reach the nations, Eden will be restored, and God will pierce the dragon. The themes of the serpent, the dragon and the sea will also be visited as these visions unfold.

The woman in verse 2 is described as being in *agony*. This word is used in the New Testament to refer to trial and persecution (Mt. 8:29; Mk. 5:7; Lk. 8:28; 2 Pet. 2:8). In Revelation, it refers to a torment sent either from the devil (9:5) or from God (11:10; 14:10; 20:10). Hence the woman is being tormented and attacked as she waits to give birth. The faithful Jewish community experienced much persecution and hardship in the times leading up to Christ. Other Scriptures referring to the circumstances of childbirth shed light on the meaning here. Jesus compared the pain of his disciples as they contemplate his death to that of a mother about to give birth (Jn. 16:19-22). In that account, the disciples take the role of the mother (the faithful community of Jewish believers) in whose midst the Messiah was born and would be resurrected.

The vision continues: *And another sign appeared in heaven: behold, a great red dragon, with seven heads and ten horns, and on on his heads seven diadems* (verse 3). The same dragon spoken of by Isaiah (Isa. 27:1; 51:9) is shortly to be revealed as the ancient serpent, Satan himself (verse 9). The "dragon" in the Old Testament is the evil sea monster who symbolizes the kingdoms trying to destroy Israel, in particular Egypt. God defeats Pharaoh, portrayed as a sea dragon (also identified as Rahab, the proud or overbearing one) at the Exodus, but which also appears at later points in history (Ps. 74:13-14; 89:10; Isa. 31:7; 51:9; Ezek. 29:3; 32:2-3; Hab. 3:8-15). In Jer. 51:34, Babylon is identified with a sea monster. Isaiah (27:1) prophesies that at the end of history, God will again destroy this Egyptian dragon who lives in the sea. That the same evil spirit possessing Egypt resides in the latter-days dragon is evident from the numerous allusions to the Exodus in Revelation — for instance, in the trumpet and bowl plagues and the reference to the Red Sea deliverance in 15:3. Egypt and Babylon, homes of the Old Testament dragon, become types or prophetic forerunners of the spiritual dragon of the last days. Yet the dragon is not just a figure of speech standing for evil governments. He is in fact the very real evil force behind all human kingdoms which persecute the church (12:9; 20:8-10). His *seven heads and ten horns* indicate the comprehensive and global nature of his power (the numbers seven and ten referring Biblically to fullness or completion). The ten horns are those of the fourth, terrifying beast in Daniel's vision (Dn. 7:7, 24). His red color is the same as that of the harlot and the beast, which in 17:3-6 are linked with the fact the harlot is drunk with the blood of the saints. The crowns on his head show that he works through earthly kingdoms. They are also a blasphemous and rebellious imitation of Christ's true kingship. In 19:11-16, Christ pictured as the true King who wears many diadems. The contrast between these two pictures shows the dragon's false authority as he attempts to oppose Christ.

The battle is engaged: *His tail swept down a third of the stars of heaven and cast them to the earth. And the dragon stood before the woman who was about to give birth, so that when she bore her child he might devour it* (verse 4). This fulfills the vision of Daniel that a powerful enemy would throw "some of the stars" of heaven to earth (Dn. 8:10). Stars can represent God's people (Dn. 12:3), but these heavenly stars are angelic forces who are seen by Daniel as representing those people (Dn. 10:20-21; 12:1). This is very similar to the role of the angels of the seven churches or the twenty-four elders in Revelation. The dragon's attack wounds some of the faithful, as represented by their guardian angels. The battle in heaven mirrors the battle on earth. When the saints are being persecuted, their angels and God himself are pictured as being attacked. But here, the dragon has a particular goal in mind: to devour the child the woman bore. Here in one phrase is summed up all the ways the devil tried to destroy Jesus, from the attack of Herod on the children of Bethlehem, to the temptation in the wilderness, to the attempt of the citizens of Nazareth to throw him off the cliff, and so on right up to the cross.

The condensation of Christ's life into a brief phrase is very clear in the next verse: *She gave birth to a male child, one who is to rule all the nations with a rod of iron, but her child was caught up to God and to his throne* (verse 5). Ps. 2:9 prophesies that the coming Messianic king will break the nations "with a rod of iron." At the cross, it seemed that the dragon had at last succeeded in his mission to devour the child. Yet at that very moment, the child was *caught up to God.* This clearly describes the resurrection and ascension of Christ. The faithful Christians at Thyatira are told they will rule the nations "with a rod of iron" even as Christ himself does (Rev. 2:27). Christ is referred to as the *male child* specifically because Psalm 2 identifies him as the Lord's "son" (Ps. 2:7, 12). It was at the very point of the resurrection and ascension, not at some date in the distant future, that Christ received the "rod of iron" prophesied in Ps. 2:9 and took up his kingdom rule. Now, seated at the right hand of the Father's throne, he has begun to exercise his authority over the nations of the world. The fulfillment of his rule will come at the end of history, when he wields the "rod of iron" with absolute and consummate power (Rev. 19:15).

As the child was caught up to God, *the woman fled into the wilderness, where she has a place prepared by God, in which she is to be nourished for 1,260 days* (verse 6). The woman in verses 1-2 is portrayed from a heavenly perspective, possibly because there she represents the faithful "cloud of witnesses" of Old Testament saints constituting the covenant line of the Messiah. Now she is pictured as on earth, emphasizing her present existence as the body of Christ, God's people of every nation. The *wilderness* in the Bible represents the place of refuge or protection, primarily as the place where God sheltered the Israelites from the wrath of the Egyptians (Exod. 16:32). Both Moses and Elijah, who together represent the church in chapter 11, took refuge in the wilderness (Exod. 2:15; 1 Kings 17). God hid David in the wilderness (1 Sam. 23:15; 24:1), and there he encountered John the Baptist (Mt. 3:1) and Jesus (Mt.

4:1). The prophets, particularly Isaiah, speak of a time (clearly at the end of history) when God will bring his deliverance to Israel in the wilderness (Isa. 32:15; 35:1-10; 40:3-8; 41:17-20; 43:19-20; 51:3; Jer. 31:2; Ezek. 34:25-31; Hos. 2:14-15). The church (restored or spiritual Israel), in which these prophecies are fulfilled, will be kept by God in the wilderness, but ultimately delivered by him from it at the return of Christ. There is a strong parallel between the place prepared here for believers in the wilderness, and Jesus' promise that he goes to the Father to "prepare a place" for them (Jn. 14:3). Traditionally, we have understood this latter "place" to be heaven, but in the light of the parallel to Revelation, could it be that the "place" God prepares is simply the place of his presence, whether on earth or in heaven? In this "place," believers are kept spiritually safe regardless of what other troubles they may suffer. Spiritual safety means God's protection against deception and compromise in the face of the devil's continuous attacks. In this sense, the wilderness is equivalent to the picture of the temple in 11:1-2, and the period of the protection (*1,260 days*) is exactly the same as in those verses (1,260 days = 42 months). This verse very clearly indicates the time frame in view, which commences with the child's being caught up to the throne (Christ's resurrection and ascension, verse 5). It ends with his return, as the last of the visions of this section makes clear (14:14-20). *This is the same time period each of the seven series of judgments (seals, trumpets and bowls) depicts.* In the wilderness experience of the church age, she will be kept faithful even while enduring suffering, persecution and possibly death. Her protection is primarily spiritual in nature. The church will suffer because the Babylonian harlot (wicked world governments throughout the church age) also resides in the wilderness (17:3). According to Deut. 8:15-16, the wilderness was a place of "fiery serpents and scorpions" (= Rev. 9:10, 19), yet also the place where God brought water from the rock and fed his people with manna. The number of days comes from the time of tribulation prophesied by Daniel (7:25; 12:7), and alludes to the forty-two years (including two years prior to the sending out of the spies) the children of Israel spent in the wilderness, during which they had forty-two encampments. It is also modeled on the forty-two months of Elijah's ministry of judgment, on which the ministry of the church is itself patterned in chapter 11. And finally, it may be modeled on the approximately three and a half years of Christ's earthly ministry. Following these forty-two months, the church will be ushered into the heavenly kingdom in the same way the children of Israel entered the earthly promised land. Like all other numbers in Revelation, the period of 1,260 days or 42 months is to be understood in a figurative rather than literal sense, as the comparison to time periods of different literal lengths (months vs. years) in the Old Testament shows.

WARFARE IN HEAVEN (12:7-12)

The next verses (7-12) continue the warfare vision of verses 1-6. They describe a war being fought in heaven which accompanies that being fought on earth: *Now war arose in heaven, Michael and his angels fighting against the dragon* (verse 7a). It is not surprising that events in heaven parallel those on earth, when we consider that the seven letters were written to the angels of the churches who represented them in the heavenly sphere. Revelation continually portrays events in the heavenly realm which have direct impact on events on earth. For instance, the three sets of seven judgments come from the throne room of God (6:1; 8:1; 15:1). Daniel's vision identifies Michael as the powerful angel representing God's people (Dn. 10:13, 21; 12:1). In this role, he assists the Son of man in the battle against the demonic rulers of Persia and Greece, nations which oppress God's people. In the vision, Michael stands beside the Son of man to fight for him even as he did in Daniel's vision. Now he fights no longer as representative of Israel as a nation, but on behalf of the new covenant people of Christ from every nation. The power behind Daniel's demonic rulers of Persia and Greece is now revealed to be Satan himself. But he is vanquished: *And the dragon and his angels fought back, but he was defeated, and there was no longer any place for them in heaven* (verses 7b-8). The heavenly war exactly mirrors that on earth. The moment Christ was resurrected from the dead, divine power was released in the heavens. Michael and his angels became too strong for the devil and his forces. As a result, *the great dragon was thrown down, that ancient serpent, who is called the devil and Satan, the deceiver of the whole world - he was thrown down to the earth, and his angels were thrown down with him* (verse 9). This is another illustration (as in 11:18) of the Biblical principle of the punishment fitting the crime. Even as he unjustly threw the stars onto the earth (verse 4), so he now suffers the same punishment. The dragon is described as *the devil* (which means "slanderer"), *Satan* (which means "adversary"), and *that ancient serpent* (the deceiving serpent of the Garden). According to Gen. 3:5, the serpent opposed and slandered God by questioning his motivation for giving the command not to eat the fruit. He deceived Adam and Eve by implying their rebellion would have a positive result for them (Gen. 3:4-5).

The vision continues: *And I heard a loud voice in heaven, saying, "Now the salvation and the power and the kingdom of our God and the authority of his Christ have come, for the accuser of our brothers has been thrown down, who accuses them day and night before our God"* (verse 10). The voice explains the significance of the events which have just been described. It represents the multitude of the saints in heaven, for God is addressed as *our God*, and reference is made to *our brothers*. The meaning of Christ's ascension to heaven (verse 5) and the devil's expulsion from it (verses 8-9) are that Christ's kingdom and authority *have come*. This is the fulfillment of the prophetic word regarding the inauguration of the Messiah's rule in Ps. 2:7-9 ,which has been alluded to in verse 5. Those verses are the only place in the Old Testament where "Lord" and Christ" occur together as they do here. According to the Psalm, the coming King will inherit the nations and possess the ends of the earth. The resurrection and ascension are the pivotal moments of history. The present inauguration of the Messianic kingdom is emphasized by the word *now*. Christ begins his rule over the earth at the ascension, and not at some indeterminate future date. The power and reality of the kingdom are present now. This has happened because *the accuser of our brothers has been thrown down.* It is clear from Job 1:6-11, 2:1-6 and Zech. 3:1-2 that Satan had a mandate to accuse the saints. He had a legal point, for sin incurs the death penalty, yet God had welcomed Old Testament saints (from Enoch to Elijah) into his presence. However, he had not yet executed just punishment for peoples' sin (Rom. 3:25). But now, the death of Christ has satisfied the anger of God against the sins of all faithful believers of both covenants (Rom. 3:25; 8:1; 8:33-34, 38). The resurrection sealed God's approval of Christ's sacrifice, and with the ascension, Satan has no basis left for his accusations. As a result, at the moment of the resurrection, he is evicted from the counsel of God. Jesus links the fall of Satan from heaven with the fact that the disciples' names are written in heaven, and that they are now empowered with the authority of the kingdom (Lk. 10:17-20). Jesus also taught that at the moment he was lifted up, the ruler of this world would be cast out (Jn. 12:31). The power of the kingdom is now released into the earth, even though its consummated form awaits the Lord's return.

The assurance is now given to the saints on earth that their present suffering will issue in eternal glory: *And they have conquered him by the blood of the Lamb and by the word of their testimony, for they loved not their lives even unto death* (verse 11). This verse expresses one of the major themes of Revelation — God's assurance to the saints that their suffering is like the suffering of Christ on the cross. Far from being a sign of their defeat, it is actually a sign of their victory. Nothing (from mild suffering to death) can take away from persecuted Christians their most precious possession — God's eternal reward. And so the command is given: *"Therefore, rejoice, O heavens and you who dwell in them! But woe to you, O earth and sea, for the devil has come down to you in great wrath, because he knows that his time is short!"* (verse 12). The *short* time is to be identified as (1) the "little time" of 6:11 during which deceased saints wait for the rest of the redeemed to join them in glory; (2) the forty-two month period during which the outer court is trampled (11:1-3); (3) the same period in which the witnesses give testimony but are attacked (11:4-13); and (4) the time the church is in the wilderness (12:6). We will discover in chapter 20 one further way of referring to the same time period: the "millennium." All these expressions refer in different ways to the church age. During this time, from the resurrection to the Lord's return, the church bears faithful witness, suffers in various ways, but is ultimately vindicated. This is the time of the devil's wrath. The time seems *short* to Satan because it is short compared to the eternity he will spend in the lake of fire (20:10). It also seems short because he faces the same prospect as do believers (though from a different perspective): Christ may return at any moment, and he is not aware of that moment, which God alone knows (Mt. 24:36). But even in this time of Satan's wrath, his power is limited (20:2; Mk. 3:27), and the power of God's kingdom, the same power that raised Jesus from the dead (Eph. 1:19-20) is available to his church.

THE WOMAN IN THE WILDERNESS (12:13-18)

Verse 13 picks up the story where it was left in verse 6, with the woman fleeing into the wilderness: *And when the dragon saw that he had been thrown down to the earth, he pursued the woman who had given birth to the male child.* The woman (the church) is persecuted because of her association with the male child (Christ). The story of the flight continues: *But the woman was given the two wings of the great eagle so that she might fly from the serpent into the wilderness, to the place where she is to be nourished for a time, and times, and half a time* (verse 14). According to Exod. 19:4, God bore Israel "on eagles' wings" into the wilderness and away from the Egyptians. In Deut. 32:10-12, God is pictured as an eagle who finds Israel in the wilderness and cares for them there. John sees the end-times fulfillment of this vision, with the church as the true spiritual Israel taking the place of the old physical Israel. But perhaps the most significant Old Testament background here is the prophecy of Isaiah that God will come to his people "in the wilderness," where a voice is crying "Prepare the way" (40:3-11). This passage is interpreted by John the Baptist as referring to his last-days ministry preparing the way for the Messiah (Jn. 1:23). According to Isaiah's prophetic word, "they who wait for the Lord.... shall mount up with wings like eagles" (40:31). John's vision of the woman given the wings becomes a clear picture of the church protected by God in the wilderness between Christ's resurrection and return. This is confirmed by the fact that the wilderness is defined here as *the place where she is to be nourished for a time, and times, and half a time.* The time reference is identical to the three and a half years of 11:2 (see 13:5), and the 1,260 days of 11:3; 12:6, previously identified as the church age.

Now comes Satan's response to the woman's flight: *The serpent poured water like a river out of his mouth after the woman, to sweep her away with a flood* (verse 15). Like almost all other visions in the book, this one is to be interpreted in light of the Old Testament. The primary reference is to the Red Sea, which Satan used as a barrier to prevent the children of Israel (the old covenant "woman") to reach freedom. Satan will try to keep the church from gaining freedom by any obstacles he can place in the way. He will attempt to destroy the church from within (using deception) and from without (using persecution). The church will successfully cross the end-times Red Sea into the wilderness, where she resides under God's protection until Christ's rturn. Isaiah prophesies that the restoration of end-times Jerusalem will involve God once again drying up the rivers and the deep (44:27), so that when they "pass through the waters.... and through the rivers, they shall not overwhelm you" (43:2). The Old Testament (significantly in Daniel, from which so much of Revelation is drawn) uses "flood" to speak of the advance of an enemy army (Dn. 11:10, 22, 26, 40). It is also used as a figure of speech for the persecution of God's people by enemies from whom the Lord delivers them (2 Sam. 22:5; Ps. 66:12; 69:1-2; 124:4-5). Daniel (9:26) prophesies an end-times "flood" through which God's enemies will attempt to destroy his people.

The picture of the Red Sea continues in verse 16: *But the earth came to the help of the woman, and the earth opened its mouth and swallowed the river that the dragon had poured from his mouth.* The Red Sea (the literal river) parted and allowed the Israelites through, but the figurative "river" (the Egyptian army) was subsequently "swallowed up" as the course of natural earthly events resumed: "the earth swallowed them" (Exod. 15:12). Later, the earth "swallowed up" Dathan and Abiram to bring an end to their rebellion against God (Num. 15:32). Significantly, the Old Testament identifies Pharaoh as a "dragon in the seas" or "sea monster," and says that the moment of God's defeat of the dragon was when he parted the Red Sea to allow Israel through but closed it back over Pharaoh and his army (Ps. 74:13-14; Isa. 51:9-10; Ezek. 29:3; 32:2-3). Isaiah sees this pattern repeating itself as he prophesies concerning the restoration of spiritual Israel (Isa. 51:11-6). God will again dry up the sea and defeat the dragon so that the "ransomed of the Lord shall return and come to Zion with singing" (Isa. 51:11). These prophetic words are fulfilled in Christ and his church.

The continuing warfare of the devil against the church is summarized as follows: *Then the dragon became furious with the woman and went off to make war on the rest of her offspring, on those who keep the commandments of God and hold to the testimony of Jesus. And he stood on the sand of the sea* (verses 17-18). The devil, having been frustrated in his efforts to destroy the original offspring of the woman (the male child, that is, Christ) now spends the rest of the church age making war against her offspring. They are identified as all those who *hold the testimony of Jesus* -- that is, Christians. Viewed from another perspective, the woman and her offspring represent one and the same thing — the faithful covenant community before Christ (the faithful Jewish remnant) and after Christ (the church). It may seem difficult to see the woman and her offspring as representing the same reality. However, this has a good Old Testament background. Faithful Israel was viewed as a mother, yet also as composed of her godly children (Isa. 49:14-26). Alternatively, unfaithful Israel is pictured as a female figure or mother, in whom her unfaithful children are included (Ezekiel 16; Hos. 4:5). In chapters 17-18, we meet spiritual Babylon, the modern-day equivalent of unfaithful Israel, who is also pictured as a woman, but in whom is included a multitude of wicked individuals. It is important to remember that John is seeing visions, which are to be interpreted symbolically (see on 1:1-3). The vision of the woman kept safe in the wilderness speaks of the reality of God's protection over his church as a spiritual entity, whereas the warfare conducted against the many offspring speaks of the reality of the battle which is fought not against a universal church, but against the multitude of its actual individual members in their day-to-day struggles.

THE SECOND VISION: THE DEVIL USES THE SPIRITUAL POWER BEHIND EVIL HUMAN GOVERNMENTS TO ATTACK THE CHURCH AND DECEIVE THE LOST (13:1-10)

THE BEAST ARISES OUT OF THE SEA (13:1-4)

This new vision, introduced by *And I saw* (verse 1), covers the same time span as 12:13-18, but begins to reveal the agents through whom the devil uses to attack the church. Chapter 12 has revealed the devil as the evil foe warring against the church. Chapter 13 reveals how he conducts this battle. Chapter 12 ends with the dragon standing "on the sand of the sea" (verse 18). Now from that sea a beast arises: *And I saw a beast rising out of the sea, with ten horns and seven heads, with ten diadems on its horns and blasphemous names on its heads. And the beast that I saw was like a leopard; its feet were like a bear's, and its mouth was like a lion's mouth. And to it the dragon gave his power and his throne and great authority* (verses 1-2). The vision is based on Dn. 7:2-7 and 7:19-24. Daniel saw four beasts, one like a lion, one like a bear, one like a leopard with four heads, and one with ten horns. John's beast is a composite of Daniel's four beasts. Like them, it has seven heads and ten horns in total. The *ten diadems* represent the fact that the ten horns stand for ten kings (Dn. 7:24). The *blasphemous names* are probably connected to the figure allied with Daniel's fourth beast who speaks boastful and arrogant things against God himself (Dn. 7:8, 25). The names, along with the diadems, represent a false claim to Christ's true authority.

The fact that it has *ten horns and seven heads* like the dragon (12:3) shows where it derives its being and character from. It is the dragon who directs the activities of the beast. The dragon gives permission to the beast to exercise his *power*, thus corrupting God's intention for the state (Rom. 13:1-7). That the beast represents all forms of evil human government is also shown by the fact that horns and diadems refer in Scripture to earthly kings or kingdoms. This does not suggest that all human governments are evil. It does mean that the devil is continually trying to influence them in that direction. Sadly, he often succeeds. The fact that the symbolic numbers seven and ten (representing fullness or completion) are used shows that no particular king or kingdom is in view, but that the beast represents the evil spirit behind all evil kings and governments throughout history which seek to oppress the church. The beast is a composite of Daniel's four beasts. This shows that the evil spirits behind the previous kingdoms of Daniel live on in the last kingdom. It is this kingdom which confronts the saints from the time of Christ's resurrection until his return. Apart from being a servant of the devil, the beast is a direct counterfeit of Christ, who also has seven horns (5:6), expressing his true God-given right to worldwide rulership. Both the beast and Christ have diadems. However, the beast has only ten diadems. Christ, the true King of kings and Lord of lords, has "many diadems" (19:12, 16).

John now sees a strange sight: *One of its heads seemed to have a mortal wound, but its mortal wound was healed, and the whole earth marveled as they followed the beast* (verse 3). The *mortal wound* is real, and is from the hand of God. The reason this is true is because the Greek word for "wound" (*plege*) is the same word translated "plague" eleven times elsewhere in Revelation. It always represents the judgment of God. This wound on the beast's head was inflicted by Christ at his resurrection. It is the fulfillment of Gen. 3:15: "He shall bruise your head." The reason the wound is fatal is because at the resurrection and ascension of Christ, the power of the devil and his agents received a fatal blow. His power is now limited and his days numbered. The healing is only temporary. The enemy, thrown down to the earth, exercises an authority. But this authority is limited by God's sovereign will during the three and a half year period which symbolically represents the church age. He may attack and harm the church physically, but is unable to touch their spiritual security. The phrase *seemed to have a mortal wound* is (literally) "seemed as slain." It is almost identical to the description of Christ in 5:6, "a Lamb standing, as though it had been slain." This is another confirmation that the beast represents the satanic counterfeit to Christ. In 13:14, the beast's recovery is even pictured as a resurrection — his wound was mortal or fatal, "yet he lived." There are in fact numerous parallels between Christ and the beast. Both were slain but lived. The followers of both have their respective names inscribed on their foreheads (13:16; 14:1). Both are pictured with ten horns (5:6; 13:1). Both exercise respective measures of authority over every "tribe, language, people and nation" (5:9; 7:9; 13:7). Both receive worship across creation (5:8-14; 13:4, 8). Both have a final coming, one to eternal destruction and the other to eternal victory (17:7-18; 19:11-16). Christ comes as a servant of God, and is used by God to extend his kingdom. Behind the beast, however, is the devil himself. He works through his agents to use human governments (the "kingdom of the world," 11:15) against the kingdom of God. Whenever an evil kingdom rises, the devil is at work in another manifestation of the beast. This is a caution against closely identifying the beast with any one person, government or political movement. The parallel to Christ shows that both Christ and the beast are spiritual powers or realities exercising respective measures of authority, yet even the beast is restrained under God's sovereign direction throughout the church age.

THE LOST WORSHIP THE BEAST (13:5-10)

The lost multitudes are deceived by the beast's apparent recovery: *And they worshiped the dragon, for he had given his authority to the beast, and they worshiped the beast, saying, "Who is like the beast, and who can fight against it?"* (verse 4). Their words, *"Who is like the beast?"*, are a demonic mockery of similar words rightly used toward God in the Old Testament ("Who is like you, Lord, among the gods?" Exod. 15:11; see Ps. 35:10; 71:19; Isa. 40:18; Mic. 7:18). The devil continues to empower the beast: *And the beast was given a mouth uttering haughty and blasphemous words, and it was allowed to exercise authority for forty-two months. It opened its mouth to utter blasphemies against God, blaspheming his name and his dwelling, that is, those who dwell in heaven* (verses 5-6). The time frame, as in chapters 11 and 12, alludes to the church age. This is a time limit ultimately determined by God himself (*it was allowed*). The mouth uttering great boasts is the same as that of the demonic figure representing the beast in Dn. 7:8, which had "a mouth speaking great things" (things against God). The beast utters *blasphemies against God.* Exactly as in Dn. 7:25 ("he shall speak words against the Most High"), the beast speaks words against God while he wars against the saints for three and a half years. *Those who dwell in heaven* are probably all the saints, both dead and living. This group is opposite to those who "dwell on earth" (verse 8 and many other places in Revelation). The latter group are those who refuse to acknowledge God. That God's temple (or dwelling) is under attack takes us back to 11:1-2, where the outer court of the sanctuary (representing the place of the saints' dwelling on earth) is trampled by the enemy during the same forty-two month period as in this verse.

The warfare during the church age continues: *Also it was allowed to make war on the saints and to conquer them. And authority was given it over every tribe and people and language and nation, and all who dwell on earth will worship it, everyone whose name has not been written before the foundation of the world in the book of life of the Lamb who was slain* (verses 7-8). As in verse 6, the beast's authority is only exercised by divine permission (***allowed.... authority was given***). In John's vision, all that Daniel saw concerning the Son of man takes place also with reference to the beast. Both are granted authority by God (Dn. 7:14; Rev. 13:7) over those on earth who will worship them (Dn. 7:10; Rev. 13:8), and these events are associated with a book (Dn. 7:10; Rev. 13:8). John sees that the beast is a demonic counterfeit of Christ, though one allowed by God and ultimately under his control. The book of life appears five times elsewhere in Revelation, and always refers to the record of saints whose names were entered into the book of God's eternal kingdom before the foundation of the world (3:5; 21:27). The names of the lost were never entered in this book.

Believers are now exhorted to pay attention to what John is saying: ***If anyone has an ear, let him hear: If anyone is to be taken captive, to captivity he goes; if anyone is to be slain with the sword, with the sword must he be slain. Here is a call for the endurance and faith of the saints*** (verses 9-10). This is the same exhortation given to each of the seven churches in chapters 2-3 (see further on 2:7). There it echoed the words of Jesus and of Isaiah. Both of them turned from straightforward teaching which any-one could understand, and began instead to teach and act in parables and prophetic actions which would draw the attention of believers, but further harden the hearts of the lost. Those who have ears will hear, and those who do not will be further hard-ened by the prophetic message. In presenting these visions, John draws attention to their shock value. These are images meant to jar believers out of their worldly complacency, and warn them of the threat at hand. At the same time, they further harden the hearts of "earth-dwellers" who cannot make any sense of them.

Even as the exhortations given to the seven churches were directed toward believers, so also is this appeal. Believers will suffer as the beast makes war on them, and in some cases appears to conquer them. Yet they are to persevere in faithfulness in spite of suffering, because they know their names are written forever in the book of life which has just been mentioned. Meanwhile, the judgment of God on the unbelievers who persecute them (and presently seem triumphant) is certain. They are destined for ***captivity*** and ***to be slain with the sword***. These words of judgment are taken from Jer. 15:2 and 43:11, where they are addressed to disobedient Israel in exile. Those who are unfaithful and have mocked God will not escape judgment. In those days also, there was a remnant of faithful saints. Jeremiah's words assured them that the judgment of

God would eventually come on the lost, as surely as his salvation would come to them on a day when their fortunes would be restored (Jer. 31:23). In the meantime, and throughout history, the saints need *perseverance and faith*. Trial and persecution will happen, but believers must persevere in their faith and not give in. The words "faith" and "faithful" in Revelation refer either to the faith of Christ or to the faith of the saints in the face of persecution (1:5; 2:10, 13, 19; 3:14; 14:12; 17:14).

THE THIRD VISION: THE STATE USES ITS RELIGIOUS ALLIES TO PERSECUTE THE CHURCH AND DECEIVE THE LOST (13:11-18)

THE SECOND BEAST ARISES (13:11-15)

The vision progresses as a second beast is revealed: *Then I saw another beast rising out of the earth. It had two horns like a lamb and it spoke like a dragon* (verse 11). This vision deals with the same time period as the previous vision. Here the emphasis is on a second beast, which allies with the first beast. Daniel's four beasts also rose "out of the earth" (Dn. 7:17). Like the Lamb of 5:6 and the first beast, it too has horns, symbolizing the reality of its power. The fact it has *two horns like a lamb* suggests its role is not only to be a deceptive representative of Christ, but to mimic the two witnesses, two lampstands and two olive trees (11:3-4), all of which represent the church. The fact that this beast is later called the "false prophet" (16:13; 19:20; 20:10) confirms its religious nature. The first beast speaks loudly against God (verses 5-6), but the second beast is far more subtle, using deceptive means to make the claims of the first beast appealing even to those within the church. Its goal is to conform the church to the idolatrous institutions and practices of pagan culture, and to turn it away from the commandments of God's Word. Its appearance as a lamb imitating the church is deceiving, for it speaks *like a dragon*. This emphasizes the fact that Satan is as deceptive in his ways now as he was in the garden.

The second beast acts as an agent of the first beast: *It exercises all the authority of the first beast in its presence, and makes the earth and its inhabitants worship the first beast, whose mortal wound was healed. It performs great signs, even making fire come down from heaven to earth in front of people* (verses 12-13). The second beast gives religious support to the first beast. The beast is a religious counterfeit of Moses, who also performed signs (Exod. 4:17, 30; 10:2). He is equally a counterfeit of Elijah, reproducing his ability to call down fire (1 Kgs. 18:38-39; 2 Kgs. 10:1-14). These allusions are hardly coincidental, as Moses and Elijah are presented together in 11:3-7 as representative of the church. The beast, therefore, is the demonic counterfeit to the church. The beast is also a counterfeit to the true apostles. Like them, he persuades people to worship his master on the basis of his apparent resurrection (see Ac. 17:31). Like them, he performs signs and wonders (see Ac. 4:12; 2 Cor. 12:12). Daniel warns that a last-days deceiver will infiltrate the church and turn people away from God (Dn. 11:30-37). The second beast is at work within the church when leaders begin to take their direction from the values of the pagan culture they live in rather than from the Word of God.

And his deception will prevail powerfully among the lost: *And by the signs that it is allowed to work in the presence of the beast it deceives those who dwell on the earth, telling them to make an image of the beast that was wounded by the sword and yet lived* (verse 14). As the true church stands in the presence of the Lord (11:4), so false religion stands *in the presence of the beast*. The *image* alludes to Daniel's golden statue: "King Nebuchadnezzar made an image of gold" (Dn. 3:1). Both images are religious counterfeits of the one true God. Multitudes of those who do not know Christ will be swayed by the apparent reasonableness and legitimacy of the false prophets. False religions will multiply, while those holding the true faith will appear narrow, and be called bigoted and intolerant for their refusal to compromise with the spirit of the world. Yet all this is *allowed* under the sovereign plan of God, in order to harden the hearts of the rebellious. This expression, referring to divine permission, appears also in the next verse: *And it was allowed to give breath to the image of the beast, so that the image of the beast might even speak and might cause those who would not worship the image of the beast to be slain* (verse 15). The reference to Daniel continues with this verse. Even as the people of Babylon were commanded to "worship the golden image" (Dn. 3:5), so the people of spiritual Babylon are commanded to worship the image of the beast. As in Daniel, those who refused would be *slain*. The ability of the second beast to *give breath* suggests a counterfeit to the role of the Holy Spirit, pictured in the Bible by the same figure of speech (Gen. 1:1; Jn. 20:22; see Jn. 3:8; Ac. 2:2). Even as the Holy Spirit empowers the church to bear true witness throughout the forty-two months of the church age (13:5), so also the demonic spirit represented by the second beast empowers counterfeit believers to bear false witness during that time.

THE MARK OF THE BEAST (13:16-18)

The false prophet has a further task: Also it causes all, both small and great, both rich and poor, both free and slave, to be marked on the right hand or the forehead, so that no one can buy or sell unless he has the mark, that is, the name of the beast or the number of its name (verses 16-17). The false prophet seeks the help of the state in enforcing worship of the beast. The mark is the exact satanic counterpart to the "seal," which represents the name of God written on the foreheads of believers (7:3; 14:1). Neither are to be understood literally. The seal and the mark are figurative or symbolic ways of signifying ownership (see on 7:3). To be in someone's name also denotes ownership. The "name" of the Lord denotes God's ownership of us. That is why we are baptized "in the name" of Jesus (Ac. 10:48), and why God will give us what we ask "in his name" or as those under his authority (Jn. 14:13). The metaphor may be rooted in the contemporary practice of branding slaves or tattooing devotees of certain gods. They were marked with the name of their owner. In addition, the word "mark" (Greek *charagma*) refers to the seal of the emperor and the impression of his head on coins. Only those who submit to (are "owned by") the idolatrous practices of the pagan culture in which they live will enjoy its economic benefits, i.e. be allowed to **buy or sell**. Christians were under increasing pressure to conform to Roman practices of emperor worship. To be identified with the emperor's mark was to agree to worship him. Although we are not asked to worship our political leaders, there are many ways in which we are under pressure to compromise our faith in order to gain acceptance within our culture. These pressures may soon exclude non-compromising Christians from certain areas of employment or social acceptance. Christians are already coming under legal sanction for failing to compromise with certain social beliefs or practices. Like the Christians at Smyrna whose poverty was linked with their profession of faith (2:9), true believers can be expected to suffer economic as well as physical and political persecution. The latter phenomena are visible in many nations of the world today. The mark of the beast's ownership is placed on the *forehead* and **right hand**. If the *forehead* represents our beliefs, the **right hand** represents our conduct as a result of those beliefs. This is a satanic counterfeit of commitment to God and his law. The law of God is understood in Exod. 13:9 as a "sign on your hand and as a memorial between your eyes [=forehead]" (also Exod. 13:16; Deut. 6:8; 11:17). The "blasphemous names" written on the heads of the first beast, along with its ten diadems, signify its false claims to kingship (13:1). The fact that the beast's name is written on unbelievers signifies their agreement with those false claims and their refusal to worship the true God.

The number of the beast is now revealed: *This calls for wisdom: let the one who has understanding calculate the number of the beast, for it is the number of a man, and his number is 666* (verse 18). Many attempts have been made to interpret the meaning of this number. This has often been done by use of "gematria," an ancient system which substituted letters of the alphabet for numerals. Each letter stood for a number. Our modern numerical system is actually a product of much later Arabic mathematicians. The problem is that no clear identification can be made by means of gematria which would link 666 with any particular name. In spite of hundreds, if not thousands, of attempts over the centuries at altering spellings and adding titles, nothing has come of any of them. Some (often preterists seeking to prove that Revelation describes almost exclusively first century events) have tried to identify 666 with the Roman emperor Nero. This requires using a Hebrew transliteration of the title "Nero Caesar." This, however, was only one of his many titles. The effort requires a creative reworking of the Hebrew spelling. Finally, it ignores the fact that the readers of Revelation spoke and read Greek and not Hebrew. In fact, it was not Nero, but his successor Vespasian who conquered Jerusalem in AD 70, the event around which the preterist interpretation is constructed. Between the sixteenth and early nineteen centuries, according to one study, over one hundred names were proposed as candidates for 666. Innumerable names in recent decades have been suggested and in due course discarded, including Kaiser Wilhelm, Adolf Hitler, Henry Kissinger, Saddam Hussein, various Russian dictators and a few popes. All such attempts fail because they do not understand the symbolic use of numbers in Revelation (twenty-four elders, seven seals, trumpets and bowls, two witnesses, seven heads, ten horns, a thousand years and so on). *Numbers are interpreted not by gematria, but by their Biblical significance.* The Bible has an amazing way of interpreting itself, if we will allow it to. According to verse 17, the number of the beast is equivalent to the name of the beast. There, both constitute his mark written on the foreheads of the lost. In the verse immediately following this (14:1), believers are pictured with the *name of the Lord written on their foreheads.* The name of the Lord refers to a supernatural spiritual reality (God or Christ). The name or number of the beast must refer to the opposing demonic reality (Satan or the beast). *No human being, alive or dead, can therefore be identified with 666.* This is supported by a correct understanding of the phrase *for it is the number of a man*. The indefinite article (a) is best translated here "*for it is the number of humanity.*" Or more specifically, fallen humanity. It is the number of fallen humanity because fallen humanity is under the ownership of the devil and his agents. The definite article "the" would have been used if a specific individual were in mind.

How then are we to understand the number? If the number seven (used repeatedly in Revelation) refers to completeness and is God's number, the number six is the number of man. Man was created on the sixth day, but without the seventh day of rest he would not have come to completion. Hebrews 4:1-10 teaches that Adam and Eve entered God's original rest. However, following the fall, they lost that position. Israel failed to enter it. Only in Christ is it restored. The sixth seal, the sixth trumpet and the sixth bowl portray God's final judgment on the followers of the beast, whereas the seventh component in each series portrays the eternal kingdom of Christ, or a judgment which ends in the establishment of the eternal kingdom. The use of three sixes points to a level of fallenness beyond that of fallen humanity. *It points to the demonic reality out of which fallen humanity emerged.* The three sixes signify the demonic counterfeit of the Trinity (the dragon, the beast and the false prophet) and the fallen humanity that trinity controls.

In support of the concept of the demonic trinity, consider the following parallels:

The beast as counterfeit of the Son. The Son receives authority from the Father (2:27; 3:21), while the beast receives authority from the dragon (13:4). The beast has crowns (13:1), and so also does Christ (19:12). The beast appears as slain and is resurrected (13:3), as is also the case with Christ (1:18; 5:6). The Son of man steps forward to receive kingdom authority from God as a result of which people from all tribes and nations serve him as his kingdom advances in power (5:6-14; Dan. 7:13-14). The beast rises to receive kingdom authority from the dragon, as a result of which the whole world and its fallen expressions of government follow him (13:1-3).

The second beast or false prophet as counterfeit of the Spirit. The Spirit is the breath of God (Gen. 1:1; Jn. 20:22; Ac. 2:2). The false prophet gives breath to the statue of the beast (13:15). The Spirit glorifies the Son (Jn. 16:14). The false prophet glorifies the beast (13:12-15). The Spirit empowers the church to bear true witness and be the instrument for the advancement of God's kingdom (Ac. 1:8). The false prophet empowers unbelievers to use ungodly religious institutions to advance the kingdom of darkness and counteract the true witness of the church (13:11-18).

The warning *this calls for wisdom* puts believers on guard against the continual deceptive work of the beast throughout history. We need God's wisdom to interpret the Bible. Yet such a task should not be difficult. The Bible is not meant to be so complicated no one can understand it. Given that no one else has yet been able to come up with a concrete historical identification for 666, futurists might resort to a twenty-first century supercomputer! But John is not posing a complex mathematical problem for us here. The real solution is one every believer from John's day until now can easily grasp. He is pointing to a reality which any Spirit-filled believer can readily understand: the work of Satan and his agents is present among fallen humanity in every age, even within the visible church, and must be guarded against with all possible vigilance.

THE FOURTH VISION: THE LAMB AND THE 144,000 ON MOUNT ZION (14:1-5)

The next vision transports John from contemplating the work of the beast, the counterfeit Christ, to Mount Zion, where the true Son of man appears in all his glory: *Then I looked, and behold, on Mount Zion stood the Lamb, and with him 144,000 who had his name and his Father's name written on their foreheads* (verse 1). *Zion* is used 155 times in the Old Testament, and for the most part refers to God's eternal city as the place of his presence. One significant passage in this regard is Ps. 2:6-7: "As for me, I have set my King on Zion, my holy hill. I will tell of the decree: The Lord said to me, "You are my Son; today I have begotten you."" Paul quotes this passage and affirms that it has been fulfilled in Christ: "What God promised to the fathers, this he has fulfilled to us their children by raising Jesus, as also it is written in the second Psalm, 'You are my Son, today I have begotten you'" (Ac. 13:33). According to Paul, therefore, Christ is already reigning from the heavenly Mount Zion. The Messianic promise of Psalm 2 concerning end-times Zion is also seen as fulfilled in Rev. 2:26-27 and 12:5. Other passages affirm that God's promise of Israel's salvation at Mount Zion has begun fulfillment through Christ in the church. For instance, the whole of Joel chapter 2 is about the judgment and restoration of Zion. This is the passage from which Peter quotes in his first sermon in Ac. 2:16-21. Peter says that what was prophesied then is happening now (see also Heb. 1:1-5). According to Heb. 12:22-23, Mount Zion is the "assembly of the firstborn enrolled in heaven," suggesting it is the present residence of deceased saints. *Mount Zion* thus has a two-fold reference. It refers to God's inaugurated presence through the resurrected and ascended Christ in the church age, and it refers to the fulfilled reality of his presence in the eternal kingdom.

The *144,000* John sees on Mount Zion with the resurrected Christ are the same group as the 144,000 sealed, pictured in 7:4. There we saw that these are the faithful saints of all ages, Jews of the old covenant and the church of every nation of the new covenant. The names of God and the Lamb *written on their foreheads* are identical to the seal on the foreheads of chapter 7. Both "seal" and "name" carry the meaning of protection and ownership, and thus refer to all those under Christ's lordship, not some limited number. The actual number, symbolic in nature as with all other numbers in Revelation, speaks of the complete number of God's people. The twelve tribes and the twelve apostles represent the covenant community through the ages. The two twelves are multiplied together, and then multiplied by one thousand to give the idea of completeness (see 2 Pet. 3:8 for use of one thousand as an indefinitely large number). This number stands in stark contrast to the number of the beast mentioned in the preceding verse, which through its triple sixes expresses that which falls short of God and his plan for his creation. The group is also pictured in immediate contrast to those worshipping the beast and with his name written on their foreheads (13:14-17). Even as the lost worship the beast and go to destruction, so the saved worship the Lamb and are destined for glory.

Following a pattern in Revelation (4:1; 5:1; 6:1, etc.), after John has seen the vision, he now hears something connected with it: *And I heard a voice from heaven like the roar of many waters and like the sound of loud thunder. The voice I heard was like the sound of harpists playing on their harps, and they were singing a new song before the throne and before the four living creatures and before the elders. No one could learn that song except the 144,000 who had been redeemed from the earth. It is these who have not defiled themselves with women, for they are virgins* (verses 2-4a). The picture is similar to that of 5:8-10 and 15:2-3, where the heavenly beings or the company of the redeemed sing a new song and use harps to celebrate God's victory. The *new song* they sing is the "new song" of the Old Testament, which was always an expression of praise for God's victory over the enemy (Ps. 33:3; 40:3; 98:1; Isa. 42:10). John sees the entire company of redeemed saints, but from a heavenly or eternal perspective, given that from his earthly perspective most were yet to be born. The sound is so loud because it emanates from such a large host. This group is described as **these who have not defiled themselves with women, for they are virgins.** Their chastity is not to be understood literally, for nowhere does Scripture assign a negative value to sexual relationships within the marriage covenant. Further, this would limit the group to a relatively small number of men only (literally "male virgins"), whereas as we have seen, it actually stands for the entire group of the redeemed. Believers are described as **virgins** because they have remained loyal as a bride betrothed to Christ. The symbolism of a pure bride is explained by the similar description of the church in 19:7-9 and 21:2. Paul writes to the Corinthians: "I betrothed you to one husband, to present you as a pure virgin to Christ" (2 Cor. 11:2). The Old Testament similarly refers to "virgin Israel" (2 Kgs. 19:21, Isa. 37:22, Jer. 14:17; Lam. 2:13, Am. 5:2). Faithful believers are those who have refused to commit acts of sexual immorality (Greek *porneia*) with the harlot Babylon (17:16), whose immorality is about to be explicitly referred to (13:8). The reference is not simply to wrong sexual acts, but to compromise with the values of the pagan culture and the demonic forces behind it. For the same broad meaning of *porneia*, see on 2:14-15, 21-23; 14:8; 17:1-2.

Believers are further described: **It is these who follow the Lamb wherever he goes. These have been redeemed from mankind as firstfruits for God and the Lamb, and in their mouth no lie was found, for they are blameless** (verses 4b-5). This alludes to Jesus' simple command that believers should follow him in the way of the cross (Mt. 4:19; Lk. 9:59; Mk. 8:34-38). In the Old Testament, the firstfruits were what was holy and set aside for God, the rest being common or profane. "Firstfruits" continues the imagery of virgins, indicating that believers are those set aside as clean and belonging to God, whereas the rest of fallen humanity is unclean and unsuitable for an offering. Israel is described similarly in Jer. 2:3, where God's people coming out of Egypt are described as "holy to the Lord, the firstfruits of his harvest." Jeremiah points out, however, that Israel has gone away from God. Now this description finds more lasting fulfillment in the spiritual Israel of the new covenant. The distinction here is not between a smaller group of believers as firstfruits, to be followed by a larger harvest later, but rather between the redeemed as a whole and the lost as a whole, the harvest referring to the judgment of God at the very end of time. Only what is clean belongs to God. The fact that *no lie* was found in their mouths is probably an allusion to the description of Jesus in Isa. 53:9: "There was no deceit in his mouth." This contrasts genuine believers (the true Israel) with the unbelieving Jews of Philadelphia, who "say that they are Jews, and are not, but lie" (3:9). Refusal to lie is not just a reference to truthfulness in general. It is the refusal to betray Christ, no matter what the cost.

THE FIFTH VISION: JUDGMENT OF THE WICKED AND REWARD OF THE FAITHFUL
(14:6-13)

The time of this new vision is immediately prior to the final judgment. The destiny of the redeemed has just been described in verse 1-5, but now the focus is on the fate of the lost: *Then I saw another angel flying directly overhead, with an eternal gospel to proclaim to those who dwell on earth, to every nation and tribe and language and people. And he said with a loud voice, "Fear God and give him glory, because the hour of his judgment has come, and worship him who made heaven and earth, the sea and the springs of water"* (verses 6-7). The angel John sees preaches the Gospel in its dimension of judgment (as in Rom. 1:16-3:21; 2 Cor. 2:14-16). The angel is similar here to the eagle (an angelic being) pronouncing judgment in 8:13. Both fly *directly overhead* (lit: "in mid-heaven"). Both speak with a *loud voice*. Both address *those who dwell on the earth* (a term whose twelve occurrences in Revelation are used to describe those hardened in unbelief). The angels announce *the hour of his judgment*. The last judgment is at hand. The exhortations to *fear God* and *worship him* are final appeals to unbelievers to turn from their rebellious ways. The content of this verse is parallel to that of 11:13, where following the sixth trumpet the survivors were terrified and gave God glory. Yet, as we saw there, their terror was a human fear, not genuine awe of God. Nowhere in Revelation, at the end of any of the four sets of judgments, is there an indication of a last-minute mass conversion, though of course there may be some who do respond. The allusion in both places is likely to God's dealings with Nebuchadnezzar, who gave glory to God (Dn. 2:46-47; 4:34-37) while continuing to worship idols (3:1), and whose kingdom represents the forerunner of the harlot Babylon of verse 8.

A second angel now follows, declaring the downfall of Babylon: *"Fallen, fallen is Babylon the great, she who made all nations drink the wine of the passion of her sexual immorality"* (verse 8). This message of judgment again suggests that the gospel preaching of verse 7 is primarily judgmental rather than saving. The title *Babylon the great* is drawn from Nebuchadnezzar's proud description of the city he ruled (Dn. 4:30). Now spiritual Babylon will fall, even as Nebuchadnezzar did. We should not think that these end-times events are going to occur in a particular middle-eastern locale, for the reference to Babylon here is symbolic of all evil world governments under the control of the beast. Physical Babylon disappeared forever in a previous judgment of God, and will never rise again (Jer. 50:39-40, 51:26, 64; Isa. 13: 19-22). The conflict is now played out between spiritual Babylon and the church, not physical Babylon and Israel. That the nations were "made to drink" of her wine refers to her compelling the participation of the nations in her corrupt political, economic and social system in return for economic and political security. This is clear from 18:3, where their intercourse with the harlot is equated with their participation in her commercial affairs. Here, the economic and social connotations of *porneia* come into stark relief. The picture in this verse is drawn directly from Jer. 51:7, where the prophet speaks of the nations going mad from drinking Babylon's wine.

A third angel now appears with a further message of judgment: *"If anyone worships the beast and its image and receives a mark on his forehead or on his hand, he also will drink the wine of God's wrath, poured full strength into the cup of his anger, and he will be tormented with fire and sulfur in the presence of the holy angels and in the presence of the Lamb"* (verses 9-10). As is the case elsewhere in Revelation, the punishment fits the crime (see 11:18; 16:6; 17:14; 18:6, 7-8). Because the nations have selfishly drunk of Babylon's wine (verse 8), they will also drink *the wine of God's wrath*. In the Old Testament, drinking the wine of God's anger is a figure of speech for suffering God's anger (Ps. 60:3; 75:8; Isa. 51:17, 21-13; 63:6; Jer. 25:15-18). The wine of God's anger is mixed in *full strength* and will last forever, whereas the deceptively positive effects of Babylon's wine are only temporary. Worshipers of the beast will suffer the torment of *fire and sulfur*. As elsewhere in Revelation, *fire* is figurative for judgment (1:4; 2:18; 4:5; 8:5, 7-8; 15:2; 19:12). Torment is not just physical, but includes spiritual and psychological suffering, as in 11:10, where it is linked with the witnesses' preaching. In 18:7, it is linked with mourning.

The angel concludes his dire message: *"And the smoke of their torment goes up forever and ever, and they have no rest, day or night, these worshipers of the beast and its image, and whoever receives the mark of its name"* (verse 11). The picture of fire, sulfur and smoke is drawn from Isaiah's prophecy concerning the destruction of Edom: "And the streams of Edom shall be turned into pitch, and her soil into sulfur; her land shall become burning pitch. Night and day it shall not be quenched; its smoke shall go up forever" (Isa. 34:9-10). The destruction of Edom, which is complete, becomes a prophetic picture of the final destruction of unbelievers. According to Rev. 20:10, 15, this torment of the "lake of fire" is eternal. Into it will be cast the devil and his emissaries, as well as the earth-dwellers who have followed them. Though it is a complete and total destruction, it does not refer to a judgment followed by personal annihilation. The word "torment" is used in Revelation (9:5; 11:10; 12:2; 18:7, 10, 15; 20:10), and elsewhere in the New Testament (Mt. 4:24; 8:6; Lk. 8:28; 2 Pet. 2:8), of *conscious suffering, never of personal annihilation.* The smoke that ascends is that of their continuing torment, not their completed destruction. Even as the worship of God by the living creatures (4:8) and the entire community of the redeemed (7:15) continues "day and night" forever, so also, *day or night,* does the torment of the lost. Even as the blessedness of the righteous is everlasting, so also is the suffering of the wicked (Rev. 22:14-15). The smoke of unbelievers' torment goes up *forever and ever,* just as the righteous will reign "forever and ever" (22:5). The eternal restlessness of unbelievers (verse 11) contrasts with the eternal rest of believers enjoying eternity with God (Heb. 4:9-11). The two run in exact parallel, as all these verses affirm.

This message of impending judgment calls for a response: *Here is a call for the endurance of the saints, those who keep the commandments of God and their faith in Jesus* (verse 12). The judgment pictured in verses 6-11 is a motivation for faithful believers to persevere in spite of present sufferings. An almost identical exhortation is given in 13:10 ("Here is a call for the endurance and faith of the saints"), following a portrayal of the church's suffering. Faith brings endurance in the face of suffering, along with "wisdom" (13:18) to understand the identity and nature of the beast. The present sufferings of believers are not to be compared to the future sufferings of the lost. Believers persevere not just to receive their eternal reward, but because they desire to see the name of God glorified (14:1-5; 15:3-4). The *commandments of God* refer to the entirety of God's truth in Old and New Testaments, whereas *faith in Jesus* refers to believers' trust in Christ as the cornerstone of all Biblical revelation.

The vision concludes: *And I heard a voice from heaven saying, "Write this: Blessed are the dead who die in the Lord from now on." "Blessed indeed," says the Spirit, "that they may rest from their labors, for their deeds follow them!"* (verse 13). Those who *die in the Lord* refers to all those who have remained faithful unto death, and is not a reference only to those who have died for their faith. The interjection by the Spirit brings divine assurance that faithful believers will be rewarded. The *labors* and *deeds* (Greek *erga*) are not just random good works. *Labors* most often in the New Testament refers to the lifestyle of faith which perseveres through hardship: "Therefore, my beloved brothers, be steadfast, immovable, always abounding in the work of the Lord, knowing that in the Lord your labor is not in vain" (1 Cor. 15:58). Similarly, Paul says: "For we are his workmanship, created in Christ Jesus for good works (*erga*)" (Eph. 2:10). Our works represent our life as lived for Christ.

THE SIXTH VISION: THE FINAL JUDGMENT (14:14-20)

The fifth vision announces the coming judgment, whereas the sixth vision describes the actual judgment taking place: *Then I looked, and behold, a white cloud, and seated on the cloud one like a son of man, with a golden crown on his head, and a sharp sickle in his hand* (verse 14). The allusion here is to Daniel's vision of the Son of man (Dn. 7:13). Jesus said he would come "on the clouds of heaven" to judge and to save (Mt. 24:30). He clearly identified himself as the Son of man who would come at the final judgment both to judge and to redeem (Mt. 24:27-51; Mk. 13:26; Lk. 21:27). In the context of verses 6-13 as well as verses 14-20, it seems likely that Christ's role of judgment rather than salvation is being emphasized here. *The golden crown* further identifies Christ as King. The vision continues: *And another angel came out of the temple, calling with a loud voice to him who sat on the cloud, "Put in your sickle, and reap, for the hour to reap has come, for the harvest of the earth is fully ripe." So he who sat on the cloud swung his sickle across the earth, and the earth was reaped* (verses 15-16). The fact that the angel gives a command to Christ does not indicate that the angel is superior to Christ, merely that he comes with a command from the Father. This could mean that Christ, even in his ascended state, still does not know the final hour until he is informed by the Father. This would fulfill Jesus' words: "But concerning that day or that hour, no one knows, not even the angels in heaven, nor the Son, but only the Father" (Mk.

13:32). The vision of the harvest as *fully ripe* underlines the fact that God alone knows the exact hour at which judgment must begin.

The vision of harvest is repeated in verses 17-20, though in an expanded form. The reality of judgment is explicit in these verses: *Then another angel came out of the temple in heaven, and he too had a sharp sickle. And another angel came out from the altar, the angel who has authority over the fire, and he called with a loud voice to the one who had the sharp sickle, "Put in your sickle and gather the clusters from the vine of the earth, for its grapes are ripe." So the angel swung his sickle across the earth and gathered the grape harvest of the earth and threw it into the great winepress of the wrath of God. And the winepress was trodden outside the city, and blood flowed from the winepress, as high as a horse's bridle, for 1,600 stadia* (verses 17-20). Reference to the angel with *authority over the fire* reminds us of 8:3-5, where the angel throws fire (representing God's judgment) from the heavenly temple onto the earth. Reference to the *great winepress of the wrath of God* takes us back to the pouring out of God's wrath on the lost mentioned in verse 10. The question must then be asked whether there are two harvests being portrayed, one of the saved (verses 14-16) and one of the lost (verse 17-20)? It is more likely that both harvests are depictions of judgment. Several reasons can be given for this. First, both visions feature an angel coming from the temple to reap, and elsewhere in Revelation such orders from God's presence bring only judgment (6:1-5; 9:13; 16:7, 17). Second, the phrase, "the hour to reap has come" (verse 15), should be seen against the background of the nine other occasions in the book in which "hour" occurs, all of which refer to divine judgment. Third, both pictures appear to be fulfillment of Joel 3:13: "Put in the sickle, for the harvest is ripe. Go in, tread, for the winepress is full. The vats overflow, for their evil is great." This does not take away from the fact that the final harvest, as Jesus taught, will be both of the saved and the lost (Mt. 9:37-38; Mk. 4:26-29; Jn. 4:35-38). It simply illustrates the fact that in Revelation, at the end of each series of judgments and visions, a description of the final judgment of the lost is featured (see 6:12-17; 11:13-19; 16:17-21; 19:17-21; 20:7-10).

The vision concludes with the winepress being *trodden outside the city, and blood flowed from the winepress, as high as a horse's bridle, for 1,600 stadia.* The *city* (fifteen times in Revelation) is the new Jerusalem, God's holy city. The same picture occurs in 20:8-9, where the lost are judged outside the "beloved city" they have come to attack.

In Zech. 14:2, God is pictured as standing on the Mount of Olives outside Jerusalem to destroy the last-days enemy armies. Joel 3:2, 11-12, 14 (where the vision of the winepress judgment occurs) speaks of God's last-days judgment on the nations in the "valley of Jehoshaphat" outside Jerusalem. The words of the prophets are fulfilled not in the physical Jerusalem, but in the eternal new Jerusalem. The number *1,600* is figurative, speaking of a completed and final world-wide judgment (four, the number of the earth, squared and then multiplied by ten squared to express completeness).

THE SEVENTH VISION: THE SAINTS GLORIFY GOD FOR HIS VICTORY (15:1-4)

Strictly speaking, verse 1 is the introduction to the seven bowl judgments. However, this introduction is interrupted in verse 2 by a different vision before being resumed in verse 5. The vision related in verses 2-4 serves primarily as a conclusion to 12:1-14:20. It also serves as a transition to the bowl judgments (on which see below). The vision commences: ***Then I saw another sign in heaven, great and amazing, seven angels with seven plagues, which are the last, for with them the wrath of God is finished*** (verse 1). The words are very similar to 12:1: "And a great sign appeared in heaven." This is an indicator another major section of the book is about to be introduced. The ***seven plagues*** referred to are said to be ***the last.*** Some take ***last*** (Greek *eschatos*) in a simple chronological fashion, the meaning being that the bowl judgments come last in historical order before the return of Christ. However, our analysis of Revelation has shown that the series of plagues and signs all describe the same realities from different perspectives. Therefore, it is unlikely that the bowls come later in history than the visions which precede them. The word "last" probably refers instead to the *order in which John saw the visions.* The bowl judgments are the last of the four series of sevenfold judgment visions. This vision is then expanded on in chapters 17-19 in the description of Babylon and her judgment by God.

This interpretation is reinforced by the appearance of the phrase "after this" (lit: "after these things") in verse 5, which elsewhere in Revelation (4:1; 7:1, 9; 18:1; 19:1) indicates the order in which John saw the vision, rather than the chronological order in which the events related in the vision occurred. The bowls go back in time before the events related in chapter 14. The final judgment has already been described three times, at the end of the seals (6:12-17; 8:1), the trumpets (11:15-19), and again in 14:8-11 and 14-20. The word *plague* is used in the sixth trumpet (9:20) and the fourth bowl (16:9). It is also used in relation to plagues that will come upon anyone at any time in history who refuses to heed the warnings of the book (22:18). Therefore, we cannot say the plagues about to be related only occur at the very end of history.

Two other interpretations are possible of the phrase "last" plagues. In light of the fact that the bowl judgments are a clear reflection of the original plagues of Exodus, it is possible that John may refer to them as the seven *last* plagues in contrast to the seven *original* plagues of Exodus. Alternately, the "last" days, in the eyes of the New Testament, are the days beginning with the ministry of Christ (see on 4:1). In this sense, we could say that the seven bowl judgments are those which occur at varying times throughout the "last days" or the church age, from the resurrection of Christ until his return.

What then is the meaning of the phrase *with them the wrath of God is finished?* The verb *finished* (Greek *teleo*) also carries the meaning of "filled up." The same idea (but using a different verb) occurs in both 15:7 and 21:9, where it refers to the fact that the seven bowls are "filled up" with the wrath of God or the seven plagues. The appearance of this idea in verse 1 in connection with the bowls is hardly coincidental. The meaning would then be that in the seven bowl plagues the wrath of God is pictured as being "filled up." This may mean that the bowls portray the wrath of God more intensely than conveyed in the previous sets of judgments. This might also explain why God revealed this vision last of all.

In verses 2-4, this vision is interrupted by another one: *And I saw what appeared to be a sea of glass mingled with fire -- and also those who had conquered the beast and its image and the number of its name, standing beside the sea of glass with harps of God in their hands* (verse 2). This draws us back to the series of seven visions commencing at 12:1, and serves as their conclusion. The last judgment has been portrayed in 14:14-20, and John now beholds the saints in heaven celebrating the final triumph of God. John sees *a sea of glass mingled with fire.* The Red Sea was the Biblical barrier to freedom for the people of God. Its evil character is alluded to in 12:15, where the serpent attempted to swallow the woman up. The Red Sea is pictured in the Old Testament as the dwelling place of the sea monster or dragon (Isa. 51:9-11;

Ps. 74:12-15; Ezek. 32:2). It is no surprise that the beast (like the four evil beasts of Dn. 7:3) arises out of the sea (13:1), where he is met on the shore by the dragon. Significantly, in the new heaven and new earth, there is no longer any sea (21:1). Like the heavenly "sea of glass" in 4:6, the sea here has been calmed by the power of God. The fire mixed with glass signifies the judgment of God on the wicked. This is in line with the significance of fire elsewhere in Revelation (8:5, 7; 9:17, 18; 11:5; 14:18; 16:8; 17:16). The Red Sea allusion is confirmed by the fact that John sees at this calmed sea *those who had conquered the beast and its image and the number of its name.* These saints have refused to compromise with the demands of the world system by resisting the beast and its image, and by refusing to identify with its name. Even as with the children of Israel in the days of Moses, so now God has made the saints triumphant over the forces of evil.

Even as Moses and the people sang a song of victory on the shores of the Red Sea, so the saints are pictured singing the heavenly fulfillment of that song: *And they sing the song of Moses, the servant of God, and the song of the Lamb, saying, "Great and amazing are your deeds, O Lord God the Almighty! Just and true are your ways, O King of the nations! Who will not fear, O Lord, and glorify your name? For you alone are holy. All nations will come and worship you, for your righteous acts have been revealed"* (verses 3-4). The church, the new Israel, has passed through the sea of evil and come to the place of freedom. The group of believers here is the same as in 14:1-5, that is, the totality of believers of all ages, all those who have "conquered the beast" (verse 2). The song is identical to the "new song" of the heavenly beings in 5:9-10, as well as that of the multitude of the redeemed in 14:3. The song is new, in that it is not only the *song of Moses* but also the *song of the Lamb.* The contents of the song do not actually come from Exodus 15, though they do reflect Deut. 32:4, which is part of another passage recording a song of Moses. The opening words of the song *Great and amazing are your deeds, O Lord God the Almighty!* allude to Ps. 111:2-3. The title *Lord God the Almighty* is found often in Haggai, Zechariah and Malachi to describe God as the one who is sovereign over the history of his people. The crowd of the redeemed are celebrating the culmination of God's sovereign activity from their heavenly vantage point. The phrase *Just and true are your ways* underlines the fact that God's actions are rooted in his moral character and are not just expressions of brute power. He is addressed as *King of the nations* to emphasize his sovereignty and the fact that history ends with all the kingdoms subject to him (11:15). To this they add the refrain *Who will not fear you, O Lord, and glorify your name?* The redeemed saints are singing the song of Jeremiah 10:7: "Who would not fear you, O King of the nations?" The reason for worshiping God is given in the next words of the song *For you alone are holy.* The Hebrew word for "holy" derives from the idea of being set apart. The holiness of God consists in the fact that his moral attributes are totally different from those of his fallen creation. God deserves to be worshiped as the One totally different, set apart and above us in every possible respect.

The last part of the song expresses the result of God's holiness: *All nations will come and worship you.* The phrase *all nations* does not suggest that every single person on earth will bow in worship. It is a figure of speech expressing the fact that there will be people from every nation who will do so. In the same way, the statement that the beast has authority over every nation (13:7) does not mean that every single person will be lost, but that there are those from every nation who will be. Revelation is clear from beginning to end that only some will be saved, while others will certainly be lost. The final phrase of the saints' worship, *For your righteous acts have been revealed,* is taken from Ps. 98:2: "He has revealed his righteousness in the sight of the nations." It is a testimony to the unity of God's revelation in Scripture that John sees the heavenly saints praising God largely in the words of the Old Testament. It is fitting that Psalm 98 is quoted here, for that Psalm commences (verse 1) with a reference to the song of Moses at the Red Sea, just as in Rev. 15:3. It continues (verse 5) by exhorting the saints to praise God with harps, just as in Rev. 15:2. These Old Testament verses are quoted with a purpose. They are part of the portrayal of the fact that the deliverance of the Israelites at the Red Sea is a typological or prophetic anticipation of the deliverance of the new covenant saints. Having been delivered from spiritual Egypt and from the hand of the latter-day Pharaoh or dragon, these saints will experience their own sojourn in the wilderness (the forty-two months). After this, they will be delivered into the Promised Land (the heavenly Mount Zion or the new Jerusalem). We have already seen how the trumpet plagues are modeled on the plagues of Egypt, and this song takes us back to that theme. We will encounter it again as we turn to the seven bowls.

7

THE SEVEN BOWLS

(15:5-16:21)

The angels come forth from heaven (15:5-8)

The first five bowls (16:1-11)

The sixth bowl: (1) the enemy gathers his forces (16:12-15)

The sixth bowl: (2) Armageddon and the beginnings of the last judgment (16:16-21)

THE ANGELS COME FORTH FROM HEAVEN
(15:5-8)

John resumes the introduction to the bowl judgments he began in 15:1: *After this I looked, and the sanctuary of the tent of witness in heaven was opened, and out of the sanctuary came the seven angels with the seven plagues, clothed in pure, bright, linen, with golden sashes around their chests* (verses 5-6). This new vision describes the fourth and last set of seven judgments. The angels seen in verse 1 are described in more detail. The phrase *tent of witness* occurs 140 times in the Old Testament, almost always in Exodus and Deuteronomy. Hence, the *sanctuary of the tent of witness in heaven* is the heavenly equivalent of the earthly tent of Moses. The *witness* originally referred to the ten commandments placed within the tent (Exod. 32:15), which themselves stood for the whole of God's law. The earthly tent was an expression of God's presence with Israel and both his mercy and his judgment toward them. The heavenly tent John sees here expresses only God's judgment on the wicked. The witness includes not only the Old Testament law but also the "testimony [lit: "witness"] of Jesus" (see 19:10). The "testimony of Jesus" is the church's testimony to Jesus. God is about to reveal his just punishment of those who have rejected the testimony he has given in his Word concerning Jesus. That testimony has been faithfully proclaimed by his church. Chapter 11 speaks of the two witnesses (representing all faithful Christians of the church age) giving their testimony to Christ in the temple (signifying God's presence on earth in the church). Yet their legal testimony is rejected, which leads eventually to the final legal judgment depicted in the opening of the heavenly temple (11:19), a scene parallel to the opening of the same temple here. *The seven angels* come out of the temple with *the seven plagues*. The background to this text is clearly the plagues of Egypt. There is also an allusion to Lev. 26:14-33, where God warns the Israelites in four different verses that he will strike them seven times. This is translated in the Greek Old Testament as "I will further bring upon you seven plagues" (Lev. 26:21). That the angels are *clothed in pure, bright linen, with golden sashes around their chests* identifies them closely with Christ, who is similarly described in 1:13.

The vision continues: *And one of the four living creatures gave to the seven angels seven golden bowls full of the wrath of God who lives forever and ever, and the sanctuary was filled with smoke from the glory of God and from his power, and no one could enter the sanctuary until the seven plagues of the seven angels were finished* (verses 7-8). Golden bowls were associated with the service of the tabernacle (1 Chron. 28:17; 2 Chron. 4:8, 22). John previously saw golden bowls full of incense (5:8), which represented the prayers of the saints. The bowls here, full of God's wrath against unbelievers, are the answer to the saints' prayers for justice (6:9-11; 8:3-5). Isaiah spoke of the cup of God's wrath and "the bowl, the cup of staggering" (Isa. 51:17). This cup was drunk first by Jerusalem, but was soon to be poured out on Babylon, Israel's tormentor (Isa. 51:23). Now the same cup will be given to spiritual Babylon, which will drink "the cup of the wine of the fury of his wrath" (Rev. 16:19). The heavenly sanctuary or temple is *filled with smoke from the glory of God and from his power.* The same phenomenon occurred in the earthly tabernacle and temple (Exod. 40:34-35; 1 Kgs. 8:10-11; 2 Chron. 5:13-14; Isa. 6:4). Ezekiel likewise saw an angel clothed in linen standing by four cherubim in the heavenly temple (Ezek. 10:9), which was also filled with the cloud of the glory of God (Ezek. 10:2-4). God's presence within his temple is such that *no one could enter the sanctuary* until the plagues were finished (verse 8).

THE FIRST FIVE BOWLS (16:1-11)

The bowl judgments commence: *Then I heard a loud voice from the temple telling the seven angels, "Go and pour out on the earth the seven bowls of the wrath of God"* (verse 1). This verse alludes to Isa. 66:6: "A sound from the temple! The sound of the Lord, rendering recompense to his enemies." The pouring out of God's wrath in the Old Testament is a figurative expression for God's judgment of those who have violated his covenant and persecuted his people (Ezek. 14:19; Jer. 10:25; Ps. 69:24). The bowls are not literal, but represent the judgments of God that come in various ways on unbelievers throughout the church age. There is a great similarity between the trumpets and the bowls. These show that the bowls portray the events of world history in the same way as the trumpets, though with some variations of detail. We could compare this to the fact the four Gospels cover the same period of history, but each records the details from a different perspective. The bowl judgments emphasize more consistently the fact that the plagues fall upon hardened unbelievers dwelling in the kingdom of the beast, who practice idolatry (16:2), refuse to repent (16:9, 11) and persecute Christians (16:6). The bowls (16:5-7), like the trumpets (8:3-5), represent the answer to the prayers of the saints for justice as recorded in 6:9-11. Both trumpets and bowls present the plagues in the same order. They both strike (in sevenfold sequence) the earth, the sea, the rivers, the sun, the realm of the wicked with darkness, the Euphrates, and the entire world with the final judgment. They are both accompanied by lightning, sounds, thunders, earthquake, and great hail. Both trumpets and bowls are rooted in the Exodus plagues. The plagues of Exodus serve as typological judgments, prophetically foreshadowing the plagues of the church age and culminating in the final judgment of the wicked.

The first bowl is poured out: *So the first angel went and poured out his bowl on the earth, and harmful and painful sores came upon the people who bore the mark of the beast and worshiped its image* (verse 2). The first bowl judgment is based on the Egyptian plague of literal boils (Exod. 9:9-11). As often in Revelation, it expresses the principle of the punishment fitting the crime. Those who receive *the mark of the beast*, which benefits them socially and economically in this life, will as a result also receive a mark of judgment in the form of the sores. Bearing in mind our comments on the figurative nature of the visions, we should not necessarily restrict the meaning to physical boils. The reference is to any type of physical or even psychological judgment causing pain or suffering. The spread of sickness and disease, sometimes in plague-like form, is a constant characteristic of human history, down to the present day. This does not mean that all disasters or sicknesses are an expression of the judgment of God, although the bowl judgments particularly highlight the punishment of unbelievers. For believers, sickness and suffering are part and parcel of living in a fallen world, and do not necessarily point to a particular degree of sinfulness or disobedience in a person. The sincere Christian also humbly recognizes his or her ongoing participation in the fallenness of this world as expressed in Rom. 3:23: "All have sinned and [continue to] fall short of the glory of God."

The second angel poured out his bowl into the sea, and it became like the blood of a corpse, and every living thing died that was in the sea (verse 3). The second bowl, like the second trumpet, is based on Exod. 7:17-21, where Moses turned the Nile into blood and its fish died. The "sea" in Revelation refers to the dwelling place both of demonic figures (13:1) and unbelievers (17:1). It also refers to the world's economic system (18:17-19), as represented by maritime commerce. The plague on the sea represents God's judgment on the world's economy, and that judgment leads to the downfall of the merchants who facilitate that commerce, as well as the consumers who benefit from it. Death need not be taken literally, but includes reference to the failure of economies and the suffering caused by it. The second trumpet pictures this plague as affecting one-third of the world, whereas here the effect is universal. The trumpets could speak of times when only part of the world's economic system is affected, while the bowls speak of times of more severe judgment. Both are features of economic history. It also reflects the fact that the bowl judgments speak of God's judgments in a more intense manner.

The third angel poured out his bowl into the rivers and the springs of water, and they became blood. And I heard the angel in charge of the waters say, "Just are you, O Holy One, who is and who was, for you brought these judgments. For they have shed the blood of saints and prophets, and you have given them blood to drink. It is what they deserve!" And I heard the altar saying, "Yes, Lord God the Almighty, true and just are your judgments" (verses 4-7). The third bowl is similar to the third trumpet, again with the apparent distinction (as not all waters appear to be affected in the trumpets) between partial and universal effect. Once more, the punishment fits the crime: as the wicked have shed the blood of the righteous, they also will be given blood to drink (for the same idea, see 11:18; 14:8-10; 17:14; 18:6, 7-8). Later, John describes God's judgment on Babylon in similar words: "In her was found the blood of prophets and of saints, and of all who have been slain on earth" (18:24). The third bowl is thus a preliminary form of that final judgment. "Drinking blood" was a figurative expression for oppression. This expression as a whole goes back to Ps. 79:3, 10, 12, where the Psalmist calls for God to avenge the blood of his people poured out like water. The third bowl, like the third trumpet, is based on the Exodus plague on the Nile, both dealing with judgment on the world's economic system. The blood is thus figurative, referring to various degrees of suffering endured by the lost. The third bowl is concluded with a declaration from the **altar** that God's judgments are right. Mention of the **altar** combined with the mention of God's judgments takes us back to 6:9-10 and the cry of the saints "under the altar." The altar itself is not speaking -- the cry **Yes, Lord God** probably represents the voice of the deceased saints pictured in chapter 6. There, they were asking God to exercise judgment on the earth-dwellers for their slaying of the saints. Now, their prayers are beginning to be answered ,as these judgments fall on the lost who have oppressed them in various ways. God's judgment on unbelievers is emphasized again.

The fourth angel poured out his bowl on the sun, and it was allowed to scorch people with fire. They were scorched by the fierce heat, and they cursed the name of God who had power over these plagues. They did not repent and give him glory (verses 8-9). *Fire*, as often in Revelation (8:7; 9:18; 14:18; 15:2; 19:20; 20:10), is a figurative way of referring to God's judgments. Frequently in the Old Testament the outpouring of God's anger is expressed in relation to fire. According to Jeremiah: "My anger and my wrath will be poured out on this place, upon man and beast... it will burn and not be quenched" (Jer. 7:20). To this Ezekiel added: "I will gather you and blow on you with the fire of my wrath, and you shall be melted in the midst of it... and you shall know that I am the Lord; I have poured out my wrath upon you" (Ezek. 22:21-22). The Exodus plague on which this appears to be modeled is that in which thunder, hail and fire struck the earth, bringing judgment on Egypt's economy. According to Deut. 32:19-27, God's fire will be kindled, as here, against idolaters and the disobedient. This fire is interpreted figuratively in Deuteronomy as pestilence, war and famine. Outside of chapter 16, cursing God is attributed to the beast alone. The blaspheming of unbelievers here shows they have taken on the characteristics of their master. In the face of dire economic judgments probably involving natural calamities also, they refuse to acknowledge God and give him glory. The fourth bowl continues the emphasis on the punishment of unbelievers prevalent in the bowl judgments. The judgments have the effect of hardening the hearts of unbelievers further, rather than driving them to repentance.

The fifth angel poured out his bowl on the throne of the beast, and its kingdom was plunged into darkness. People gnawed their tongues in anguish and cursed the God of heaven for their pains and sores. They did not repent of their deeds (verses 10-11). The *throne* represents the beast's power over his dominion. This is just the same as the way the "throne of Satan" (2:13) represented the similar demonic power behind worldly rulers oppressing the saints in Pergamum. The fifth bowl, like the fourth trumpet, is based on the Exodus plague of darkness. The *darkness* here is figurative, as with the other plagues. In Exodus, people could not see those around them, nor could they attend to normal activities. Darkness is also used figuratively in the Old Testament to describe God's judgment. Isa. 8:20-22 describes a severe famine which God will bring on disobedient Israel as a "darkness" without a "dawn." Jer. 13:16-17 speaks of the nation's coming defeat as "twilight," "gloom" and "deep darkness." In both those cases, the normal functioning of society and government broke down, as it did with the literal darkness of the Egyptian plague. This bowl thus refers to a breakdown in the functioning of the demonically-controlled systems of government in the world. This brings suffering, both psychological and economic, upon their followers. The love of money and the false security it offers is a particular idolatrous expression of the rebellion of unbelievers. Economic judgment inflicts pain and fear on those who love and trust in money and the ungodly world system. In response to the fifth bowl judgment, unbelievers *cursed the God of heaven* and *did not repent*. Like Pharaoh, their hearts were hardened, and they only cursed God further. The mention of *sores* links this judgment to the first bowl plague. This suggests again that all these plagues are characteristic of various stages of human history. The sixth trumpet judgment also highlights unbelievers' refusal to repent. It lists their sins as idolatry, murder, sorcery, sexual immorality and thefts (9:20-21). In the face of repeated and increasing judgment, they only sink further into this deep pit of sin and rebellion.

The first five bowl plagues describe human history throughout the church age, beginning with Christ's resurrection. The sixth and seventh bowls, like the sixth and seventh seals and trumpets, however, speak specifically of the final judgment. The account of the sixth bowl begins: *The sixth angel poured out his bowl on the great river Euphrates, and its water was dried up, to prepare the way for the kings from the east* (verse 12). The drying up of the Euphrates is a last-days fulfillment of the prophetic words of Isaiah and Jeremiah (Isa. 11:15; 44:27-28; Jer. 50:38; 51:36). These prophetic words were originally and literally fulfilled when the Euphrates was diverted to allow Cyrus, a king from the east (Isa. 41:2), to conquer Babylon, and after that to set Israel free from captivity (Isa. 44:26-28; 45:13; 2 Chron. 36:22-23). This prophesied event was itself patterned after the drying up of the Red Sea (Exod. 14:21-22; Isa. 11:15; 50:2; 51:10). God dries up the water, either to deliver, to judge or both. This time it is the waters of spiritual Babylon which will be dried up. The Old Testament is clear that historical Babylon was destroyed, and will never be rebuilt (Jer. 50:39-40; 51:24-26, 62-64). Babylon is therefore figurative or spiritual in nature. The Euphrates must therefore also be figurative in nature, rather than referring to the literal river. This is demonstrated by 17:1, where spiritual Babylon sits "on many waters," which refers to the spiritual Euphrates. In 17:15, these waters of the Euphrates are figuratively interpreted as "peoples and multitudes and nations and languages." This is parallel to the figurative use of "sea" when used in connection with the beast or his followers (12:15, 16; 13:1; 15:2; 17:1, 15). If the Euphrates pictures the unbelieving multitudes throughout the world who follow the beast, its drying up represents the loss of their allegiance to spiritual Babylon. What this looks like is explained in 17:16-17, when civil war breaks out in the kingdom of darkness. If Babylon and the Euphrates are spiritually universalized in Revelation, then so also are Cyrus and *the kings from the east*. These kings are not literally from the east of Babylon, and are in fact reinterpreted in verse 14 as "the kings of the whole world." An Old Testament historical example is taken as a prophetic or typological fore-shadowing of events of the last days, and is to be understood in this light. The kings of the whole world will gather together in rebellion against Babylon as part of the purpose of God that both they and Babylon be destroyed.

THE SIXTH BOWL: (1) THE ENEMY GATHERS HIS FORCES (16:12-15)

Verse 12 gives a summary statement concerning the sixth bowl. Verses 13-16 give the details of the plague. The pouring out of the bowl initiates activities by the three great opponents of God: *And I saw, coming out of the mouth of the dragon and out of the mouth of the beast and out of the mouth of the false prophet, three unclean spirits like frogs* (verse 13). The phrase *false prophet* occurs for the first time in the book. It describes the deceptive function of the second beast. Prior to this, we have seen that the dragon is the devil, and the beast is the demonic power behind evil world governments. Now we see the false prophet revealed as the demonic power behind all false religious movements. The false prophet, according to 13:11-18, deceives people into supporting the beast through supernatural or apparently spiritual activi-ties. False prophets in the New Testament function within the covenant community, either of Israel (Lk. 6:26; Ac. 13:6; 2 Pet. 2:1) or the church (Mt. 7:15; 24:11, 24; Mk. 13:22, 1 Jn. 4:1). It is thus possible that the demonic false prophet here will be active not only in the world but also among God's people, trying to entice them away from Christ. Church history affords many sad examples of such Satanic ac-tivity, down to the present day. Out of the mouths of each spirit come *frogs*, which takes us back to the Exodus plague of frogs (Exod. 8:2-14). This is the only other time frogs are mentioned in the Bible (excluding two references to the plague in the Psalms). Frogs are chosen to represent these unclean spirits simply because the bowl judgments are modeled on and fulfill the original Exodus plagues. In addition to this, they were one of the two plagues the Egyptian magicians were able to recreate, thus signifying spiritual deception similar to that of the three evil beings here. Jewish tradition held that their croaking sound confused the Egyptians, reinforcing the deception theme. That they are described as **unclean spirits** makes sense in that frogs were unclean animals (Lev. 11:9-12, 41-47). The plague of frogs in Exodus signified God's judgment on Heqt, the Egyptian goddess of resurrection, who was represented by a frog. It is significant that the false prophet testifies to the apparent resurrection of the beast (13:3, 12). This is a counterfeit of the apostolic witness of the church testifying to Christ's true resurrection. The frogs in Exodus were sent by God. Even though these frogs issue from the mouth of the enemy, ultimately they are used (and sent) by God to help bring about the downfall of the beast's kingdom.

They are now further described: *For they are demonic spirits, performing signs, who go abroad to the kings of the whole world, to assemble them for battle on the great day of God the Almighty* (verse 14). The deception of the frog spirits is aimed at the kings. This is not surprising, as the frog plague was the first to affect the king of Egypt (Exod. 8:3-4; Ps. 105:30). *The kings of the whole world* is a phrase used in Revelation to denote ungodly rulers (1:5; 6:15; 17:2, 18; 18:3, 9). The phrase may derive from Ps. 2:2: "The kings of the earth set themselves, and the rulers take counsel together, against the Lord and against his Anointed." This verse was quoted by the early church in their Jerusalem prayer meeting (Ac. 4:26). The fact that they perform signs indicates the false-religious nature of their activity. The false prophet likewise is said to perform "great signs" (13:13; also 19:20).

The purpose of the enemy's deception is to *assemble them for battle*. The same battle or war is referred to in 19:19, where the beast, the false prophet and the kings are "gathered to make war." It is also the battle mentioned in 20:8, where Satan and the nations of the world are gathered "for battle." The three synonymous phrases (16:14; 19:19; 20:8) are based on Old Testament prophecies that God would gather the nations together for the final war of history: "I will gather all the nations to Jerusalem to battle" (Zech. 14:2; see Zechariah chapters 12-14; Ezek. 38:2-9; 39:1-8). The three parallel references in Revelation are all prefaced by the definite article ("the"). This gives a different nuance to the meaning of the phrase. It is not just "for battle" but rather "for that battle." It is for that war of the end the Bible has prophesied and that we all know about because it is prophesied by Ezekiel and Zechariah. Given that the three passages in chapters 16, 19 and 20 all refer back to "that" battle the prophets were foretelling, it means that all three passages are referring to the same war. This will have great significance for our understanding of the millennium. The battle of 20:8, which takes place at the end of the millennium, is the same battle alluded to in chapters 16 and 19. This proves that the millennium itself covers the same time period as that ending in the great battle of chapters 16 and 19 -- namely, the church age.

The war will be fought by spiritual Babylon, not a literal Babylon which will never be rebuilt. Likewise, it will be fought against spiritual Jerusalem, the church, not the literal, historical Jerusalem. The phrase *the great day of God* also refers to this last battle and is taken from Joel 2:11, 31 (quoted in Mt. 24:29; Mk. 13:24; Ac. 2:20) and Zeph. 1:14. Joel refers to a historical judgment against literal Jerusalem, but at Pentecost Peter reinterprets it as a future event. The same battle is also referred in the sixth seal judgment as the "great day" of the wrath of God and the Lamb (6:17). This demonstrates once again that the three series of judgments, as well as the seven visions of conflict, all recount the same basic events of history, which are again retold in chapters 19 and 20. This war, as 19:19 makes clear, is against God himself, but is also, as 20:9 shows, against the saints. Satan will make one last effort to destroy God's authority and wipe out the saints, but he will fail.

Because this war is directed against the saints, an exhortation is addressed to them: *Behold, I am coming like a thief! Blessed is the one who stays awake, keeping his garments on, that he may not go about naked and be seen exposed!* (verse 15). The same exhortation is given to the Laodiceans (3:18). It was as relevant to believers then as it is to believers now and to those in the last generation before Christ returns. The language here shows the close link between the letters and the visions. It is rooted in the Old Testament imagery of nakedness as symbolizing God's judgment on Israel for her participation in idolatry (Isa. 20:4-5; Ezek. 16:36; 23:29; Nah. 3:5). In spite of the pressure to deny Christ and conform to the idolatrous practices of the world around, believers are to stand firm in light of the certainty of their final triumph. The *garments* are later identified as "fine linen... the righteous deeds of the saints" (19:8).

THE SIXTH BOWL: (2) ARMAGEDDON AND THE BEGINNINGS OF THE LAST JUDGMENT
(16:16-21)

The account now comes to its peak: *And they assembled themselves at the place that in Hebrew is called Armageddon* (verse 16). The literal Hebrew words are Har-Magedon, or the "mountain of Megiddo." The reference is not to a literal geographical location. The Old Testament prophecies, taken literally, suggest the battle will be held right outside Jerusalem (Joel 2:1, 32; Mic. 4:11-12; Zech. 12:3-4; 14:2, 13-14). Yet Megiddo was a two day's journey from Jerusalem. Not only that, Megiddo is a plain, and the town called Megiddo sits at most on a very small rise of land, whereas the Hebrew word *har* refers to a mountain. John is likely combining two significant places in Old Testament history into one symbolic location. The plain of Megiddo was the site of two famous battles (Judg. 5:19; 2 Kgs. 23:29; 2 Chron. 35:22). It became a symbol for the place where righteous Jews were attacked by wicked nations. Eventually, it also became a prophetic symbol for the Jewish people of the last battle. In the conflict with Barak and Sisera, God said he would "draw out" Sisera (Judg. 4:7) to the "waters of Megiddo" (Judg. 5:19). In the same way, he gathers the pagan kings here for battle at the mountain of Megiddo. At Megiddo, the righteous King Josiah was defeated by the Pharaoh (symbolic of the dragon) on his way to the Euphrates! The mountain referred to is likely Mount Carmel, which was not far from Megiddo. Mount Carmel was the location of another of the Old Testament's greatest battles (1 Kgs. 18:19-46). There Elijah (symbolic of the church in Rev. 11:3-7) defeated the prophets of Baal.

John joins the two somewhat close but separate locales into one symbolic place -- the mountain of Megiddo or (in Greek transliteration) *Armageddon*. Consider the parallels between the two Old Testament references and the composite figurative Armageddon. Both feature the defeat of kings oppressing God's people (Judg. 5:19-21; Rev. 16:14; 19:17). Both feature the destruction of false prophets (1 Kgs. 18:40; Rev. 19:20). Even though Josiah is considered a "good" king, both feature the death of kings who are misled or deceived (2 Kgs. 23:29; 2 Chron. 35:20-25; Rev. 16:13-14). Ezekiel refers to the last battle occurring not in or near Jerusalem, but on the mountains of Israel (38:8; 39:2-8). This may form part of the allusion here. In fact, Ezek. 38:16 sees the whole land of Israel being the battleground, thus showing even the prophets did not have one clear locale in mind. It is no surprise that Armageddon is a figurative reference, considering that the battle is fought not between literal Babylon and literal Israel but between spiritual Babylon (the evil world system) and spiritual Israel (the world-wide body of Christ). The locale for Armageddon is thus worldwide in nature.

The outcome of the battle is not given here, but is clearly stated in 17:14; 19:14-21; and 20:7-10. Directly following the battle, *The seventh angel poured out his bowl into the air, and a loud voice came out of the temple, from the throne, saying, "It is done!"* (verse 17). The seventh bowl describes the final destruction of the world system. The hailstones of verse 21 link this judgment with the Exodus plague of hail (Exod. 9:22-35). The fact that the voice comes *from the throne* suggests it is either God or Christ speaking. The cry *"It is done"* echoes Christ's cry on Calvary, "It is finished." This time, however, the words (ironically if it is Christ speaking) have a reverse meaning: what is finished is not the work of salvation, but the process of God's judgment. The voice of judgment has an accompaniment: *And there were flashes of lightning, rumblings, peals of thunder, and a great earthquake such as there had never been since man was on the earth, so great was the earthquake* (verse 18). These cosmic effects occur first in God's appearance at Sinai. There, all four elements are present (Exod. 19:16-19). They are signs warning of God's judgment on any who approach. Isaiah says the judgment of God will be accompanied by thunder, earthquake and great noise (Isa. 29:6). Jesus saw earthquakes as symbolic of judgments in this present age (Mt. 24:7; Mk. 13:8; Lk. 21:22). The elements appear earlier in Revelation (4:5; 8:5; 11:19). That this is the last judgment is indicated by the statement there had never been an earthquake like it. This fulfills the prophetic vision of Daniel: "And there shall be a time of trouble, such as never has been since there was a nation till that time" (Dn. 12:1). Daniel's time of trouble occurs immediately prior to the resurrection and last judgment (Dn. 12:2). Daniel's words are a prophetic application of the words describing the original Exodus plague on which this bowl judgment is based: "There was... very heavy hail, such as had never been seen in all the land of Egypt since it became a nation" (Exod. 9:24). This shows again how the plagues of Revelation are firmly rooted in the plagues of Egypt. Daniel prophesies a recurrence of these plagues in the last days, which for John began with the death and resurrection of Christ and continue until his return.

The account reaches its climax: *The great city was split into three parts, and the cities of the nations fell, and God remembered Babylon the great, the make her drain the cup of the wine of the fury of his wrath* (verse 19). The prophets foresaw a devastating earthquake accompanying God's final act of judgment (Hag. 2:6; Zech. 14:14; see Heb. 12:26-27). The reference *Babylon the great* is quoted from Dn. 4:30, where the earthly Babylonian king was facing judgment. Now spiritual Babylon is about to fall, along with the *cities of the nations,* all of which are part of the worldly political and economic system described as Babylon. The judgment is universal, and not limited to a literal Middle Eastern locale. Earthly Babylon was destroyed forever (Jer. 51:26), never to rise again (Jer. 51:64; see Jer. 50:39-40; 51:24-26, 62-64; Isa. 13:19-22). Babylon's punishment, as elsewhere in Revelation, fits the crime. As she has given the saints and prophets blood to drink (see 16:6), so she must now drink the wine of God's wrath. With this plague, however, the last judgment is imminent.

The picture of the world's total destruction concludes: *And every island fled away, and no mountains were to be found. And great hailstones, about one hundred pounds each, fell from heaven on people; and they cursed God for the plague of the hail, because the plague was so severe* (verses 20-21). Nearly identical descriptions of the last judgment are found in the parallel accounts of 6:14 ("and every mountain and island was removed from its place"), and 20:11 ("earth and sky fled away, and no place was found for them"). This shows again that the same events are referred to in all three places. The "last days of the last days" plague of hail, unlike the Egyptian plague, is universal in extent. The hail comes down from heaven like the fire of 20:9, describing the same cataclysmic event, bringing God's final judgment on the lost. The cursing of the people does not necessarily indicate that they survived the plague, but that they cursed God during it. In contrast to the cursing of verses 9 and 11, no time is now left for repentance. Even as they face final doom, lost humanity, with hearts irredeemably hardened, has time only to curse the Creator who made them and sent his Son to save them. This proves the justice of God's judgment upon them.

8

THE FINAL JUDGMENT OF BABYLON AND THE BEAST

(17:1-19:21)

*The relationship of Babylon and the beast
(17:1-18)*

*The destruction of Babylon and the rejoicing of
the saints (18:1-19:10)*

*Christ reveals his sovereignty in his final defeat
of the beast and his allies (19:11-21)*

THE RELATIONSHIP OF BABYLON AND THE BEAST (17:1-18)

This section, divided into three parts, amplifies the contents of the sixth and seventh bowls. Chapter 17 is the first part of this section. It explains the relationship between Babylon and the beast. The position and power of the woman portrayed here is dependent on her relationship with the beast. Chapter 18:1- 19:10 describes the fall of Babylon and the consequent rejoicing of the saints. The section concludes in 19:11-21 with a description of the last battle immediately preceding the final judgment.

DESCRIPTION OF THE GREAT PROSTITUTE (17:1-6A)

The vision commences: *Then one of the seven angels who had the seven bowls came and said to me, "Come, I will show you the judgment of the great prostitute who is seated on many waters, with whom the kings of the earth have committed sexual immorality, and with the wine of whose sexual immorality the dwellers on earth have become drunk"* (verses 1-2). The presence of the bowl angel indicates that the vision about to be given relates to the bowl judgments. The content of the vision is God's judgment of *the great prostitute.* This indicates that the vision is an amplification of the sixth and seventh bowl judgments, which relate the climactic final days of history and the fall of Babylon. The angel speaks to John in words taken from God's judgment on historical Babylon: "O you who dwell by many waters, rich in treasures, your end has come" (Jer. 51:13). The fact that Babylon sits on *many waters* signifies her authority over the nations, for "sitting" in Revelation (3:21; 4:2, 4; 5:1; 14:14; 18:7) indicates possession of authority, no matter of whom it is used. The Greek word for *sexual immorality* (*porneia*) refers in Revelation primarily to self-serving participation in economic and religious activities. The primary reference is to the Old Testament thought of people breaking their marriage covenant with God by pursuing other gods. Hosea says that Israel has forsaken the Lord to "inquire of a piece of wood... for a spirit of whoredom has led them astray" (Hos. 4:12). Idolatry and immoral activity are closely connected in Revelation (see 2:14, 20-21; 9:21; 14:8). The nations and their inhabitants have become dependent on Babylon's promises of economic security and thus turned their back on the true security that comes alone from God. This becomes very clear in 18:3, 9-19, where the ideas of sexual immorality and drunkenness noted here in verse 2 are used to describe the world economic system.

Babylon is thus to be defined as a demonically-inspired and empowered economic and religious system which exists throughout the church age. It uses the power of the state to oppress the saints.

Next, John is transported: *And he carried me away in the Spirit into a wilderness* (verse 3a). The phrase *in the Spirit* refers again to John's commissioning as a prophet (for similar phrases see Ezek. 2:2; 3:12, 14, 24; 11:1; 43:5). The background to this seems to be Isaiah 21, where an "oracle" comes "from the wilderness" (Isa. 21:1), proclaiming "Fallen, fallen is Babylon" (21:9). The very same words are spoken by the angel in 18:2, this time concerning spiritual Babylon rather than historical Babylon. The Old Testament prophesies that historical Babylon will be made like a wilderness when she is judged (Isa. 13:20-22; Jer. 50:12-13; 51:26, 29, 43). This is also the fate of spiritual Babylon. It is in the wilderness where the "great red dragon, with seven heads and ten horns" (12:3) persecutes the saints (12:13-17). Yet the wilderness is also the place where the church is kept by God. It signifies the present church age, where God has delivered the church from Egypt, but not yet delivered it into the promised land of the new Jerusalem.

In the wilderness, John sees the same sight as in chapter 12: *And I saw a woman sitting on a scarlet beast that was full of blasphemous names, and it had seven heads and ten horns* (verse 3b). The description of the beast indicates its close relationship to the dragon. It is the same beast portrayed in 13:1 which, like the dragon, has seven heads and ten horns. The meaning, as in 13:1, is drawn from Daniel's vision of the four beasts, which between them had seven heads and ten horns (Dn. 7:3-7, 20, 24). The *blasphemous names* connote the beast's false claims to divine status. The numbers seven and ten signify completeness, and so the heads and horns represent the fullness or complete nature of the beast's power to oppress the saints. The scarlet color of the beast indicates its persecuting nature, and links it again with the scarlet dragon of 12:3. The color is also linked with the fact it is drunk with the blood of the saints (see verse 6). The fact that the woman sits on the beast indicates that, though she is not to be identified with the beast, she is closely allied with it. The woman represents the ungodly world system in its political, social and economic dimensions, all of which are used to oppress the saints. The beast represents the supernatural demonic power which energizes this system. The description of the woman indicates her close relationship to the dragon and the beast. This woman dwelling in the desert persecutes the saints (verse 6) and deceives the earth-dwellers (verse 8). It is in the desert that John sees the downfall of the beast and his allies (verses 13-14) as well as that of the woman Babylon (verses 15-17). On the Biblical principle of the punishment fitting the crime so often used in Revelation (see also 11:18; 16:6; 18:6, 7), Babylon is judged in the very same place in which she persecuted the saints.

That the woman represents particularly the economic power of the state is clear from verse 4, where the richness of her attire shows how she seduces through the promise of wealth: *The woman was arrayed in purple and scarlet, and adorned with gold and jewels and pearls, holding in her hand a golden cup full of abominations and the impurities of her sexual immorality* (verse 4). The *scarlet* represents her persecution of the saints. Isaiah and Jeremiah also speak of prostitutes in red clothing which, as here, symbolizes their spilling of the saints' blood (Isa. 1:15-23; Jer. 2:34). The picture of the *golden cup full of abominations* is rooted in Jeremiah's description of Babylon as a golden cup making the earth drunk and driving the nations insane (Jer. 51:7-8). The *impurities* include idolatrous practices. In 16:13-14 and 18:2, demons are referred to as "unclean" or "impure," and it is demons who are the power behind idolatry (1 Cor. 10: 19-20). The *abominations* in the woman's cup also describe idolatry, for the word is used frequently in the Old Testament in that connection (Deut. 29:17; 2 Kgs. 23:24; 2 Chron. 34:33; Jer. 16:18). There is a clear connection in Revelation (see 2:18-29) between ungodly forms of economic activity (including simply the worship of money) and idolatrous practices (with their sexual connotations), often represented in the concept of *porneia*, and the woman represents both.

The nature of the woman is revealed: *And on her forehead was written a name of mystery: "Babylon the great, mother of prostitutes and of earth's abominations." And I saw the woman, drunk with the blood of the saints, the blood of the martyrs of Jesus* (verses 5-6). In Revelation, a name or mark on the forehead is a sign of allegiance and of character. A person belongs either to God (7:3; 14:1) or to the devil (13:16; 14:9). In this case, the name on the forehead indicates allegiance to the world system, behind which the beast operates as an agent of the devil. The title *Babylon the great* comes from Dn. 4:30. There it appears in the context of Nebuchadnezzar's boastful independence of God, which led to his downfall. The *mystery* is a reference to Dn. 4:9. There it describes the "mystery" of the king's dream, which warned of disaster to come if he continued in a prideful attitude toward God. This "mystery" is now connected with the mystery of the fall of spiritual Babylon, which likewise exhibits an arrogant and rebellious attitude toward God. The mystery was prophesied to be fulfilled in the "days of the trumpet call to be sounded by the seventh angel" (Rev. 10:7). It has up till now been known only to God, but through John he is revealing it to those with the wisdom to understand. The concept of "mystery" in the New Testament is linked with the idea of the fulfillment of Old Testament prophecy in an unexpected manner (see on 1:20 and 10:7; Rom. 11:25; 16:25-27; 1 Cor. 15:51; Eph. 3:4; Col. 1:26-27). A central part of the mystery is that the establishment of the kingdom of God and the fall of spiritual Babylon are not to come with military force and power, as was often assumed by Jewish readers of Old Testament prophecy. Instead, they are to come through the sufferings of Christ and those who follow in his footsteps. A further aspect of the mystery is that the fall of Babylon will occur through a self-destruction or kind of civil war which begins even before the events surrounding the return of Christ. This will be revealed in verses 15-18 of this chapter.

The woman is also called ***mother of prostitutes and of earth's abominations.*** This demonstrates her role in promoting idolatry and false religion. Babylon is consciously contrasted with another woman, the church. Babylon is described as a woman in the desert, and also as a city (17:10). The church is described as a woman who lives in the desert (12:1), and also as a bride (19:7-8; 21:2, 10) who is a city (21:2). These contrasts make it clear that, even as the church exists throughout the world from Pentecost to the Lord's return, so also does spiritual Babylon. Babylon, as portrayed in Revelation, is not to be identified with any one geographical location or as existing at any one particular time only in history. The two women are in complete opposition to each other: Babylon is pictured as ***drunk with the blood of the saints.*** Those who do not submit to Babylon's economic and spiritual idolatry will suffer in various ways: exile (1:9), imprisonment (2:10) and even death (2:10, 13). All of these sufferings were beginning to occur as John wrote, and they will continue throughout the church age. "Drinking blood" was a figure of speech encompassing all forms of oppression, not just death.

THE BEAST AND THE SEVEN KINGS (17:6B-10)

John's response is recorded: ***When I saw her, I marveled greatly*** (verse 6). Daniel was fearful, alarmed and dismayed on receiving the vision of God's judgment on

Nebuchadnezzar (Dn. 4:5, 19). That vision is a prophetic foreshadowing of John's vision of the destruction of spiritual Babylon, so it is not surprising that his reaction was similar to Daniel's — one of astonished perplexity. He might have been appalled at the picture of Babylon drinking the blood of the saints, or wondered how such a picture of Babylon's magnificent appearance and triumph over the saints could fit with the angel's pronouncement of Babylon's judgment (verse 1). The angel, however, brings both clarity and reassurance: *But the angel said to me, "Why do you marvel?" I will tell you the mystery of the woman, and of the beast with seven heads and ten horns that carries her. The beast that you saw was, and is not, and is about to rise from the bottomless pit and go to destruction* (verses 7-8a). The angel will unfold the judgment about to come in spite of the woman's apparent magnificence and power. God has been described four times as the One who was and is and is to come (1:8; 4:8; 11:16; 16:5). This description is now applied to the beast, but only in order to mock him. The beast *was, and is not, and is about to rise... and go to destruction.* The *is not* refers to the defeat of the beast at the cross. He is still active, in that his wound was healed (13:3), but his power is restricted and exercised only with God's permission. The beast's apparent resurrection is evident in the fact he still operates in the world in spite of Christ's triumph over him. This apparent resurrection will be confirmed further at the end of the age when he is released briefly from the bottomless pit. Though he will arise again (*is about to rise*), and briefly appear to succeed in conquering the church, in fact he will rise only to go to his doom (he will *go to destruction*). The language of the angel mirrors what Daniel saw in his vision — the beasts came up from the sea (Dn. 7:3, 17) and went to destruction (7:11, 26). The beast's rising from the bottomless pit shows his close relationship to the devil, for that is the devil's dwelling place (9:1, 2, 11). At the very end of the church age, the beast will rise from the bottomless pit (11:7) and appear to bring devastating defeat to the church. But his victory is illusory, for he will soon be destroyed. A similar pattern is applied to Satan in 20:1-10. He was active on earth, but through Christ's triumph was bound in the bottomless pit. He will then be released for a brief time before going to destruction. The same events are being described, first with respect to the beast and then with respect to the devil.

The earth-dwellers will be amazed by the exploits of the beast: *And the dwellers on earth whose names have not been written in the book of life from the foundation of the world will marvel to see the beast, because it was and is not and is to come* (verse 8b).

They will marvel at the beast's apparent triumph, which deceives them into believing that he is invincible. A day will come when the power of the beast and of the devil will appear as strong as it was on the day Christ was crucified. True believers, however, will be protected from such deception, because God has written their names *in the book of life.* This happens through their identification with the saving death of Christ. The book is identified closely with the Lamb (13:8 and 21:27). True believers will not be deceived by these dire events: *This calls for a mind with wisdom: the seven heads are seven mountains on which the woman is seated; they are also seven kings, five of whom have fallen, one is, the other has not yet come, and when he does come, he must remain only a little while* (verses 9-10). There are seven heads in total on the four beasts of Dn. 7:4-7. This is the background to the *seven heads* of the beast here and in 13:1. The image of a sea beast or dragon is used throughout the Old Testament to symbolize a wide variety of evil kingdoms spanning centuries of time (Ps. 74:13-14; 89:10; Isa. 27:1; 30:7; 51:9; Ezek. 29:3; 32:2-3; Hab. 3:13-14). Seven is the number of completion (=the full number), and so these heads are representative of all kingdoms which oppose Christ and are controlled by the beast. The *seven heads* are also identified as *seven mountains.* *Mountains* in Revelation carry the meaning of strength. In 8:8 and 14:1, mountains also refer figuratively to kingdoms, as is the case in the Old Testament (Isa. 2:2; Jer. 51:25; Ezek. 35:3; Dn. 2:35, 45; Zech. 4:7). The reference is not to a particular geographical location with seven literal mountains (such as Rome, which was built on seven hills). Daniel prophesied that in the last days, the power of an evil state would arise, but those who are "wise among the people" (like those *with wisdom* here) would gain understanding, even though many of the righteous would be slain (Dn. 11:33-34). In Daniel's prophecy, the righteous will be purified in the ensuing suffering, but the wicked will continue in their ignorance (11:35, 12;10). What John sees here is the last-days fulfillment of Daniel's prophecy. Through reading these prophetic warnings, even believers who have lost their first love will be shaken out of their stupor and restored as they realize the urgency of the situation. In the meantime, unbelievers will mock the warnings and go from bad to worse. Thus is fulfilled what the angel speaks in 22:11: "Let the evildoer still do evil, and the filthy still be filthy, and the righteous still do right, and the holy still be holy."

The way in which the information regarding the seven kings is given is deliberate. Five are fallen, one is, one is yet to come, but he too will fall. This continues the way in which the beast was mocked in verse 8. The beast and the kings are compared to God, who was, is and is to come. The beast and the kings will meet an end, while only God lives forever. The reference to various kings shows clearly that no one king or kingdom is being referred to. *Seven* signifies the full number of evil kings throughout the church age. The number is figurative, as are all other numbers in Revelation. It occurs 45 times in Revelation outside of 17:3-11, representing the idea of fullness or completion, rooted in the seven days of creation. Sometimes the number denotes completion connected with God the creator (the seven spirits/eyes/torches of fire = the Holy Spirit in 4:5; 5:6), but at other times it simply connotes the idea of totality (the seven churches and their seven angels in chapters 2-3, the various sets of seven plagues). The seven kings or kingdoms thus represent the oppressive power of governments through the ages which seek to destroy the church. They convey the same idea as the four kingdoms with seven heads in Daniel 7, which combine the number of the earth and the number of totality. They speak of the full number of wicked kingdoms throughout the history of the world. Both Babylon and Rome are examples, but many others are included up to the present day. They collectively represent the beast-inspired power of ungodly world government. The dragon of 12:3 also had seven heads and ten horns, symbolizing the fullness of his authority throughout world history. The beast, like the Lamb, exercises his perversion of earthly governments throughout history, not just through a few select kings at its end.

The fact that five kings have fallen simply signifies some have come and gone. Six is the number of man, and thus the sixth king (*one is*) describes the reign not of one literal king or nation, but of a succession of evil men throughout the church age. There is always an expression of fallen humanity behind whatever kingdoms prevail at any given time. One last manifestation of evil is yet to come, but will be short-lived (*he must remain only a little while*). This is the time period referred to as the "three and a half days" in 11:9, and the "little while" of 20:3. The many evil kingdoms of human history can be referred to in Revelation as one kingdom (the "kingdom of the world," 11:15) because in the last analysis, all are manifestations of the power of the beast which controls them.

Some have argued that seven Roman emperors are referred to here. This argument is usually made in support of the preterist understanding that Revelation refers almost exclusively to historical events of the first century. This view ignores the symbolic nature of numbers in Revelation, but also presents a further problem. The sixth Roman emperor was Nero, who died in 68, over twenty years prior to John's vision. Attempts made to identify Nero as 666 by means of the ancient numerological system known as gematria have universally failed (see on 13:18). John wrote in the reign of Domitian, who was the twelfth emperor. This frustrates any attempt to identify the seven kings with first century historical figures. Others, coming from a dispensationalist perspective, identify the five kings with five literal empires, Egypt, Assyria, Babylon, Persia and Greece, the sixth being Rome (which would fit historically with the first century context), and the seventh a kingdom which will arise during the final seven-year tribulation. However, this violates the historical identification of the empires in Daniel 7, which this vision is presented as fulfilling. If we compare Dn. 7:6 and 8:8, 21, it is clear that Greece is the third kingdom, not the fifth, and thus Rome cannot be the sixth. Furthermore, the sixth and seventh empires are pictured in 18:9 as mourning the downfall of the prostitute who is spiritual Babylon. This leads to the question as to how Rome, as the supposed sixth empire, could be understood to have survived to see that day, which clearly has not yet come. How also could the eighth, unidentified empire be one of the seven? And how are we to account for all the various world empires which have arisen since the days of John? But if we keep in mind the figurative nature of numbers in Revelation, we will avoid all such pitfalls. It is a trap to try to identify figurative and pictorial expressions in Revelation with actual historical situations.

THE EIGHTH KING (17:11)

There is a slight shift in the image here. The beast, which in 13:1 and 17:3 was seen as having seven heads, is now identified with the seven heads: *As for the beast that was and is not, it is an eighth but it belongs to the seven, and it goes to destruction* (verse 11). The beast is pictured as being both an eighth head and as belonging to the seven. This signifies that the beast is separate from the world governments he controls. However, his full power and authority are present in each of them. This also reflects a Hebrew idiom in which two consecutive numbers stand for what is *representative of all numbers*, rather than referring to literal numerical realities. For instance, see Prov. 6:16: "There are six things that the Lord hates, seven that are an abomination to him" (also Prov. 30:15, 18, 21, 29). This does not mean there are only six (or seven) things the Lord hates, but alludes to *all the things* displeasing to him. Significantly, the same sequence occurs with the numbers seven and eight: "Give a portion to seven, or even to eight, for you know not what disaster may happen on earth" (Eccl. 11:2). An even closer parallel to our text is found in Mic. 5:5: "when the Assyrian comes into our land.... we will raise against him seven shepherds and eight princes of men." The fact that the numbers seven and eight as used here reflect this kind of Hebrew idiom means that they actually refer to an *indefinite number representative of all evil rulers*. The seven kings and the beast refer to the whole span of ungodly human government over the ages.

However, there may be something even more indicated here. The number eight, like seven, carries a figurative meaning. It is the number of resurrection. Christ died on the sixth day of the week and rested in the tomb on the Sabbath. He rose from the dead on the third day. Counting the day of his death as the first day (= sixth day of the week) places his resurrection on the eighth day. We have seen that the beast is associated with resurrection (13:3), but one which demonically mimics the true resurrection of Christ. His number, 666 (13:18), shows that his imitation falls short, both of fullness or completion and thus of God (seven), and also of resurrection (eight). As such, the fact that the beast is the eighth points to his continued activity in the future, despite his past reversal at the cross. The fact that he is one of the seven shows how he manages to exercise his powers throughout history after his apparently fatal wound. These are the events of church history described in 13:3-18. At present, this power is restricted under God's sovereign plan. Yet a time will come when that power will be so strong that earth dwellers will believe he has triumphed over Christ and the church. This is the time of the height of the beast's resurrection, and it may be that his description here as the *eighth* places the emphasis on his future, rather than present activity. The battle fought at the cross will be fought again - but this time, the beast will not return.

CIVIL WAR IN THE KINGDOM OF DARKNESS (17:12-18)

The angel now turns to the meaning of the ten horns: *And the ten horns that you saw are ten kings who have not yet received royal power, but they are to receive authority as kings for one hour, together with the beast* (verse 12). The ten horns come from the fourth beast of Daniel (Dn. 7:7-8, 19-20, 23-24). As with other numbers in

Revelation, ten is figurative, referring to a large number of kings who are great in power. Similarly, the seven horns of the Lamb (5:6) are figurative for the fullness of his power. This figurative sense suggests that the horns or kings are to be identified with the "kings of the earth" of verse 18 (and also 16:14, 16; 17:2; 18:3, 9; 19:19), who are likewise under the beast's control. Both Satan (12:3) and the beast (13:1) are described as having ten horns, referring to their control over these earthly rulers during the church age. The fact that the ten kings *have not yet received royal power* seems to link them with the seventh beast, which likewise has not yet come, and signifies that brief time immediately prior to Christ's return, when the beast and his agents appear to triumph over the church (11:7-10; 20:3b, 7-9). This is supported by the reference to the very short duration (*one hour*) of their reign. The hour was the shortest period of time measured in the ancient world. The *one hour* is also the time of Babylon's judgment (18:10, 17, 19). That this refers to the very last stage of history could also be confirmed by the fact that the ten horns of Daniel's vision were only on the head of the fourth and final beast. The *royal power* they receive is ultimately given by God, as is shown clearly by verse 17 ("God has put it into their hearts"). Everywhere else in Revelation where clauses of authorization or permission appear, it is clear that God is the subject (for instance, 6:2, 4, 8; 7:2; 9:1, 3, 5; 13:5, 7; 16:8). This emphasizes the fact that God himself is in ultimate control of history, no matter what the immediate circumstances suggest. The reality of his authority is a comfort to believers. Even in their suffering, his eternal plan is being outworked.

The kings submit to the beast's authority: *These are of one mind, and they hand over their power and authority to the beast. They will make war on the Lamb, and the Lamb will conquer them, for he is Lord of lords and King of kings, and those with him are called and chosen and faithful* (verses 13-14). The war fulfills Daniel's vision of the horn making war with the saints and prevailing over them (Dn. 7:21). Yet the final outcome of the battle reverses the prophesied temporary victory of the beast. The Lamb will overcome him even as he has tried to overcome the saints. This is yet another illustration of the "eye for an eye" principle of divine retribution which occurs throughout Revelation (11:18; 14:8-10; 16:6; 18:6, 7-8). The mention of the faithful saints is yet another assurance that the prayers of the saints in 6:9-11 will be answered.

The angel now interprets the meaning of the waters: *And the angel said to me, "The waters that you saw, where the prostitute is seated, are peoples and multitudes and nations and languages* (verse 15). Jeremiah prophesied against earthly Babylon as the one dwelling by "many waters" (51:13). This prophetic condemnation, fulfilled literally in the fall of historical Babylon, reaches its ultimate fulfillment in the judgment of spiritual Babylon. The original waters were those of the Euphrates and the canals surrounding Babylon. These were the avenues for her commerce, and also a protective feature which God would cause to dry up in the day of her destruction (Jer. 51:36). But this is no longer the judgment of a particular historical city. The angel interprets the waters on which the woman sits as the nations of the world. The formula repeated here, *peoples and multitudes and nations and languages*, originates in Daniel's description of the nations subject to earthly Babylon (Dn. 3:4, 7; 4:1; 5:19; 6:25; 7:14). Isaiah also uses the expression "many waters" for "many nations" (Isa. 17:13).

But as with earthly Babylon, the waters of spiritual Babylon will also dry up (as prophesied in the sixth bowl judgment of 16:12). How this will happen is now described: *And the ten horns that you saw, they and the beast will hate the prostitute. They will make her desolate and naked, and devour her flesh and burn her up with fire* (verse 16). The images of the prostitute's destruction are borrowed from the pictures of God's judgment against another prostitute — unfaithful Israel. Israel's enemies will hate her, devour her with fire and leave her naked (Ezek. 16:37-41; 23:25-29, 47). Ezekiel saw the prostitute Israel drinking from a cup (23:31-34), as does the prostitute Babylon in Rev. 17:4. For similar pictures see Jer. 10:25 and Hos. 2:3. The Old Testament prophecies were fulfilled in a preliminary manner when earthly Babylon destroyed Jerusalem, but will reach a second and final fulfillment when spiritual Babylon is herself judged. This shows that unbelieving national Israel is an enemy of God as much as overtly pagan cultures. National Israel no longer constitutes God's covenant people, even though God will still have mercy on the Jewish people before the Lord returns (Rom. 11:11-32). The "kings of the earth" of 17:2 (or the "kings from the east," 16:12) turn against Babylon. They represent the political or military aspect of the world system, which turns against spiritual Babylon, the economic-religious arm of the same. The result is a kind of worldwide civil war in the kingdom of darkness. This should not surprise us as Satan's kingdom is built on destruction. He cannot help but destroy even those he uses. Most of us can think of many sad examples of this we have witnessed in our own experience.

The Babylonian prostitute is modeled on Jezebel, who represents the spirit of idolatry, a spirit still active in the churches (Rev. 2:20-24). Here are some of the many parallels:

Both were heavily made up (2 Kgs. 9:30; Rev. 17:4).
Both were queens (1 Kgs. 16:31; Rev. 17:18; 18:7).
Both practiced witchcraft (2 Kgs. 9:22; Rev. 18:23).
Both were greedy (1 Kgs. 21:7; Rev. 18:11-19).
Both persecuted the saints (1 Kgs. 18:4; Rev. 17:6).
God avenged on both the blood of his servants (2 Kgs. 9:7; Rev. 19:2).

The comparison of Babylon to Jezebel suggests a warning to those who may be operating in deception even within the church, as for instance, was occurring in John's own day at Thyatira (2:20-23). Jezebel is a powerful spirit linking false religion with the pursuit of wealth, political power and sensuality. No wonder she is used as a model for spiritual Babylon. Contained within this picture is a warning to deceived believers, such as those in Thyatira. They have compromised with the Jezebelic spirit in order to avoid the cost of the cross. The angel appeals to them to come out of Babylon lest they be destroyed along with her (see 18:4). This is also a solemn reminder that the unbelieving church (false members of the covenant community), along with unbelieving national Israel and unbelieving pagan cultures, all form a part of spiritual Babylon.

Even though the beast and the kings join together in a common cause, God himself is the ultimate author of the events: *For God has put it into their hearts to carry out his purpose by being of one mind and handing over their royal power to the beast, until the words of God are fulfilled. And the woman that you saw is the great city that has dominion over the kings of the earth* (verses 17-18). The meaning of Daniel's prophecy concerning the fourth beast and the ten horns (Dn. 7:19-28) is now explained. The means of Babylon's downfall fulfills the words of Jesus: "And if Satan has risen up against himself and is divided, he cannot stand, but is coming to an end" (Mk. 3:26). Daniel prophesied that the end-times kingdom was to be a divided kingdom (Dn. 2:41-43). He and other prophets saw that at the end of history, evil men would take up the sword against each other (Dn. 11:40-43; Ezek. 38:21; Hag. 2:22; Zech. 14:13). The "mystery" of Babylon (17:5), which is now revealed, is the way in which all these prophecies will come to fulfillment through spiritual Babylon's destruction. The concept of "mystery" in the New Testament relates to something unexpected, often the unexpected way in which Old Testament prophecy is fulfilled (see on 1:20; 10:7; 17:5-6) Here, the element of shock may be the way in which Babylon's allies turn against her and bring about the sudden downfall of the system which had seemed utterly impregnable. Babylon is described as *the great city,* a phrase drawn from Nebuchadnezzar's prideful description of historical Babylon. Her domain is universal, for she represents the worldwide political, economic and religious system controlled by the beast.

Revelation presents contrasting parallels between the two women of Revelation, the bride of Christ and the Babylonian prostitute. One is a bride (21:9), the other a prostitute (17:1). Both possess jewels and linen. But the attire of the prostitute conceals her corruption (17:4; 18:16), whereas that of the bride reveals God's glory (21:2, 9-23). Both are seen in a desert and referred to as a city (12:14 and 21:2; 17:3, 18), yet the character of each is diametrically opposed to that of the other. Both are universal, spiritual realities. The prostitute does not refer to a particular "end-times" location any more than does the bride of Christ.

THE DESTRUCTION OF BABYLON AND THE REJOICING OF THE SAINTS (18:1-19:10)

The first part of the vision concerning Babylon (chapter 17) has dealt with the relationship between Babylon and the beast. Now a new vision is introduced.

THE DESTRUCTION OF BABYLON (18:1-8)

After this I saw another angel coming down from heaven, having great authority, and the earth was made bright with his glory (verse 1). The vision of chapter 18 explains in detail God's judgment on Babylon, thus fulfilling the angel's promise to do so (17:1). The *great authority* of the angel emphasizes the significance of his message of judgment. The angel cries out: *And he called out with a mighty voice, "Fallen, fallen is Babylon the great! She has become a dwelling place for demons, a haunt for every unclean spirit, a haunt for every unclean bird, a haunt for every unclean and detestable beast* (verse 2). The certainty of the coming judgment is underlined by the fact it is related in the past tense: *Fallen, fallen.* This is similar to the Hebrew "prophetic perfect" tense, where events of the future are related as having already occurred because of the certainty that God's word will come to pass. She may have an appearance of beauty and glory (17:4; 18:16), but the true demonic nature of Babylon is now revealed: she is nothing more than a *dwelling place for demons.* Earthly Babylon is again a prophetic foreshadowing of spiritual Babylon. Isaiah (13:20-22; 34:11) prophesied that earthly Babylon would become the dwelling place of howling creatures, hyenas, jackals and wild goats (or goat demons). The description of the prostitute continues: *For all nations have drunk the wine of the passion of her sexual immorality, and the kings of the earth have committed immorality with her, and the merchants of the earth have grown rich from the power of her luxurious living"* (verse 3). These statements show that economics, rather than literal immorality, is at the root of the ungodly union between Babylon and the earthly powers. Greed for riches is a form of idolatry, and thus promotes other forms of idolatry. It leads on, of course, to immoral conduct of every sort. The abortion "industry" is an example of this in our own culture. The picture is drawn from Isaiah's description of Tyre prostituting herself "with all the kingdoms of the world" (Isa. 23:17). The nations drinking of the wine represents their willingness to submit to Babylon in order to secure economic security.

Before the downfall of earthly Babylon, faithful Jewish believers were exhorted to leave lest they be caught in the coming disaster (Isa. 48:20; 52:11; Jer. 50:8; 51:6). Now in similar words, Christians are exhorted to leave spiritual Babylon: *Then I heard another voice from heaven saying, "Come out of her, my people, lest you take part in her sins, lest you share in her plagues; for her sins are heaped high as heaven, and God has remembered her iniquities* (verses 4-5). Although Christians can hardly "leave" the society in which they live, they are called to maintain their values while living within it, no matter what the consequences may be from a social or economic perspective. They are in fact witnesses within the world, as 11:3-7 makes clear, but witnesses who refuse to compromise (16:15). Paul also quotes Isa. 52:11 in his exhortation to the Corinthians not to be yoked with unbelievers and the ungodly values they hold ("go out from their midst;" 2 Cor. 6:17). The sins of Babylon are heaped *high as heaven* even as earthly Babylon's judgment "reached up to heaven" (Jer. 51:9).

Retribution, however, is coming, as the words of the angel continue: *Pay her back as she herself has paid back others, and repay her double for her deeds; mix a double portion for her in the cup she mixed* (verse 6). The pronouncement of the angel reflects and fulfills the words of the Psalm: "O daughter of Babylon, doomed to be destroyed, blessed shall he be who repays you with what you have done to us!" (Ps. 137:8). This is another illustration of the Biblical principle of an "eye for an eye" punishment, which occurs often in Revelation (11:18; 14:8-10; 16:6; 17:4; see also on 18:20-21, 22-23a). The idea of repaying her double seems to violate this, but in fact translates a Hebrew phrase meaning to "give back the duplicate." The eye for an eye punishment theme is continued in the next words of the angel: *As she glorified herself and lived in luxury, so give her a like measure of torment and mourning, since in her heart she says, 'I sit as a queen, I am no widow, and mourning I shall never see.' For this reason her plagues will come in a single day, death and mourning and famine, and she will be burned up with fire; for mighty is the Lord God who has judged her"* (verses 7-8). This is the ultimate fulfillment of the words of Isaiah concerning earthly Babylon: "You said, 'I shall be mistress forever,'.... you lover of pleasures, who say in your heart... 'I shall not sit as a widow'" (Isa. 47:7-8). Spiritual Babylon will fall, as did earthly Babylon, "in one day" (Isa. 47:9). Her judgment will be by fire. This makes her just like earthly Babylon, of which Isaiah wrote, "They are like stubble; the fire consumes them; they cannot deliver themselves from the power of the flame" (Isa. 47:14).

THE MOURNING OF THE KINGS, MERCHANTS AND MARINERS (18:9-19)

The theme of the next verses (9-19) is the mourning of those who have profited from association with spiritual Babylon. They mourn because they realize their own fate is linked with her's. The downfall of Tyre, as recorded in Ezekiel 26-28, serves in these verses as a prophetic model for the downfall of spiritual Babylon. This shows that more than one ungodly nation can serve as a spiritual forerunner of the last-days world system. It also shows us that we should not locate the end-times judgment in literal Babylon or in literal Tyre, both of which are long since destroyed. The laments here are those of the kings of the earth (verses 9-10), the merchants of the earth (verses 11-17a) and the mariners (verses 17b-19). These are the same three groups who mourned over Tyre (Ezek. 26:16-18; 27:26-36).

The first group of mourners are identified: *And the kings of the earth, who committed sexual immorality and lived in luxury with her, will weep and wail over her when they see the smoke of her burning* (verse 9). The connection between immorality and luxury shows once again that the meaning of immorality (Greek *porneia*) in Revelation is primarily economic. According to Ezek. 27:33, Tyre "enriched the kings of the earth." *Smoke* and *burning* have been linked with the fate of the beast's followers in 14:10-11. The description of the kings continues: *They will stand far off, in fear of her torment, and say "Alas! alas! You great city, you mighty city, Babylon! For in a single hour your judgment has come"* (verse 10). Perhaps they fear the same judgment is coming on them. The kings who mourned the fall of Tyre likewise trembled and were appalled at these events (Ezek. 26:16-18). The *one hour* refers back to the time frame of the alliance of the beast and the kings in 17:12, and describes the speed with which the downfall will come. Their use of the word *judgment* makes clear that they perceive the hand of God in her downfall. The kings, who previously were part of the conspiracy against Babylon (17:16), realize too late they have been duped by the enemy, who used them for his own purposes. They have unwittingly brought destruction on themselves. Satan uses unbelievers as pawns in his hands, and then dispenses with them once their usefulness to him is finished.

A second group of mourners now appears: *And the merchants of the earth weep and mourn for her, since no one buys their cargo anymore, cargo of gold, silver, jewels, pearls, fine linen, purple cloth, silk, scarlet cloth, all kinds of scented wood, all kinds of articles of ivory, all kinds of articles of costly wood, bronze, iron and marble, cinnamon, spice, incense, myrrh, frankincense, wine, oil, fine flour, wheat, cattle and sheep, horses and chariots, and slaves, that is, human souls* (verses 11-13). Like the kings, their mourning is self-centered, focussing on the economic loss they have suffered. Verses 12-13 contain a list of 29 products, of which 15 appear also in Ezek. 27:7-25. The gold, precious stones and various kinds of cloth stand at the beginning of the list and are associated with the clothing of the prostitute in 17:4 and 18:16. The loss of the merchants and the mariners receives more attention than that of the kings, and this may be in order to emphasize the powerful influence of money on human hearts. This illustrates the truth of Paul's statement that the "love of money is a root of all kinds of evils" (1 Tim. 6:10). It is not that material things are evil in themselves, but it is the wrong valuing of them that is the issue. This is shown by the fact that the items on this list appear in descending order of value, starting with gold and silver, but the last item on the list is the most precious in God's sight, *slaves, that is, human souls*. The greatest temptation to Christians to compromise with the world system is probably economic in nature, as is suggested in the letters to the seven churches. "Immorality," as defined in Revelation, begins with economic and social compromise with the world system as manifested in the pagan cultures in which for the most part Christians must live.

The merchants have lost what Babylon offered: *"The fruit for which your soul longed has gone from you, and all your delicacies and your splendors are lost to you, never to be found again"* (verse 14). The splendors are literally the "bright things." The same word is used in 15:6; 19:8; 22:1, 16 in connection with the brightness given by association with God's glory. By contrast, the "bright things" of the world are false and will soon pass away. Like the kings, the merchants mourn: *The merchants of these wares, who gained wealth from her, will stand far off, in fear of her torment, weeping and mourning aloud, "Alas, Alas, for the great city that was clothed in fine linen, in purple and scarlet, adorned with gold, with jewels, and with pearls! For in a single hour all this wealth has been laid waste"* (verses 15-17a). The kings focussed on Babylon's might (verse 10), but the merchants focus on its material wealth. The city is described as a woman clothed in her wealth, figuratively described in terms of six luxurious products. The list may also have behind it the portrayal of the king of Tyre in Ezek. 28:13, who is often thought to be representative of Satan: "You were in Eden, the garden of God; every precious stone was your covering." Gold, purple, scarlet, linen and precious stones were all parts of the high priest's garments (Exod. 28:5-9, 15-20). This would suggest a false-religious aspect of the woman's character, which constitutes a demonic substitute for the true glory of God. And to be sure, Babylon is deliberately contrasted here with Christ's pure bride or city (21:2, 9-23), which is also adorned with precious stones and gold, and whose stones are based on the garments of the high priest in Exod. 28:17-20.

The third and final lament now comes forth: from the mariners. Their cry is also economic in nature: *And all shipmasters and seafaring men, sailors and all whose trade is on the sea, stood far off and cried out as they saw the smoke of her burning, "What city was like the great city?" And they threw dust on their heads as they wept and mourned, crying out, "Alas, alas, for the great city where all who had ships at sea grew rich by her wealth! For in a single hour she las been laid waste"* (verses 17b-19). As in Ezek. 27:30-32, the mariners cast dust on their heads and mourn over their economic losses. Her downfall represents their own loss, thus showing that both merchants and mariners are in fact a part of the Babylonian system themselves. Money again plays a central role in the lament. Interestingly, the laments over loss of money (verses 11-19) take up far more space than the lament over loss of power (verses 9-10).

THE PRONOUNCING OF GOD'S JUDGMENT ON BABYLON (18:20-24)

The laments having finished, the angel addresses the saints: *"Rejoice over her, O heaven, and you saints and apostles and prophets, for God has given judgment for you against her!" Then a mighty angel took up a stone like a great millstone and threw it into the sea, saying, "So will Babylon the great city be thrown down with violence, and will be found no more"* (verses 20-21). The command to the saints to rejoice could be construed as a continuation of the merchants' cry of woe. But, given their content, it is probably better seen as a resumption of the address of the mighty angel to the saints recorded in verses 1-8. The words are based on Jeremiah's declaration that "the heavens and the earth, and all that is in them" will rejoice at the fall of earthly Babylon (Jer. 51:48). Even as the world rejoiced over the sufferings of the church (the earth-dwellers rejoiced at the death of the two witnesses in 11:10), so now the church rejoices at the downfall of the evil world system. The eye for an eye punishment is once again visited on the lost (11:18; 14:8-10; 16:6; 17:14; 18:6, 7-8). Taken together with 19:1-5, 18:20 is the climax of the response to the saints' cry for vindication in 6:10 ("how long before you will judge and avenge our blood...."). The joy of the believers does not come out of a desire for revenge, or from the destruction of Babylon. Instead, it is rooted in satisfaction that God has exercised his justice, and that by refusing to let sin remain unpunished, he has vindicated his own righteous character in the process. God's judgment comes in force and power. The angel takes up a great stone and throws it into the sea. The change in terminology from stone to *millstone* may reflect Jesus' saying that those causing his little ones to stumble would be better off "to have a great millstone fastened around his neck and to be drowned in the depth of the sea" (Mt. 18:6). Babylon will be *thrown down with violence.* The violent nature of God's judgment corresponds to the way in which Babylon treated others. This demonstrates again, as in the previous verse, the Biblical principle of the punishment fitting the crime. The picture is taken from Jer. 51:63-64, where Jeremiah commands his servant to tie a stone to a record of his prophecies against Babylon and throw it into the Euphrates. The prophet declares that in this manner

Babylon will sink, never to rise again. A similar prophetic picture is found in Ezek. 26:12, which says that the "stones" of Tyre will be "cast into the midst of the waters." Ancient Babylon and ancient Tyre both stand as prophetic forerunners of end-times spiritual Babylon.

The angel's announcement of judgment continues: *And the sound of harpists and musicians, of flute players and trumpeters, will be heard in you no more, and a craftsman of any craft will be found in you no more, and the sound of the mill will be heard in you no more, and the sound of the mill will be heard in you no more, and the light of a lamp will shine in you no more, and the voice of bridegroom and bride will be heard in you no more* (verses 22-23a). Here again, the punishment fits the crime. Even as Babylon has discriminated against Christians and removed them from the workplace, leaving them in poverty (2:9), so now will God remove her own tradespeople. The persecution of Christians has robbed them of their earthly joys (6:10; 13:16-17; 16:6; 17:6). Now those joys of daily life, of music and culture, of bride and groom, will be taken from Babylon. The reason for the judgment is given: *For your merchants were the great ones of the earth, and all nations were deceived by your sorcery. And in her was found the blood of prophets and of saints, and of all who have been slain on earth"* (verses 23b-24). The world is judged for three things. First, it has exalted itself and pursued the idol of earthly wealth (*your merchants were the great ones*), instead of worshiping God alone. Second, it has indulged in *sorcery*, a particularly evil form of idolatry. Idolatry, sorcery and sexual immorality are linked in Rev. 9:20-21 and Gal. 5:19-21. Jezebel was judged for immorality and sorcery (2 Kgs. 9:22), as was earthly Babylon (Isa. 47:9-15). Third, it has persecuted and *slain* the saints. The paragraph opened (verse 20) with a reference to Jer. 51:48 (rejoicing over the fall of historical Babylon). It ends (verse 24) with a reference to Jer. 51:49 and another instance of eye for eye punishment: "Babylon must fall for the sake of Israel, just as for Babylon have fallen the slain of all the earth." In the Old Testament, Nineveh also was judged because she was a bloody city (Nah. 3:1). Babylon, Tyre and Nineveh are all used in this chapter as prophetic forerunners of spiritual Babylon. This shows again that spiritual Babylon cannot be confined to a specific nation at a specific time. It represents the evil world system controlled by the beast and opposed to the church from the resurrection until the Lord's return. The judgment against spiritual Babylon is now given not on behalf of earthly Israel but on behalf of spiritual Israel, the church.

REJOICING IN HEAVEN (19:1-8)

The rejoicing over Babylon's downfall is now pictured from a heavenly perspective (19:1-8). With its announcement of the beginning of God's reign and the sound of thunder, it draws us back to the similar events described by the seventh trumpet (11:15-19). As with the seventh trumpet, history has reached its conclusion. John sees the entire assembly of the saints: *After this I heard what seemed to be the loud voice of a great multitude in heaven, crying out, "Hallelujah! Salvation and glory and power belong to our God, for his judgments are true and just; for he has judged the great prostitute who corrupted the earth with her immorality, and has avenged on her the blood of his servants"* (verses 1-2). Their praises are in stark contrast to the various laments of chapter 18. The saints were exhorted to rejoice in 18:20, and these verses bring the response to that exhortation. The saints rejoice because God has vindicated himself by showing his justice and taking all glory and power to himself. This verse represents the final answer to the cry of the saints in 6:10 that their blood be avenged. Both 6:10 and this verse echo the words of the Psalmist: "Why should the nations say, 'Where is their God?' Let the avenging of the outpoured blood of your servants be known among the nations before our eyes!" (Ps. 79:10).

The fact that Babylon's judgment is now complete is reinforced: *Once more they cried out, "Hallelujah! The smoke from her goes up forever and ever"* (verse 3). This phrase is borrowed from God's judgment on Edom: "Its smoke shall go up forever" (Isa. 34:10). Edom joins Babylon, Tyre and Nineveh as prophetic forerunners of spiritual Babylon. All the nations of the world have been caught up in her evil grip, which is now destroyed forever. In her corporate destruction is included the individual destruction of her many followers throughout the ages. Babylon can be referred to as a corporate entity in just the same way the Body of Christ is, though both can also be viewed as the collection of all the individuals who are part of her. Individuals wishing to be saved must come out of Babylon (18:4).

The vision continues: *And the twenty-four elders and the four living creatures fell down and worshiped God who was seated on the throne, saying, "Amen. Hallelujah!"* (verse 4). The elders and living creatures are heavenly beings who appeared first in chapter 4. The two Hebrew words Amen and Hallelujah comprising the cry mean "trust" and "praise." Both appear in Ps. 106:48, where the people praise God for his deliverance of Israel from captivity. This praise is echoed by the heavenly beings on account of God's deliverance of spiritual Israel. The voice from the throne continues: *And from the throne came a voice saying, "Praise our God, all you his servants, you who fear him, small and great"* (verse 5). Those who fear God are first revealed in the seventh trumpet as "your servants, the prophets and saints, and those who hear your name" (11:18). The seventh trumpet records the same events as are described here. *All you his servants* includes the saints of all ages.

A response now comes forth: *Then I heard what seemed to be the voice of a great multitude, like the roar of many waters and like the sound of mighty peals of thunder, crying out, "Hallelujah! For the Lord our God the Almighty reigns. Let us rejoice and exult and give him the glory, for the marriage of the Lamb has come, and his Bride has made herself ready; it was granted her to clothe herself with fine linen, bright and pure" -- for fine linen is the righteous deeds of the saints* (verses 6-8). The cry of the multitude is another parallel to the seventh trumpet's declaration that "the Lord God Almighty.... (has) begun to reign" (11:17). Many passages in the Old Testament speak of God's reign in relation to the triumph of earthly Israel (Ps. 93:1; 96:10; 97:1). Other passages speak of a future fulfillment of God's reign (Isa. 52:7; Zech. 14:9). God has always reigned supreme, but his judgment of spiritual Babylon and final vindication of the saints demonstrates his reign publicly and universally in its fully completed form. The entire section, from 17:1-19:6, has dealt with the nature and fall of Babylon. But now these events are shown to be divine preparation for something far more significant and of far greater eternal value. The suffering of the saints has prepared for them a greater weight of glory. Now the *marriage of the Lamb has come*. The bride is clothed in *fine linen*. The high priest was clothed in linen, and the mention of the garments here may be suggesting the status of new covenant believers as the new priesthood, replacing the old. The fact that Babylon also is attired in "fine linen" (18:16) points to her standing as a demonic counterpart to the church, the true bride of Christ. The righteous deeds of the saints are to be contrasted with the unrighteous acts of Babylon (18:5). The emphasis in verse 7 is on the bride preparing herself, but in verse 8 the clothes are given to her by God. Both aspects are true. A Spirit-filled life is the necessary response to God's gift of justification. Its absence suggests the reality of justification is not present. The clothes are given, but the bride must put them on. The emphasis, however, must always remain on the sovereignty of God. Without his gift of justification and without his giving us the power represented by his grace, no good works are possible on our part. It is a consistent theme in Revelation that God gives white clothes to his godly saints (3:5-6, 18; 6:11; 7:13-14). Even if believers have prepared themselves, this preparation ultimately comes from God: "And I saw the new Jerusalem, coming down out of heaven from God, prepared as a bride..." (Rev. 21:2). Although in one sense the bride can be said to prepare herself, in reality it is ultimately God who prepares her by enabling her to perform good works and live a righteous life. The background to this passage is found in Isa. 61:10: "He has covered me with the robe of righteousness... as a bride adorns herself with her jewels." The next verse makes clear that this is all God's work: "So the Lord will cause righteousness and praise to sprout up before all the nations" (Isa. 61:11).

JOHN AND THE ANGEL (19:9-10)

The angel continues to speak: *And the angel said to me, "Write this: Blessed are those who are invited to the marriage supper of the Lamb." And he said to me, "These are the true words of God"* (verse 9). The word *invited* or "called" refers to the sovereign hand of God in salvation, and appears frequently with this meaning in Paul's letters. The "called" are the "elect" or "chosen ones" (Rev. 17:14). The bride now appears not as a corporate entity, as in verses 7-8, but as the sum total of all the individuals she comprises. In a parallel manner, Babylon is presented both as a corporate entity (the prostitute), and also as composed of individuals (the earth dwellers, kings, merchants, mariners and so on). The same idea is present in 12:17, where the woman is the church, and the "offspring" are her individual members.

John responds to the angel's message: *Then I fell down at his feet to worship him, but he said to me, "You must not do that! I am a fellow servant with you and your brothers who hold to the testimony of Jesus. Worship God." For the testimony of Jesus is the spirit of prophecy* (verse 10). The angel rebukes John for worshiping him instead of God alone. In spite of this, John repeats his error in 22:8, thus showing how easy it is to fall into what is actually a form of idolatry. In the limits of our own experience, we may not be tempted to worship angels we have not encountered, yet how often do we place Christian leaders and Christian media personalities on pedestals which should be reserved only for the Lord? And of course there are many other forms of idolatry. The angel identifies himself with John and his brothers. Even more obviously, the greatest Christian leader is only a brother in Christ. The *testimony of*

Jesus is linked to *the spirit of prophecy*. Capital letters are not used in the middle of a Greek sentence. Therefore, the latter phrase could mean "the Spirit of prophecy," that, is the Holy Spirit inspiring prophecy which is the testimony to Jesus. Alternately, it could refer to the spirits of the people who are prophesying or bearing prophetic witness. If the reference is to the Holy Spirit, the meaning is that the Spirit inspires believers to testify to Christ. If the reference is to the human spirit, the meaning is that each of us as believers carries within our spirit the ability to testify to Christ. Of course, it is that only by the power of the Holy Spirit working in our human spirits that we are able to witness to Christ. The most comprehensive way of understanding the phrase is that the Holy Spirit has placed within our spirits the ability to testify to who Christ is. The reference includes all those who bear witness to Jesus, and thus includes all God's people, not just a few who may be gifted in prophecy. The reference to *a spirit of prophecy* thus means that we are a prophetic people. A prophetic people point others to Christ by our words and by our lives, as lived in obedience to Scripture and God's law. No one in the body of Christ is excluded. All have received the empowering of the Spirit which has given us life in our own spirits and the ability to witness to Christ. Elsewhere, the New Testament identifies a separate prophetic office (Ac. 13:1; 1 Cor. 12:29). But here the body of Christ *as a whole* is pictured as a prophetic community. The Spirit was poured out on *all believers*, who as a result will prophesy (Ac. 2:17). The fact that the entire church is represented by Elijah and described as "prophesying" (11:3, 6, 10) also supports this interpretation. The broad Biblical basis of prophecy is the declaration of the presence of the kingdom of God in the words and Christ-like lives of believers. In declaring the arrival of God's kingdom in Christ, we fulfill a prophetic function. The Biblical gift of prophecy, or office of prophet (Ac. 11:28; 13:1; 21:9-11; 1 Cor. 12:10, 29; 13:2; Eph. 4:11) is a specialized and much smaller area within the larger understanding of God's people in their entirety as prophetic. The prophetic spirit which characterizes believers points us toward Jesus and away from ourselves. That truth applies even to the angel himself, so there is no basis for glorying in anything or anyone other than Christ.

CHRIST REVEALS HIS SOVEREIGNTY IN HIS FINAL DEFEAT OF THE BEAST AND HIS ALLIES (19:11-21)

The destruction of Babylon, as recorded in chapters 17 and 18, was not a complete defeat of the forces of evil. As 17:12-18 shows, God's agents in defeating Babylon were the beast and his allies. It therefore remains for these last foes of God to be vanquished. In this section, Christ and his armies are described (verses 11-16), the imminent destruction of the enemy is announced (verses 17-18), and the scene is climaxed by the defeat of the beast, the false prophet and their followers (verses 19-21).

THE RIDER ON THE WHITE HORSE (19:11-16)

A new vision commences: *Then I saw heaven opened, and behold, a white horse! The one sitting on it is called Faithful and True, and in righteousness he judges and makes war. His eyes are like a flame of fire, and on his head are many diadems, and he has a name written that no one knows but himself* (verses 11-12). *White* in Revelation speaks of righteousness, purity and also God's vindication of the saints who are robed in white (see verses 7-8). The one on the horse is called *Faithful and True*, which speaks of God's faithfulness in fulfilling his promises to vindicate the saints and judge the wicked. God's own words or promises are themselves described as "trustworthy [=faithful] and true" in 21:5 and 22:6. The rider, Christ, judges righteously, a description of God himself in the Psalms (Ps. 9:8; 72:2; 96:13; 98:9). This shows again how Christ is frequently identified with God in Revelation. The judgment of God as prophesied in the Old Testament, symbolized here by fire, is now carried out by Christ, whose eyes are like *a flame of fire* (verse 12). Fire is frequently associated with judgment in Revelation (9:18; 14:18; 19:10). The picture of Christ is borrowed from Daniel's depiction of the Son of man. His eyes are "like flaming torches" (Dn. 10:6). Daniel's Son of man, like Christ, comes to judge God's enemies. On Christ's head are *many diadems*. This phrase contrasts Christ as the true King with the false kingly claims of the dragon (on whose head were seven diadems, 12:3) and the beast (on whose horns were ten diadems, 13:1). Christ's diadems are unnumbered, as opposed to the limited number on the heads of his enemies.

But how do we understand the comment that his name is known only to himself? The fact is that verses 11, 13 and 16 all identify Christ in one way or another ("Faithful and True," The Word of God," "King of kings and Lord of lords"). The answer may be found in a parallel to the name of the prostitute. In 17:5, her name is stated to be a "name of mystery." Yet her name is immediately revealed in the very next phrase as "Babylon the great." What is hidden in both cases is not the actual name, but the *true meaning or significance* of the name. What is hidden or mysterious is the fact that *Christ's description as the King of kings must be understood in light of the cross, rather than Jewish expectations of a conquering Messiah.* This is in line with the New Testament's use of the word "mystery" as Old Testament prophecy fulfilled in an unexpected way (see on 1:20 and 10:7; Rom. 11:25; 16:25-27; 1 Cor. 15:51; Eph. 3:4; Col. 1:26-27). Even believers do not now fully comprehend the meaning of his name, even as they do not fully comprehend in this life what it means to follow him in the way of the cross. The name refers at its heart to Christ's identity as Son of God. In eternity, this identity will be revealed to his people in a way they now know only incompletely. According to the Old Testament, to "know" a name implies having control over the person. The mysterious or unknown nature of Christ's name here points to his absolute sovereignty over the world. No one has control over him. He reveals his name (or identity) in a real but incomplete way in this age to believers. Meanwhile, unbelievers, who know nothing of his name now, will know it fully only in judgment.

The vision continues: *He is clothed in a robe dipped in blood, and the name by which he is called is The Word of God. And the armies of heaven, arrayed in fine linen, white and pure, were following him on white horses* (verses 13-14). The allusion here is to Isa. 63:1-6, where God comes as judge, with blood on his garments as he treads the wine press of his anger, a thought completed in verse 15. The name *The Word of God* refers to the fact that the rider will judge according to God's own words. The phrase "the Word of God" appears four other times in Revelation. Each time it occurs in connection with the "testimony" (6:9) or the "testimony of Jesus" (1:2, 9; 20:4). This shows that the life and teaching of Christ is the primary and climactic place where the Word of God is truly revealed. Hence, it is entirely appropriate that *The Word of God* is identified here as his name. In addition, the phrase the "words of God" in 17:17 and 19:9 (and similar phrases in 21:5 and 22:6) refer to the fulfillment of prophecy, so that in this name of Christ is also revealed the fact that in him all Biblical prophecy is fulfilled. The saints, described as the *armies of heaven*, accompany Christ into battle. This has already been stated in 17:14, where alongside Christ in the final war are the "called and chosen and faithful." The saints are likewise pictured as clothed in white in 19:8. The role of the saints is not military in nature. Rather, the testimony of their faith in Christ, accompanied by their persecution and unjust suffering in the world, becomes *part of the legal evidence* by which the lost and their demonic overlords are judged (for similar thoughts on the role of the saints in judgment, see Mt. 12:42; 19:28; 2 Cor. 6:2-3). As in 7:9, 14-15, the white robes probably represent purity and the priestly garments given to them in their capacity as the priests of the new Israel (see on 1:6; 5:10).

The description of Christ continues: *From his mouth comes a sharp sword with which to strike down the nations, and he will rule them with a rod of iron. He will tread the winepress of the fury of the wrath of God the Almighty. On his robe and on his thigh he has a name written, King of kings and Lord of lords"* (verses 15-16). There are four Old Testament allusions in this one verse alone. The first two allusions come from Isaiah. The first deals with the *sharp sword.* Isaiah says of the Messiah: "He has made my mouth like a sharp sword" (Isa. 49:2). The second involves the *rod*: "He shall strike the earth with the rod of his mouth" (Isa. 11:4). The mention of the sharp sword, combined with the description of the rider as the "Word of God" (verse 11), reminds us of Heb. 4:12-13. There, the power of God's word, "sharper than any two-edged sword," leaves all creatures "naked and exposed to the eyes of him to whom we must give account." The same thought is expressed by Jesus when he said: "If anyone hears my words, and does not keep them, I do not judge him... the word that I have spoken is what will judge him on the last day" (Jn. 12:47-48). The third allusion, also dealing with the *rod of iron*, is to Ps. 2:9, where the Messiah will break the nations "with a rod of iron" (see Rev. 2:27 for the same allusion). The final allusion, dealing with the *winepress*, is to Isa. 63:1-6, which is also the background to verse 13 (see above). There, God is pictured treading the winepress of the nations in judgment, their blood spattered on his garments. One further name is added on the rider's *robe* and *thigh*, the thigh being the location of a warrior's sword (Exod. 32:27; Ps. 45:3) and the place under which the hand was placed to swear oaths (Gen. 24:2, 9; 47:29). The name, as in 17:14, is *King of kings and Lord of lords*, the absolute ruler of all kings.

THE LAST BATTLE AND THE LAST JUDGMENT CONCLUDED
(19:17-21)

The vision of Christ concludes as John sees another vision: *Then I saw an angel standing in the sun, and with a loud voice he called to all the birds that fly directly overhead, "Come, gather for the great supper of God, to eat the flesh of kings, the flesh of captains, the flesh of mighty men, the flesh of horses and their riders, and the flesh of all men, both free and slave, both small and great"* (verses 17-18). This angel, like the angel coming down from heaven in 18:1, brings a message of judgment. In both cases, birds are associated with the judgment (see 18:2). The first angel announced the fall of Babylon. This angel declares the fall of the beast and the false prophet, the demonic powers behind Babylon. The invitation to the birds to *gather for the great supper of God* contrasts with the invitation given to the saints to the "marriage supper of the Lamb" (verse 9). The Old Testament background to the vision is found in Ezek. 39:17-20, referring to the destruction of Gog and Magog, the last days foes of God's people: "Speak to the birds of every sort... 'Assemble and come... to the sacrificial feast that I am preparing for you... and you shall eat flesh and drink blood. You shall eat the flesh of the mighty, and drink the blood of the princes of the earth... And you shall be filled at my table with horses and charioteers, with mighty men and all kinds of warriors,' declares the Lord God." The birds are seen by John as flying *directly overhead*, the same location as the eagle in 8:13 who announced the last three trumpets. This once more demonstrates that both passages describe the same set of events. Ezekiel prophesies that through these events the name of the Lord will be revealed to Israel and to all nations (Ezek. 39:7). In the same way, the name of Christ, now hidden (verse 12), will then be made fully known.

The vision comes to its climax: *And I saw the beast and the kings of the earth with their armies gathered to make war against him who was sitting on the horse and against his army* (verse 19). The description of the last battle begun in 16:16-21 is concluded here. The wording is almost identical to the depiction of the same battle in 16:14 and 20:8. There, the spirits of demons (16:14) and Satan (20:8) gather the kings together. This partially accounts for the passive sense of the verb here (*I saw the beast... gathered*). More fundamentally, the evil forces have been gathered under the sovereign hand of God. The reference, as the wording in verses 17-18 makes clear, is to Ezekiel's prophecy of the last battle (chapters 38-39). The specific texts alluded to are Ezek. 38:2-9 and 39:2. God will gather Gog and Magog, along with other nations, for the last battle against true Israel. Gog and Magog are referred to explicitly in the parallel description of the battle in 20:8. A further allusion here (also as in 16:14 and 20:8) is to Zech. 14:2: "For I will gather all the nations against Jerusalem to battle..." That day will be a "unique day, which is known to the Lord, neither day nor night" (Zech. 14:7). On that day, "living waters shall flow out from Jerusalem" (Zech. 14:8). These are the same living waters Ezekiel saw coming from the new creation temple (Ezek. 47:1-12). The fact that the same battle is clearly depicted in chapters 16, 19 and 20 proves that the battle of chapter 20, which clearly takes place *after the millennium*, shows that the events of chapter 16 and 19 *also take place after the millennium*. Even futurist interpreters of Revelation agree that *the events leading up to the battles of chapters 16 and 19 describe portions of the church age*. This proves that the millennium occurs at the same time as the church age. We shall see in fact it is simply another term for it.

The three parallel texts, Rev. 16:14; 19:19 and 20:8, all have the definite article before the word "war," so that the literal translation is "gathered to make *the* war." This is not a general reference to any battle, but a specific reference to *the* battle - the great battle of all ages prophesied by Ezekiel and Zechariah. This is the same battle referred to in 11:7-10 (for parallels, see also on those verses). There, the beast arises from the abyss to "make war" on the two witnesses, who represent the church throughout the world. His apparent victory is cut short by the resurrection of the witnesses and the judgment of God as expressed in the seventh trumpet (11:13-19). Here, that same judgment is described: *The beast was captured, and with it the false prophet who in its presence had done the signs by which he deceived those who had received the mark of the beast and those who worshiped its image. These two were thrown alive into the lake of fire that burns with sulfur* (verse 20). Judgment comes upon the beast for his attempt to take the place of God and of Christ in rulership of the earth. Judgment comes upon the false prophet for his deceiving attempts to bolster the authority of the beast through demonic supernatural signs and false religions, thus attempting to counterfeit and counteract the work of the Holy Spirit through the church. The fact that they *were thrown alive into the lake of fire* suggests that their punishment is eternal. This becomes clear in the further declaration of 20:10: "They will be tormented day and night forever and ever." Their followers, those who worship the beast and its image and receive its mark, will likewise be "tormented with fire and sulfur.... And the smoke of their torment goes up for ever and ever" (14:10-11). That Ezekiel's Gog and Magog are symbolic of the last-days forces of the beast and false prophet is confirmed by the fact that fire and sulfur are also part of God's judgment on them (Ezek. 38:22). Allusion is also made here to Dn. 7:11: "And as I looked, the beast was killed, and its body destroyed and given over to be burned with fire." In Dn. 7:10, a "stream of fire" comes forth from *God's throne*, and then in verse 11 the beast is thrown into *the fire*. In Rev. 20:10, the same event, the judgment of the enemy and his associates in the *lake of fire*, is described once more, immediately followed by the vision of the *"great white throne"* in verse 11 depicting the final judgment.

The vision closes with the statement: ***And the rest were slain by the sword that came from the mouth of him who was sitting on the horse, and all the birds were gorged with their flesh*** (verse 21). The sword is not literal, but represents the judgment of God's Word (as in verse 15; see Heb. 4:12-13). The actual punishment is described in 20:15, which refers to the same event: "And if anyone's name was not found written in the book of life, he was thrown into the lake of fire."

9

THE MILLENNIUM

(20:1-15)

THREE WAYS OF UNDERSTANDING THE MILLENNIUM

Three major views exist concerning the millennium.

Postmillennialism generally interprets the passage symbolically and sees the millennium as an indefinite period of prosperity and advancement for the church which occurs toward the end of the church age and culminates in Christ's return. Postmillennialists are often forced into taking a preterist understanding of the book as a whole, in order to remove all the apparent references in Revelation to ongoing tribulation and persecution. These they all take to refer to events of the first century. This creates an enormous chasm between chapters 6-19, thought to refer to events preceding the fall of Jerusalem, and chapter 20 which catapults us without warning into the latter part of the church age. Postmillennialism made its first clear appearance in the seventeen century, and became popular in the nineteenth century due to optimism surrounding the Second Great Awakening of the 1830s, and even more fundamentally, the general prevalence of the liberal ideas of human progress which permeated the Victorian age. It was championed first by the famous Puritan John Owen, and later by the great Reformed theologian Charles Hodge. Postmillennialism merged gradually into the social gospel, in which social reform was presented as the key to an earthly Christian utopia. Some postmillennialists (B.B. Warfield in particular) even suggested that before the Lord's return, no unsaved people would be left on earth. The calamities of world wars and economic depression deflated the postmillennial camp. A minority of Reformed teachers, and a very small number of Biblical scholars hold this view today, usually combining it with a position called theonomy, the belief that God's laws can and will be imposed on the nations of the earth before the Lord returns. The reliance of this view upon a preterist understanding is a major difficulty, as is shown by the reasons for rejecting preterism set out in the introductory section of this book. The other major problem with this view is that the Gospels, Paul and Revelation itself point to the ongoing reality of tribulation throughout the church age. Not only that, Revelation indicates that the very last days before the return of Christ will bring difficult and testing days during which the church's very survival may appear to be in question (see 11:7-10). This is the polar opposite of a postmillennial understanding. It is backed up by Jesus' description of the last days as being times of famine, earthquake and war in which his disciples will be hated, false prophets will abound and lawlessness will increase (Mt. 24:3-14). Families will be divided against themselves (Lk 12:53) and will betray one another (Mt. 10:21). Believers will be hated by all, and only those who endure to the end will be saved (Mt. 10:22). The word "tribulation" is used consistently throughout the New Testament to characterize the struggles of Christians in the present age. There is no evidence in Revelation to support a view which suggests the very opposite to be the case. Over and over again, the text paints a picture of a church called to suffer by walking in the way of the cross.

Premillennialism interprets the passage literally. The thousand years refers to a literal period of time of that duration. It takes two forms.

Classical or historic premillennialism has been advocated by a number of teachers and scholars, and its history goes back as far as the early church fathers such as Justin Martyr and Irenaeus. It sees Christ's return as occurring prior to a thousand year reign on earth. It understands Revelation in a somewhat similar manner to that presented in this book, but tacks onto it the concept of a literal millennial rule of Christ following his return. The primary reason for this understanding is the way in which chapter 20 appears to suggest such a millennium follows the last battle portrayed in chapter 19. This view does not attach any particular significance to the place of Israel, and it rejects the concept of a rapture. Many credible Biblical scholars and teachers have advocated this view, including George Eldon Ladd, D.A. Carson and John Piper. This view, however, fails to find a cogent reason for why such a millennium should occur. Why is there need for such an intermediate state? How could there be a further rebellion of the nations when Christ himself is ruling from an earthly throne, and when only the saved enter the millennium, the lost having been destroyed at the end of chapter 19? As we explore the text of chapter 20, we come to the conclusion that John is not referring to a literal millennium at all.

Dispensational premillennialism (commonly known as dispensationalism) is by far the most common form of premillennialism existing today. As explained in the introductory section of this book, this view originated in the serendipitous meeting of a Bible teacher looking for justification for his views on Israel and a charismatic vision in which God revealed to a young lady in Scotland that Christ was going to return secretly for his church prior to his general return. The Bible teacher, John

Nelson Darby, was in the process of developing a viewpoint founded on the idea that God has two covenants and two peoples, Jews and Christians. God deals completely separately with each at different periods or "dispensations" of history. Darby believed that God sent Christ to establish a literal earthly kingdom, and that the foundation of this kingdom was laid in the four Gospels, which are directed to the Jews and not to the church. When the Jews crucified Christ instead of crowning him, God came up with a Plan B, which was the cross, the resurrection and the creation of the church. The New Testament, from part way through Acts onward, applies to the church. The church, however, is only a "parenthesis" in the purposes of God, which deal mainly with the Jewish people. Darby was puzzling over how to remove the church from the equation so that God could revert to his original plan as outlined in the Gospels when he struck oil with the young woman's vision. The vision supplied something the Bible did not: the concept of the rapture. Christ would return secretly and take the church out, so that God could fulfill his original plan to have Christ rule over the Jewish nation from Jerusalem in an earthly millennium in which the whole system of temple sacrifice existing at the time of Jesus would be restored. Dispensationalist theologians such as Lewis Sperry Chafer and John Walvoord had their teaching popularized in the 1970s by Hal Lindsey in the best-selling book *The Late Great Planet Earth*. Later, Jerry Jenkins and Tim Lahaye produced a series of novels and fictional films illustrating the same ideas, revolving around the theme *Left Behind.*

According to dispensationalism, as opposed to historic premillennialism, a much more complicated scenario evolves. First, Christ *secretly* returns and raptures the church to heaven. This idea is based on a very doubtful interpretation of the only passages in the New Testament that could possibly be claimed in its support (1 Thess. 4:15-17; Mt. 24:38-41). The correct interpretation of those passages is set out in the introductory section of this book. Even dispensationalists must admit the rapture is not referred to in Revelation. However, it is *presumed to occur* before the visions starting at 4:1 commence. Also not mentioned in Revelation or elsewhere in the New Testament but *presumed to occur* are the restoration of all ethnic Israel to the promised land, and the resumption of Old Testament sacrifices in a rebuilt temple at the initiation of personal Antichrist. After this follows a seven-year period of tribulation, half way through which the Antichrist figure will betray the Jews. This period of time is again *not referred to in Revelation.* It is based on the seventieth "week" of

Dan. 9:27, which is interpreted incorrectly as a literal seven-year period at the end of the age. The reasons we reject this view are also outlined in our introductory section. This supposed time of tribulation is described in the visions commencing at 4:1, and ends at a *further and this time public* return of Christ (19:11). At that time, Christ will defeat the beast and false prophet (19:19-21), and inaugurate a thousand year reign on earth, based in Jerusalem. The temple, subsequently destroyed by the Antichrist, is rebuilt and the sacrificial system, complete with priests and Levites, is reinstituted. Satan is bound (20:1-3). The previously-raptured saints, having experienced the first resurrection (20:4), dwell in the new Jerusalem which hovers above the earth, but sometimes visit the earth in their immortal bodies. Satan is bound, but nonetheless the children of saved believers rebel and so the period ends with the final battle against the devil and his forces (20:7-10). The lost among the mortal humans constitute the armies fighting against Christ in battle.

There are many problems with this view, some of which have been discussed in the introductory section of this book. Here is a brief summary: (a) There is no Biblical evidence for any secret rapture of the church or for two final returns of Christ. (b) There is no evidence to support the contention that the visions of chapters 4 through 19 concern the nation of Israel. (c) There is no evidence anywhere in the New Testament that God would reinstitute a sacrificial system he once and for all abolished through the sacrifice of Christ ("He does away with the first to establish the second," Heb. 10:9). On the contrary, the church has taken the place of Israel as God's covenant people, as Revelation consistently teaches from 1:6 onward. (d) The "tribulation" is a term descriptive of the entire church age, not only a short period at its end (see on 7:14, 11:1-13, 12:1-17). (e) The millennium is best understood from the text of Revelation as a figurative expression referring to the church age, not a later, literal period of time.

Amillennialism (or, better, *inaugurated millennialism*) interprets the passage symbolically. It sees both the tribulation and the millennium as referring to the same indefinite period of time which stretches from Christ's resurrection to his return. This period of time is the "church age" in which John lived, in which we live and in which believers in the last generation before Christ's return will live. God's focus during this time is on the church, which has replaced national Israel as his covenant people, notwithstanding his promise in Rom. 11:11-32 to bring a spiritual awakening to the Jewish people before the Lord's return. This view has traditionally been known as "amillennialism," which literally means "no millennium." We do, however, believe in a millennium, one which is presently in progress. Therefore, this view is better described as "inaugurated millennialism." The millennium has begun, and will continue until the Lord's return. That event will mark the initiation of the eternal creation and the new Jerusalem. The evidence we have sought to present throughout our study leads unavoidably to the conclusion that this viewpoint is correct, and makes sense of everything that has gone before. It now remains to show in more detail that the millennium described in chapter 20 actually takes place *before* the battle depicted in 19:19-21, which *every interpretation of Revelation places at the end of the church age*. If we can prove that, the millennium must be firmly situated *within the time frame of the church age*.

The clue that the thousand years are to be symbolically interpreted lies first in the use of the verbs "show" and "make known" in 1:1: "The revelation of Jesus Christ, which God gave him to *show* his servant the things that must soon take place. He *made it known* by sending his angel to his servant John." The verb "show" (Greek *deiknumi*) occurs seven times in Revelation. Each time it is used, it refers to the showing of a pictorial vision, which God then interprets symbolically. This meaning is confirmed by verse 1b, where John continues, "He made it known by sending his angel." The verb "made known" translates the Greek verb *semaino*, which means to "symbolize or signify symbolically." This indicates that *the book as a whole* should be interpreted in that manner, including all its numbers. We have seen throughout the book that the key to understanding the symbolism is the massive number of Old Testament allusions which, over and over again, make the meaning of the visions plain (see further the discussion of this topic in the introductory section). All this suggests that the millennium is to be interpreted symbolically as an indefinitely lengthy period of time. In addition to this, notice the presence of the phrase "I saw" in 20:1 and 20:4. This phrase is repeatedly used by John elsewhere in Revelation to introduce visions of a symbolic nature (4:1; 5:1; 5:11; 12:1-3 ["appeared"]; 13:1; 14:1; 17:3). As is evident from many passages, numbers in Revelation carry a strong symbolic significance. Three numbers in particular, four, seven and twelve, and their multiples, appear many times. They connote the earth or creation (four), the number of God or of completion/totality (seven) and the number of government or God's people (twelve). Why would we assume that the number 1000 would be any different?

Throughout Revelation, what John sees and hears provides the content of each vision. The visions must then be *interpreted symbolically*, almost always using the framework of Old Testament allusions present in each vision. This vision (with words like dragon, chain, abyss, serpent, locked, sealed and beast, and with people resurrected and living for 1000 years) is no exception. Using the Scripture to interpret itself yields a coherent meaning. Otherwise, Revelation is reduced to a work of science fiction or fantasy (full of strange beasts and bizarre occurrences) whose meaning can never be properly unravelled. Authors then compound the confusion by trying to fit all this into the latest news feed from the middle east, changing their story almost continuously to fit whatever is happening currently, and never apologizing when their predictions prove wrong. No wonder this kind of eschatology is causing Christianity to lose credibility with the outside world.

Apart from everything said thus far, there are many good reasons to support the "inaugurated millennial" view we have adopted, rather than the dispensational premillennial view so prevalent particularly in North American Christianity. Its great influence demands a thorough and coherent response.

Reasons for supposing that the millennium refers to the church age

1. As elsewhere in Revelation, the visions do not occur in strictly chronological order. The vision of 20:1-10 takes us back to a time before the immediately-preceding section. The description of the thousand years (verses 1-6) is then followed by a recounting of the final battle between good and evil. If the thousand years refers to the church age, then the final battle described in verses 7-10 must be the *same battle* at the end of the church age described in 19:17-21 and 16:12-16. This would not be surprising, in that similar sets of events are frequently described multiple times in different visions in the book. But is it in fact the case? The answer is yes. All three passages clearly allude to the *same prophetic visions* of Zechariah and Ezekiel (see on 19:17-21) in which the nations of the world are "gathered together" for war against God and his armies (16:14; 19:19; 20:8). The link between the three passages is reinforced by the fact that in each, human armies are gathered together by means of demonic deception, either by spirits of demons (16:14), the beast (19:19) or Satan himself (20:8). In the two previous passages, this battle takes place at the end of the church age (and is thus different from the continuous struggle against Babylon that

occurs throughout that age). The millennium, therefore, must occur *before the end of the church age and the final battle.*

2. The fourfold ending of Revelation 20-21 corresponds to the fourfold ending of Ezekiel 37-48: (a) the resurrection of the saints (Ezek. 37:1-14; Rev. 20:4); (b) the coming of God's kingdom (Ezek. 37:15-28; Rev. 20:4-6); (c) the final battle against God and Magog (Ezek. 38-39; Rev. 20:7-10); and (d) the eternal Jerusalem or temple, portrayed as a restored garden of Eden and sitting on a high mountain (Ezek. 40-48; Rev. 21:1-22:5). On this understanding, the resurrection of the saints *in this context* refers to a *spiritual reality* exactly as described in Romans 6, which commences with the outpouring of the Holy Spirit at Pentecost (see further on verses 5-6 below). The renewed Israel of Ezekiel or John's millennial kingdom on earth represents the fact that the kingdom has arrived with the resurrection of Christ and the outpouring of the Holy Spirit. The final battle immediately precedes the return of Christ at the end of the church age, which ushers in the eternal kingdom. Hence, the "first resurrection" of 20:4-5 describes saints being born again throughout the church age (buried in baptism and raised in Christ), not a physical resurrection of deceased saints following a "secret" return of Christ to earth. The physical resurrection of deceased saints will occur only at the time of Christ's return (1 Thess. 4:16-17).

3. Ezekiel sees Gog and Magog as coming from the north (38:6), yet both Rev. 19:15-21 and 20:7-10 universalize them to represent them as the "nations of the earth." This suggests the final battle has nothing to do with events in the middle east.

4. If the millennium (20:1-6) follows the final battle (19:17-21), in which all unbelievers have been completely destroyed, where do the enemy forces come from who fight against Christ at the end of the millennium (20:7-10)?

5. In 15:1, John states that with the seven plagues or bowl judgments, the wrath of God is finished. In 16:12-16, the sixth bowl judgment concludes with the nations gathered at Armageddon, following which the seventh bowl judgment represents the end of history. It is clear that 19:17-21 picks up the narrative where 16:16 leaves off, and concludes it. This means that 19:17-21 covers the same time frame as the sixth and seventh bowl judgments, thus bringing to a definitive end the

wrath of God against unbelievers. How then could there be a further, much later judgment related in 20:7-10?

6. According to 20:3, Satan will not be allowed to deceive the nations any longer. It is argued that this refers to his previous deceptive activity during the church age through the beast and false prophet, now curtailed in the millennium because of their defeat by Christ in 19:17-21. However, in light of all the other evidence, it is far more likely that this deceptive activity of Satan refers to the period alluded to in 12:1-9. There, Satan attacked God's covenant people. At the cross, he thought he had annihilated the Messiah. Having lost the battle at the resurrection, Satan was thrown out of heaven, with his power (and deceptive ability) curtailed, though not destroyed. The title given to Satan in 12:9 ("that ancient serpent, who is called the devil and Satan") reappears in 20:2 ("that ancient serpent, who is the devil and Satan"). We conclude, therefore, that the "casting down" of the devil to earth in 12:9 and the binding and throwing of the same devil into the abyss of 20:2 are one and the same thing. This binding occurred as a direct result of the resurrection. This is taught by Jesus when he speaks of his binding the strong man though his ministry (Mt. 12:29; Mk. 3:27; Lk. 11:21-22). Ever since the judgment of the nations at Babel, the nations of the world had been handed over to the worship of pagan gods and demonic deception. Beginning at Pentecost, God initiated his plan to reclaim the nations for himself, and he did this by binding the previously unlimited deceiving powers of the devil. During the church age or millennium, Satan is restricted in his ability to deceive the nations, with the result that all those God has chosen can be saved during that period of time. He emerges out of the abyss only at the end of history, to stage one last battle against Christ and his armies, a battle described in 16:12-16, 19:17-21 and 20:7-10.

THE BINDING OF SATAN (20:1-3)

The vision commences: *Then I saw an angel coming down from heaven, holding in his hand the key to the bottomless pit and a great chain* (verse 1). Keys are mentioned in three other places in Revelation, and all four occurrences refer to the same reality. The "keys of Death and Hades" (1:18) are held by the resurrected Christ. The "key of David" (3:7) is used by Christ to protect the persecuted church (3:8-9). The "key to the shaft of the bottomless pit" (9:1) signifies God's sovereignty over the realm of

Death and Hades, including his restriction on the ability of the devil to harm and deceive the saints (9:4). The first three references show how God has restricted Satan's power during the church age. Both 9:1 and 20:1 portray good angels exercising Christ's delegated authority over the demonic realm during the church age. The "bottomless pit" (9:1-2; 20:1) represents the spiritual place in which the powers of darkness dwell. It does not represent any particular earthly geographical location. The fact that the angel allows the bottomless pit to be opened (9:1-2) shows how God permits the enemy to operate only within boundaries God himself defines. The angel of 20:1, by contrast, causes the pit to be closed, as verses 2-3 indicate: *And he seized the dragon, that ancient serpent, who is the devil and Satan, and bound him for a thousand years, and threw him into the pit, and shut it and sealed it over him, so that he might not deceive the nations any longer, until the thousand years were ended. After that he must be released for a little while* (verses 2-3). This statement refers to the effect of the work of Christ on the cross and the fact he was raised from the dead. The enemy is no longer free to bring accusation against the saints, as the blood of Christ has covered their sin. Further, Christ has taken his place of rulership in heaven (Rev. 5:6-14), and sent his Spirit to empower his church (5:6). As a result, the work of Satan is now greatly hindered, and the good news of the gospel will be preached to every nation (Mt. 24:14; 28:19). The binding took place two thousand years ago, and will be in effect for a symbolic period of *one thousand years.*

The binding of Satan can be understood in light of three declarations of Jesus, all fulfilled through his own earthly ministry, his death and resurrection. First, "How can someone enter a strong man's house and plunder his goods, unless he first binds the strong man?" (Mt. 12:29). Second, "I saw Satan fall like lightning from heaven" (Lk. 10:18). This was a prophetic declaration by Jesus fulfilled at the resurrection, as Rev. 12:9 records: "And the great dragon was thrown down... to the earth, and his angels were thrown down with him." Third, "Now is the judgment of this world; now will the ruler of this world be cast out" (Jn. 12:31). In addition to these statements of Jesus, Paul says that God "disarmed the rulers and authorities and put them to open shame, by triumphing over them in him" (Col. 2:15). Finally, Heb. 2:14-15 states that Christ took upon himself flesh and blood "that through death he might destroy the one who has the power of death, that is, the devil, and deliver all those who through fear of death were subject to lifelong slavery." This binding is the fulfillment of Isaiah's prophecy: "On that day the Lord will punish the host of heaven, in heaven, and the kings of the earth, on the earth. They will be gathered together as prisoners in a pit; they will be shut up in a prison, and after many days they will be punished" (Isa. 24:22). The actual heavenly battle and divine binding is described in Rev. 12:9. Isaiah's "kings of the earth" reappear in numerous places in Revelation as earthly followers of the devil. Shortly after, Isaiah prophesies that on that same day, the Lord "will slay the dragon that is in the sea" (Isa. 27:1). The dragon that arises out of the sea (Rev. 13:1) has already been cast out of heaven, and his days are numbered. Through Christ's death, resurrection and ascension to the right hand of God, Satan has already been bound.

The binding of Satan means that he is no longer able to **deceive the nations.** In 9:1-2, when the bottomless pit was opened, those who did not have the seal of God and who were the victims of the devil's deception came to various forms of harm, including even greater spiritual deception. By contrast, in 20:2-3, the binding of the devil in the pit results in those who are sealed and have not received the mark of the beast receiving spiritual life. Both passages portray the same set of events. The first passage shows how the binding is not absolute. Satan is still active in the world and operates through his various agents. He is identified, as in 12:9, as the **ancient serpent.** This reference to the activity of the enemy in the garden reminds us of his continuing power. Through his deception, he prevented Adam and Eve from fulfilling their God-ordained mission to extend the boundaries of the Garden to the ends of the earth. He likewise turned Israel away from God through his deceiving activity, and prevented them from their mission to be "a light for the nations, that my salvation may reach to the ends of the earth" (Isa. 49:6). But now Christ has come to fulfill the mission both Adam and corporate Israel failed to accomplish. And so this passage shows that the binding, though not complete, is nevertheless real, and operates to protect and bring to salvation those God has sealed and claimed for himself. Jesus can draw all those God has chosen to himself (Jn. 12:32), because the ruler of this world has been cast out or bound (Jn. 12:31). The binding means that Satan's activities are subject to God's will. It particularly refers to his power to affect people spiritually. The fact that Christians are sealed (7:3; 9:4) does not exempt them from persecution or even death (2:13), but it does guarantee their spiritual protection.

But at the end of the church age, there will be a further development: *After that, he must be released for a little while.* What this means is explained in verse 7 ("and when the thousand years are ended"). Until then, Satan cannot stop the progress of the gospel. And what verse 7 reveals (Satan's gathering of the nations for battle) is also forbidden until the appointed time. During the church age (the three and a half years of 11:3), the church holds the keys of Death and Hades, the keys of David, and the keys of the bottomless pit. This is what Jesus promised Peter (Mt. 16:19). These keys ensure that all those sealed by God are brought into the kingdom. But at the end of the age, the devil will be *released for a little while*. This is the period referred to as the "three and a half days" (11:9). The church will be attacked on a worldwide basis and appear to be defeated (11:9-10). The beast will be released from the bottomless pit (11:7), along with the devil (20:3). They will gather the nations together for the last battle (20:7-8), but will come to destruction. All these events are ordained in the sovereign plan of God, leading to the ultimate defeat of the devil and his agents.

THE THOUSAND YEARS AND THE FIRST RESURRECTION (20:4-6)

The vision continues: *Then I saw thrones, and seated on them were those to whom the authority to judge was committed. Also I saw the souls of those who had been beheaded for the testimony of Jesus and for the word of God, and those who had not worshiped the beast or its image and had not received its mark on their foreheads or their hands. They came to life and reigned with Christ for a thousand years* (verse 4). The focus in verses 1-3 has been the restricting of the devil's powers of deception during the church age, with the result that those sealed by God are saved. The focus shifts from earth to heaven in verses 4-6, though the time period is the same. This makes the passage as a whole very similar to 12:7-11. In both passages, Satan is cast down to earth or into the bottomless pit. He attacks the saints, but the saints gain eternal victory through their faithful testimony to Christ. Events in earth and heaven are closely intertwined. The effects of Satan's binding are now unfolded from a heavenly perspective. The saints are pictured as seated on thrones because they *came to life*. *Thrones* in Revelation always refer to spiritual realities (42 heavenly and 4 demonic), not earthly ones. The Old Testament background is Dn. 7:9-11, where "thrones were placed," "the court sat in judgment," and "the beast was killed." The phrase *came to life* represents the same truth expressed by Paul when he says that God "made us alive together with Christ... and raised us up together with him and seated us with him in the heavenly places" (Eph. 2:5-6). Christians are those who have died for Christ, or who have refused to worship the beast or receive its mark. The group portrayed here is the same as in the vision of the heavenly court in 6:9, where John saw "the souls of those who had been slain for the word of God and for the witness they had borne." The saints are referred to as *souls* in that they are in heaven, awaiting their resurrection bodies. *Beheaded* likely refers to all forms of martyrdom, as Christians both then and now died many other ways. But the group is much larger than martyrs, as it includes all those who have not *worshiped the beast or its image.* These deceased saints are included in the heavenly court of judgment. This is just as Jesus prophesied: "In the new world, when the Son of Man will sit on his glorious throne, you who have followed me will also sit on twelve thrones, judging the twelve tribes of Israel" (Mt. 19:28). That this rulership is not limited to the twelve disciples is clear from 1 Cor. 6:2-3: "Do you not know that the saints will judge the world... Do you not know that we are to judge angels?" The same promise is given in Rev. 2:26-27 and 3:21. The sitting of the deceased saints in the heavenly court is a preliminary fulfillment of these promises, which will come to full fruition at the return of Christ and the inauguration of the eternal kingdom or new Jerusalem (chapters 21-22). How exactly do these saints share in the judgment? Simply by the fact that the witness they have given to Christ stands as evidence against those who refused to accept it and even persecuted them for it, thus confirming the justice of God's righteous judgment on them.

This sheds light on the next statement: *The rest of the dead did not come to life until the thousand years were ended. This is the first resurrection* (verse 5). If all the deceased saints are portrayed in verse 4, then the *rest of the dead* must refer to all the deceased lost. The next verse makes this explicit: *Blessed and holy is the one who shares in the first resurrection! Over such the second death has no power, but they will be priests of God and of Christ, and they will reign with him for a thousand years* (verse 6). To avoid the second death, one must experience the first resurrection. Hence, the first resurrection includes all the saved of all ages. The promise of priesthood takes us back to 1:6 and 5:10, where Exod. 19:6 was quoted to describe all Christians of every age. Those who are saved become priests serving eternally in God's presence, while the lost are forever separated from him. That they are also reigning kings refers both to their victory over the second death and to their ruling with Christ in his eternal kingdom. This reign begins in the millennium, but is consummated in eternity following Christ's return and the final judgment.

By contrast, premillennialism understands the first resurrection as a physical resurrection which occurs following the secret return of Christ to rapture his church. Saints who died during the church age will be physically resurrected and live for a literal thousand years. The premillennial view sees this as the meaning of the phrase *come to life* in verse 5. The argument in favor of this is based on the fact that the "coming to life" of the rest of the dead in verse 5 refers to a physical resurrection, and so the first coming to life or resurrection must also be physical in nature. In other words, some are resurrected at the beginning of the thousand years, and others at the end.

However, there are at least six good reasons for rejecting this position.

1. The verb "come to life" (Greek *zao*) in Revelation and elsewhere can be used to refer to either a physical or a spiritual resurrection, and sometimes both in the same passage. Most occurrences in Revelation (9 out of 13) refer to a spiritual rather than physical reality. Our spiritual resurrection refers to our salvation and receiving of new life in Christ. Our physical resurrection takes place at Christ's return. Paul mixes the two meanings in Rom. 6:4-11, where he says that Christ was raised physically whereas we have been raised spiritually. We are (spiritually) dead to sin and (spiritually) alive to Christ. Elsewhere, Paul clearly states that we *have already experienced a resurrection* in our coming to Christ (Eph. 2:6; Col. 3:1). In Jn. 5:24-29, Jesus teaches that the spiritual resurrection will precede the physical resurrection. In the same way, there are two senses of the concept of death present in our passage. The deceased saints of verse 4 are clearly physically dead, while spiritually alive. In fact, they are even now in the presence of the Lord awaiting his return and their physical resurrection. However, the "second death" of verse 6, to be experienced by the lost but not the saved, is *an everlasting spiritual death*. The lost are both spiritually and physically dead. They also will be raised, but only to judgment. This leads to a neat pattern: *those who have experienced the first, spiritual resurrection will avoid the second, spiritual death*. The first, spiritual resurrection is in fact the prerequisite for avoiding the second, spiritual death. The physical resurrection, which all agree will occur at the end of the millennium, does not of itself guarantee protection against the second, spiritual death.

2. This is the only place in the Bible where a number is attached to the noun "resurrection," and it is also the only place where a number is attached to the word "death."

This signals something out of the ordinary, which is that the first resurrection and the second death are both spiritual concepts. This contrast between physical and spiritual or eternal realities is a theme in chapters 20 and 21. The contrast in 20:4-8 is between the first, physical death and the second, spiritual death. The first, physical death and the second, physical resurrection are part of the physical order of things, whereas the first, spiritual resurrection and the second, spiritual death are part of the eternal order. In addition, notice the contrast in 21:1 between the first, physical heaven and earth, and the second, eternal heaven and earth. There are similar first/ second = earthly/spiritual contrasts elsewhere in the New Testament. One example is the contrast between the "first Adam" and "last [=second] Adam" in 1 Cor. 15:22. Another is the contrast between the "first" covenant and "new [=second] covenant" in Heb. 8:6-10:9. In both cases, "first" and "second" (or equivalent word) are used to contrast opposing or fundamentally different realities, one earthly or physical, and one heavenly or spiritual.

3. According to our view, the first resurrection results *after physical death* in an intermediate state between physical death and physical resurrection. This is indeed a Biblical concept. Rev. 6:9-11 presents a similar picture of saints in heaven without physical bodies, awaiting the physical resurrection. Jesus contradicted the Sadducees by maintaining that those physically dead are spiritually alive and present with God (Lk. 20:35-38). The repentant thief on the cross would join Jesus that day in Paradise (Lk. 23:43). Paul says that to be "at home in the body" is to be "away from the Lord," (2 Cor. 5:8). His desire is not to "remain in the flesh," but to "depart and be with Christ" (Phil. 1:23-24).

4. The same idea of a spiritual resurrection is taught in Ezekiel, where the spiritual resurrection (the life coming to the dry bones, 37:1-14) occurs as the precursor to the arrival of the kingdom (37:15-28), and long before the final battle (chapters 38-39) and the new temple (chapters 40-48). On this understanding, Ezekiel is prophesying the new life in Christ as a manifestation of the worldwide preaching of the kingdom beginning at Pentecost. This new life is present in even stronger form as believers are united with Christ in heaven awaiting the physical resurrection. The end of the church age is marked by the final battle, and this leads on to the new Jerusalem.

5. Only the view we have presented makes sense of the undeniable fact that the Bible consistently teaches one physical resurrection which will take place at the Lord's return (Isa. 26:19-21; Dn. 12:2; Jn. 5:28-29; Ac. 24:15; 2 Thess. 1:7-10, and many other texts). Likewise, the Bible nowhere teaches that the Lord will return twice. Not only that, his return, far from being secret, will be witnessed by all people (Mt. 24:27, 30). Finally, the Bible teaches only one final judgment (Mt. 25:31-46; Lk. 21:34; 2 Thess. 1:5-8; Hb. 10:27-28), not one *before a millennium* and another one *after it*. This is clear in Revelation itself. The sixth bowl judgment describes the last battle (Armageddon) in 16:12-16. This description is picked up and concluded in 19:17-21, where the *final* outpouring of the wrath of God against human sin is depicted. It is final because the end of the seven bowl plagues marks the definitive end of the judgment of God: "with them the wrath of God is finished" (15:1). How could there be a *second* final judgment (20:7-10, according to the premillennial view) at the end of a literal millennium?

6. The number 1000 as used here is almost certainly figurative rather than literal. Other numbers in Revelation (4, 7, 12 and so on) all carry symbolic rather than literal significance. The Old Testament uses the number 1000 to refer to an indefinitely long period of time (Ps. 90:4; 105:8). Peter says: "With the Lord one day is as a thousand years, and a thousand years as one day" (2 Pet. 3:8). The number expresses completeness or fullness in Revelation. For instance, in 21:26, 12,000 stadia is the number of God's people multiplied by 1000 to express the idea of totality (see also 5:11; 7:4-9; 9:16; 14:1 for the idea of an indefinitely large number or a number involving some multiple of 1000 expressing totality).

THE LAST BATTLE (20:7-10)

The vision now moves to the end of the thousand year period: *And when the thousand years are ended, Satan will be released from his prison and will come out to deceive the nations that are at the four corners of the earth, Gog and Magog, to gather them for battle; their number is like the sand of the sea* (verses 7-8). The *prison* is the same reality referred to as the "bottomless pit" in verses 1-3. Up until this point, Satan has been restricted in his ability to deceive the nations (verse 3), so that the preaching of the Gospel has drawn a response throughout the church age. Now this restraint, in the sovereign purposes of God, has been removed. The result is not only that there is little or no response to the Gospel message, but that the enemy is now able to bring together an army *from the four corners of the earth* to launch a worldwide attack upon the church. The Old Testament background (as in the similar verses 16:14 and 19:19) is Ezek. 38:2-7, 39:2, as well as Zechariah chapters 12-14 and Zephaniah chapter 3. All these passages emphasize that God is the ultimate author of this gathering. It is God himself who (ultimately) brings the nations against the world-wide, spiritual Jerusalem of the last days. Although Gog and Magog come from the north, Ezekiel also includes nations of the south in the army (38:5), demonstrating the worldwide scope of the enemy's forces.

Premillennial interpreters place great weight on Ezek. 38:3: "Thus says the Lord God: 'Behold, I am against you O Gog, chief prince (Hebrew *rosh*) of Meshech and Tubal.'" The statement is interpreted as "I am against you, O Gog, chief of Russia, Moscow and Tobolsk." Thus Russia is assumed to lead a latter-days invasion of the earthly-millennial state of Israel. However, *rosh* is simply the Hebrew word for "head" or "prince/ruler." Meshech and Tubal were Hebrew designations corre-sponding to areas of modern-day Turkey, but are used by Ezekiel as representative of far-flung foreign nations (he also included the African nations of Ethiopia and Put in the enemy alliance). John follows Ezekiel in using "Gog and Magog" as an ex-pression for the nations of the earth. None of these phrases can be used to justify in-terpreting the passage as predicting a Russian invasion of Israel. Indeed, it stretches the imagination to assume that Russia will even exist at the end of a thousand-year millennial period! Understandably, these unbelieving nations from one end of the world to the other appear *like the sand of the sea* in number.

The battle comes to its final resolution: *And they marched up over the broad plain of the earth and surrounded the camp of the saints and the beloved city, but fire came down from heaven and consumed them* (verse 9). The language is again borrowed from Ezekiel, where the worldwide horde "goes up" or "comes up" (38:11, 16) against God's last-days people. The phrase *the camp of the saints* has its roots in Israel's encampments in the wilderness. The wilderness is the place the church is found in, according to 12:6, 14. It is the place of God's spiritual protection. The *camp of the saints*, also identified as *the beloved city*, describes the worldwide body of Christ. The term *saints* is used in the Old Testament to refer to Israel. In Revelation, however, the word is used 13 times, and *always refers to the church* (5:8-9; 13:7-10; 14:12, etc.).

This again points to the fact that the church has fulfilled physical Israel as God's last-days covenant people. The fact that the **camp of the saints** is equated with **the beloved city** shows that the city likewise represents the worldwide body of Christ, and is not to be identified with the earthly city of Jerusalem. Rev. 3:12 states that all Christians of every race and nation will have the name of this city written on them. The walls and foundations of this city have the names of the twelve tribes and the twelve apostles written on them (21:12-14). This shows it is composed of believers of all ages, including faithful saints of the old covenant. Although the new Jerusalem is an eternal reality, it is also present in an incomplete way now. Paul clearly identifies the "Jerusalem above" with the church (Gal. 4:26), as opposed to the "present Jerusalem" (Gal. 4:25), which is ethnic Israel, pictured as being in slavery. Heb. 12:22 teaches that believers in Christ have already come to "the city of the living God, the heavenly Jerusalem." *Spiritual Jerusalem is the worldwide body of Christ.* The nations attack the church, but *fire came down from heaven and consumed them.* They meet the same fate as the armies of Gog in Ezek. 38:22. But the allusion more closely goes back to the story of the soldiers sent to capture Elijah (2 Kgs. 1:10-14). The same story is alluded in in 11:5, where the church is fittingly described as the last-days Elijah.

Now the final act of the battle plays out: *And the devil who had deceived them was thrown into the lake of fire and sulfur where the beast and false prophet were, and they will be tormented day and night forever and ever* (verse 10). These verses are a further account of the events described in 19:17-21. They add the detail that the devil also is thrown into the lake of fire along with the beast and false prophet. There is no verb in Greek -- the phrase is literally *where the beast and false prophet.* The most natural way of translating is to supply the verb "are" or "were." This makes the point that the devil is cast into the lake of fire not *after* the beast and false prophet, *but at the same time.* Premillennialists argue that the beast and false prophet were cast into the lake of fire prior to the millennium (19:17-21). We have provided many reasons, however (see above on verse 6), to support the view that 19:17-21 and 20:7-10 describe exactly the same set of events.

In addition to these considerations, it is significant that the **lake of fire** is also called the "second death" (20:14; 21:8). According to the clear teaching of 20:10-15 and 21:8, this final, everlasting punishment of the "second death" *is not initiated until the time of the destruction of the physical creation and the introduction of the eternal creation* *following the millennium.* Put another way, the second death initiates the punishment of the **lake of fire.** Even premillennialists agree that the second death does not occur until all human life has been ended, and commences only with the great white throne judgment of 20:11-15, which occurs *following the millennium* of 20:1-6. This means that the millennium *has already been concluded* at the time of the events recorded in 19:17-21. Why? Because according to those verses, the punishment of the second death and **lake of fire** *have already commenced.* All interpreters of Revelation, including premillennialists, agree that the events of 19:17-21 describe the conclusion of the church age. Therefore, the millennium as described in 20:1-6 *must occur before the end of the church age,* because it takes place *before the punishment of the lake of fire and second death is initiated.* The punishment of the lake of fire has already been initiated in 19:20 at the close of the church age. The events of 19:17-21 and 20:1-10 must describe the same set of events. *The millennium is the church age.*

The first death (that is, physical death) occurs until the time of the destruction of the present world. All those who die as unbelievers are held until that time in the realm of "Death and Hades" (20:13; see also 2 Pet. 2:4; Jude v. 6). Meanwhile, believers are translated (the "first resurrection" of 20:5) into the presence of the Lord (Lk. 20:35-38; 2 Cor. 5:8; Phil. 1:23-24). Christ's possession of the "keys of Death and Hades" (1:18) ensures that believers do not suffer this punishment. If the punishment of the beast and false prophet in 19:20 did occur long before the events described in 20:10, the text in 19:20 would have spoken of them as *having been thrown into death and Hades rather than into the lake of fire.*

In that awful fiery place of judgment, the ungodly trinity will suffer everlasting conscious punishment, along with all unbelievers (14:10-11). The word "torment" (*basanismos*) is used in Revelation of conscious suffering (see on 14:11). The phrase *forever and ever* underlines that this conscious punishment is everlasting, which is the undeniable sense of this phrase as used elsewhere in Revelation. For instance, the phrase describes God's own eternity, and his reign, glory and power (1:6; 4:9-10; 5:13; 7:12; 10:6; 15:7). The same phrase is used to describe the everlasting reign of the saints in 22:5, which parallels the period of the punishment of the lost. It is inconceivable that the phrase has a different meaning in relation to the punishment of the lost. Otherwise, God's own reign would not be eternal, and neither would be the reign of the saints along with him. *The lake of fire and sulfur* is not necessarily literal — Satan and his agents are spiritual beings and fire is symbolic of divine judgment — but without doubt refers to punishment so terrible human words cannot fully and accurately describe it. What is certainly involved, and the worst punishment of all, is eternal exclusion from the presence of God (Rev. 21:27; 22:15).

THE GREAT WHITE THRONE JUDGMENT
(20:11-15)

The vision now comes to its climax: *Then I saw a great white throne and him who was seated on it. From his presence earth and sky fled away, and no place was found for them* (verse 11). Like the previous visions of God on his throne in chapters 4 and 5, this vision alludes to Daniel 7, where God sits on a throne and books are opened. The judgment pictured as beginning in chapters 4 and 5 now comes to its conclusion. Like previous descriptions of the final judgment in 6:14 and 16:20, *earth and sky have fled away.* These are about to be replaced by a new heaven and earth (21:1). The vision continues: *And I saw the dead, great and small, standing before the throne, and books were opened. Then another book was opened, which is the book of life. And the dead were judged by what was written in the books, according to what they had done* (verse 12). Daniel also saw books being opened, which appeared to be books of judgment (7:10). However, he also saw a book in which the names of the saved were entered (12:1). In Rev. 11:18 and 19:18, which are parallel accounts of the final judgment, the judgment of "both small and great" is also mentioned, with reference to believers in the first passage and unbelievers in the second.

The vision comes to its conclusion: *And the sea gave up the dead who were in it, Death and Hades gave up the dead who were in them, and they were judged, each one of them, according to what they had done. Then Death and Hades were thrown into the lake of fire. This is the second death, the lake of fire. And if anyone's name was not found written in the book of life, he was thrown into the lake of fire* (verses 13-15). The sea, like Death and Hades, represents demonic powers (as in 13:1), going back to its original significance as the barrier to freedom for the children of Israel. In the new creation, there will be no sea (21:1). The punishment of Death and Hades are now replaced by the eternal torment of the lake of fire. The temporary punishment following the first, physical death is replaced by the eternal punishment following the second, spiritual death. Death and Hades represent demonic powers or spheres, not geographical places. If the second death is spiritual, and spiritual, non-mortal entities such as the ungodly trinity suffer its punishment, then the nature of this death is spiritual rather than physical in nature. Its primary feature is separation from God through denial of a place in the new Jerusalem (21:27). The saints do not suffer judgment, because they have received life through identification with the Lamb and his sacrificial death, and so their names are written in the book of life, which is elsewhere titled "the book of life of the Lamb who was slain" (13:8; see similarly 21:27).

10

THE NEW CREATION AND THE SAINTS IN GLORY

(21:1-22:5)

*The holy city comes down from heaven
(21:1-2)*

All things made new (21:2-6a)

Reward and punishment (21:6b–8)

The new Jerusalem (21:9–22:5)

THE HOLY CITY COMES DOWN FROM HEAVEN (21:1-2)

In verse 1, a new vision commences: *Then I saw a new heaven and a new earth, for the first heaven and the first earth had passed away, and the sea was no more. And I saw the holy city, new Jerusalem, coming down out of heaven from God, prepared as a bride adorned for her husband* (verses 1-2). Verses 1-8 introduce the fuller description of the new Jerusalem that runs from 21:9 to 22:5. These verses also form a transition from the previous vision, in that they conclude (verses 7-8) with the theme of salvation and judgment described in 20:11-15. The section as a whole presents us with two contrasts. First, the eternal, perfect church is contrasted with the earthly, imperfect churches of chapters 2-3. Second, the bride of the Lamb is contrasted with the prostitute Babylon of chapters 17-18. Believers are to stand firm in their faith in knowledge of their certain reward.

The picture of *a new heaven and a new earth* comes from Isaiah. According to the prophet, the restoration of Israel will take place in "new heavens and a new earth" (65:17). The sea, identified in Revelation as the dwelling place of evil (13:1), of Babylon (17:1), and of the unsaved dead (20:13), will be *no more*. The only "sea" remaining is the lake of fire. The Biblical roots of this negative identification of the sea lie in the Red Sea as the barrier to freedom placed in the way of the children of Israel. The picture of the new Jerusalem as a *bride adorned for her husband* is taken from Isa. 62:1-5, where Jerusalem is described as a bride whose bridegroom rejoices over her. It is also drawn from Isa. 52:1-2, where the prophet calls on Jerusalem to put on beautiful garments and enter into freedom. Jerusalem will be restored as the Lord returns to Zion (52:7). This will begin to be accomplished by the ministry of the suffering Messiah (52:13-53:12). The immediate but limited fulfillment of this prophecy was in Israel's return from Babylonian exile. But this in no way lived up to the things Isaiah was prophesying. In Christ, God initiated the true beginning of the end of death and mourning. The complete fulfillment of Isaiah's vision comes only in the new creation as described here. The new Jerusalem does not refer to the nation of Israel, for peoples of all nations will be included in the new Jerusalem. This promise is made to all faithful Christians in 3:12. The names of the tribes of Israel are written on the gates of the new Jerusalem (21:12-13), and the names of the apostles are inscribed on the foundations of the new city's wall (21:14). The word for *new* is *kainos*, indicating a change in character or quality, not just something next in chronological order (the Greek word *chronos*). The idea of change suggests the possibility of transformation, rather than total obliteration and entirely new creation. This may be something along the lines of the resurrection body, which will be entirely different in character but still belonging to the individual who existed on earth. The renewing of the creation is linked with the idea of the resurrection of the body by Paul (Rom. 8:18-23).

ALL THINGS MADE NEW (21:3-6A)

A voice from the throne provides further elaboration of the marriage metaphor. God is now making his dwelling among his people: *And I heard a loud voice from the throne saying, "Behold, the dwelling place of God is with man. He will dwell with them, and they will be his people, and God himself will be with them as their God. He will wipe away every tear from their eyes, and death shall be no more, neither shall there be mourning, nor crying, nor pain anymore, for the former things have passed away." And he who was seated on the throne said, "Behold, I am making all things new"* (verses 3-5a). This is the same thought expressed in 7:15, where believers of "all tribes and peoples and languages" (7:9) are sheltered in God's presence, freed from all suffering and tears (7:16-17). As far back as Lev. 26:11-12, God made this promise: "I will make my dwelling among you... And I will walk among you and will be your God, and you shall be my people." Many centuries after Moses, Ezekiel confirmed the same promise: "My dwelling place shall be with them, and I will be their God, and they shall be my people" (Ezek. 37:27). This promise is echoed in Ezekiel's description of the eternal temple: "Son of man, this is the place of my throne.... where I will dwell in the midst of the people of Israel forever" (43:7). These words are fulfilled here not in a physical nation in a physical earth, but in a spiritual nation dwelling in an eternal creation. The old tabernacle was physical, and only the Jewish high priest could enter, and even then only once a year. The new tabernacle is spiritual, representing the very presence of God himself, and now every believer can enter at any time. This end-times dwelling place of God, prophesied in Leviticus and Ezekiel, is present in a beginning form in the church (2 Cor. 6:16, quoting Lev. 26:11-12), but will reach its glorious climax in the new creation. Ezekiel prophesies that Gentiles will be given an inheritance among the tribes of Israel. God promised Abraham that in him "all the families of the earth shall be blessed" (Gen. 12:3). He elaborated on this by saying: "To your offspring I will give this land" (Gen. 12:7). Paul tells us this offspring of Abraham is Christ (Gal. 3:16). A few verses later, he says that through faith in Christ, peoples of every nation inherit the blessing of Abraham (Gal. 3:28-29). This fulfills the promise given to Abraham in Gen. 12:3. The "land" is not the physical territory of Israel, but the spiritual territory of the church throughout the world, fulfilled ultimately in the eternal new Jerusalem.

The new creation will be characterized by the absence of death, mourning and pain. Isaiah prophesies of the new heavens and new earth: "No more shall be heard in it the sound of weeping and the cry of distress" (65:19; for similar words see Isa. 25:7-8). Isaiah also says that in the time the sea is dried up (see verse 1 above), the redeemed will enter Zion with joy, and all sorrow will come to an end (51:10-11). The fact that *the former things have passed away* and that God is *making all things new* fulfills another prophetic word of Isaiah: "Remember not the former things.... Behold, I am doing a new thing" (Isa. 43:18-19). And similarly: "For behold, I create new heavens and a new earth, and the former things shall not be remembered or come to mind" (Isa. 65:17). The latter words are also alluded to in verse 1 above. John's use of the present tense, *I am making all things new* does not indicate that God is doing this right now. Rather, it is a "prophetic present" tense, where the future fulfillment is so certain it can be spoken of as being already accomplished. Something similar occurs in Rom. 8:30, where our future glorification is spoken of in the past tense as something so certain it can be spoken of as already realized.

The one seated on the throne commands John: *"Write this down, for these words are trustworthy and true"* (verse 5b). These words are probably rooted in the same prophetic passage in Isaiah just alluded to, which speaks of the "God of truth" (Isa. 65:16) who will bless believers in the day he creates the new heavens and new earth. The narrative continues: *And he said to me, "It is done! I am the Alpha and the Omega, the beginning and the end"* (verse 6a). The declaration finds its roots in in the words of Jesus on the cross: "It is finished." What Jesus finished on the cross has now found its final fulfillment in the new creation. God identifies himself here as *the Alpha and the Omega.* He does the same near the beginning of the book (1:8), where he also describes himself (echoing Isa. 41:4; 44:6; 48:12) as "the first and the last." The title is repeated and expanded further in 22:13. These titles, appearing significantly at the beginning and end of Revelation, emphasize God's sovereignty over the beginning and the end of history, and over everything in between. In fact, 1:8 and the present passage are the only two places in Revelation where God himself is explicitly quoted. These words, therefore, have great significance and power. They show God's sovereignty over everything, including the trials and sufferings of the saints and their eventual reward. The glory of God and his reward for those who have persevered faithfully through trial are the central themes of Revelation.

REWARD AND PUNISHMENT (21:6B-8)

God now makes a promise to faithful believers: *"To the thirsty I will give from the spring of the water of life without payment. The one who conquers will have this heritage, and I will be his God and he will be my son"* (verses 6b-7). This promise is the fulfillment of two of Isaiah's prophetic words regarding the restoration of Israel, now realized in the new Israel, the church. First he says: "They shall not hunger or thirst... for he who has pity on them will lead them, and by springs of water will guide them" (Isa. 49:10). Later he states: "Come, everyone who thirsts, come to the waters; and he who has no money, come, buy and eat! Come, buy wine and milk without money and without price" (Isa. 55:10). These promises are given to *the one who conquers.* This is the one who refuses to compromise in the face of persecution and other adversity (see 2:26). All the promises made to the conquerors in the letters section are fulfilled in this closing section, which introduces the new Jerusalem, in which believers enter their eternal reward. Examples of these fulfilled promises include a share in the tree of life (2:7; 22:2), a share in the new temple and the new Jerusalem (3:12; 21:2, 10, 22-27), and a share in the rule of Christ (2:26-27; 3:21; 22:5). Others can be easily discovered by comparing the two parts of the book. These blessings come to ultimate fulfillment and expression in the promise of sonship: *I will be his God and he will be my son.* This promise, given originally to David for the Messiah who would arise from his line (2 Sam. 7:14; Ps. 89:26), is now inherited by every believer in Christ.

But for unbelievers, a terrible fate remains: *"But as for the cowardly, the faithless, the detestable, as for murderers, the sexually immoral, sorcerers, idolaters, and all liars, their portion will be in the lake that burns with fire and sulfur, which is the second death"* (verse 8). The *cowardly* could include professing but false believers within the church as well as outright pagans, for such people would be unwilling to suffer for Christ or remain faithful to him under trial. The *sexually immoral* throughout Revelation connotes those who participate in and profit from the ungodly cultures of the world. *Liars* is used repeatedly by John in his first letter to refer to false believers (1 Jn. 2:4, 22; 4:20). Lying or deception is the main feature of the false religion inspired by the false prophet (see 13:14). Lying was present in the garden, and it is sadly also present in the visible church, but it will be completely banished from the new Jerusalem, the eternal garden-city that is the ultimate fulfillment of what the original garden was intended to be. Whatever the lake of fire signifies, its everlasting punishment (14:10-11; 20:10), characterized by fire and sulfur (symbolic of God's judgment), must be more than simple separation from God, though that itself is surely its worst aspect.

THE NEW JERUSALEM (21:9-22:5)

The rest of the vision, which extends to 22:5, deals with a description of the eternal city, the new Jerusalem. The vision is based on Ezekiel's similar vision (chapters 40-48) of the latter-day temple, city and the land around it. But whereas Ezekiel saw a temple, a city and a land, John's vision combines all three into a picture of the end-times presence of God with his people, in which the city, the temple and the land are one. Ezekiel, like John, understood all three as depicting God's eternal dwelling place with his people (37:25-28; 48:35). The city is identified with the bride (21:2, 10), which shows that a literal city is not in mind. The themes of verses 1-8 (the bride, the dwelling place of God, the water of life and the eternal destiny of the lost) are all further developed in this section. The vision is divided into a number of sections.

1. THE INITIAL APPEARANCE OF THE CITY (21:9-14)

John first sees the bride of the Lamb: *Then came one of the seven angels who had the seven bowls full of the seven last plagues and spoke to me, saying, "Come, I will show you the Bride, the wife of the Lamb." And he carried me away in the Spirit to a great, high mountain, and showed me the holy city Jerusalem coming down out of heaven from God, having the glory of God, its radiance like a most rare jewel, like a jasper, clear as crystal* (verses 9-11). The wording is very similar to 17:1-3, where John was shown the prostitute Babylon: "Then one of the seven angels who had the seven bowls came and said to me, 'Come, I will show you the judgment of the great prostitute.... And he carried me away in the Spirit into a wilderness, and I saw a woman sitting on a scarlet beast.'" The close similarity in wording paints a deliberate contrast between the two women, one faithful and the other not. The immoral and unfaithful conduct of Babylon is contrasted with the faithfulness of the bride. Babylon's jewels (17:4; 21:18-21) symbolize her power to entice people into compromise through display of her wealth. The jewels of the bride, however, like her clothing, symbolize her godly works (19:7-8; 21:2). Both pictures are clearly symbolic, in that they do not portray a particular woman. The fact that John is *carried... away in the Spirit* links him with Ezekiel, who had similar experiences (3:12, 14; 11:1; 43:5). In fact, this verse combines two segments in Ezekiel. The first is: "The Spirit lifted me up" (Ezek. 43:5). The second is: "In visions of God he brought me to the land of Israel, and he set me down on a very high mountain, on which was a structure like a city" (Ezek. 40:2). The vision to follow is thus certainly based on Ezekiel's vision of the latter-day temple in chapters 40-48. The *great, high mountain* is in line with Old Testament expectations (as in Ezek. 40:2) that the end-times, restored Jerusalem would be located on a mountain (Isa. 2:2-3; 4:1-5; 25:6-26:2; Mic. 4:1-2).

The reference to the *glory of God* and the *radiance* of the city shows it is a fulfillment of Isaiah's prophecy: "Arise, shine, for your light has come, and the glory of the Lord has risen upon you... The Lord will rise upon you. And nations shall come to your light, and kings to the brightness of your rising" (Isa. 60:1-2). Another fulfilled prophecy is that of Zechariah: "I will be to her a wall of fire all around... and I will be the glory in her midst" (Zech. 2:5). *Radiance* translates the same Greek word used in the Greek Old Testament in Dn. 12:3, where it is prophesied that in the last days God's people "shall shine like the brightness of the sky above.... like the stars forever and ever." Paul uses the same Greek word when he speaks of Christians shining "as lights" (Phil. 2:15). Christians on earth experience the beginning fulfillment of these Old Testament prophecies, which are completely fulfilled in the eternal Jerusalem.

The description of the city continues: *It had a great, high wall, with twelve gates, and at the gates twelve angels, and on the gates the names of the twelve tribes of the sons of Israel were inscribed -- on the east three gates, on the north three gates, on the south three gates, and on the west three gates. And the wall of the city had twelve foundations, and on them were the twelve names of the twelve apostles of the Lamb* (verses 12-14). Isaiah prophesied: "In that day this song will be sung in the land of Judah: 'We have a strong city; he sets up salvation as walls and bulwarks. Open the gates, that the righteous nation that keeps faith may enter in'" (Isa. 26:1-2). Isaiah also speaks of the future Jerusalem as a bride and as a city whose walls and foundations will be adorned with precious stones (Isa. 54:1-3, 11-12). Ezekiel's temple seems to have three outer gates as well as various inner ones (chapter 40), and his city has twelve gates (48:31-34). John merges Ezekiel's city and temple into one city-temple with twelve gates. This once more points out the fact that Ezekiel's temple is symbolic rather than literal in nature. Like the gates of Ezekiel's city, each gate has the name of one tribe inscribed on it. But the foundations of the city have the names of the *twelve apostles* written on them. The church, represented by the apostles, is the foundation of restored Israel. The number twenty-four is the total of the twelve tribes and twelve apostles. This takes us back to the twenty-four elders of 4:3-4, and suggests that they are heavenly representatives of the covenant people of God throughout the ages. The church on earth is the beginning fulfillment of all the Old Testament prophecies of the restoration of Israel, in that it is pictured as God's temple (1 Cor. 3:16-17; Eph. 2:21-22; 1 Pet. 2:5). The glorified church, dwelling in the eternal city-temple, is the ultimate fulfillment of this hope.

2. THE MEASUREMENTS OF THE CITY (21:15-17)

The angel revealing the vision is described: *And the one who spoke with me had a measuring rod of gold to measure the city and its gates and walls* (verse 15). This seems to be the same figure seen by Ezekiel in his temple vision, a figure who also had a measuring rod in his hand (Ezek. 40:3). That angel continues to measure the temple as Ezekiel's vision progresses. Similarly, in Zech. 2:2, an angel measures the end-times Jerusalem "to see what is its width and what is its length." The measuring, as in 11:1-2, is a reference to God's protection. There, only the inner court (the spiritual security of believers' relationship with God) was measured, while the outer court (the interaction of Christians with the pagan world around them) is not measured, indicating that faithful believers will suffer for their faith. Here, however, the entire city-temple is measured. The inhabitants of the new Jerusalem are protected in every way.

The city is a cube: *The city lies foursquare, its length the same as its width. And he measured the city with his rod, 12,000 stadia. Its length and width and height are equal* (verse 16). Ezekiel's temple was square (Ezek. 45:2), as were the altars in the tabernacle (Exod. 27:1; 30:2), and also the breastpiece (Exod. 28:16). But perhaps the strongest allusion here is to the holy of holies in the temple, which was also a cube (1 Kgs. 6:20). There is a thread running through Scripture centering on the place of God's presence. The holy of holies was itself a symbolic replica of the garden, complete with carvings of fruit and trees, and guarded by angels. The breastpiece of the high priest was a miniature version of the holy of holies, with its precious stones pointing back to the garden (see also on verses 18-21 below). The garden-city of the new Jerusalem is the ultimate fulfillment of what was intended at Eden — that the presence of God be extended throughout the creation. Adam failed in his mission to do so, even as Israel, which was called to be a light to the nations, likewise failed. Christ, as the second Adam, succeeded in his mission, with the result that the presence of God is realized in the church, his worldwide temple. But this presence will only be brought to ultimate fulfillment in the new Jerusalem. The measurements are symbolic, the number twelve standing for the people of God in all ages, multiplied by 1,000 to reinforce the idea of completeness. Ancient Babylon was also square with a river flowing through it and a main street with a series of trees on either side. It may be that the portrait of the heavenly city here is meant to contrast it with spiritual Babylon.

The measurements continue: *He also measured its wall, 144 cubits by human measurement, which is also an angel's measurement* (verse 17). The height is again symbolic, based on the twelve tribes multiplied by the twelve apostles to represent the entire people of God. A wall of such literal height (216 feet = 64m) would scarcely be appropriate for a city 12,000 stadia (1,500 miles = 2,400 km) in height. The human measurements are *also an angel's measurement* — in other words, the human measurements are to be understood spiritually rather than literally. This is in line with the correct way of understanding all of John's visions. John sees things before him and records what he sees, but the meaning of them must be understood spiritually and in line with the Old Testament Scriptures, which are continually referenced. Here John sees a city with certain literal dimensions, but the measurements, involving multiples of twelve and one thousand, have spiritual (angelic) or symbolic meaning. The same set of numbers has two references: one human (what John actually saw in the vision), and one angelic or divine (what the meaning of those measurements is symbolically).

3. THE MATERIAL OF THE CITY (21:18-21)

John describes the composition of the wall, the foundations, the gates and the street of the city: *The wall was built of jasper, while the city was pure gold, clear as glass. The foundations of the wall of the city were adorned with every kind of jewel. The first was jasper, the second sapphire, the third agate, the fourth emerald, the fifth onyx, the sixth carnelian, the seventh chrysolite, the eighth beryl, the ninth topaz, the tenth chrysoprase, the eleventh jacinth, the twelfth amethyst. And the twelve gates were twelve pearls, each of the gates made of a single pearl, and the street of the city was pure gold, transparent as glass* (verses 18-21). The city itself, made of gold, is again linked with the Old Testament temple, which was overlaid with gold (1 Kgs. 6:20-22). The purity of the *gold* enables the city to reflect the glory of the God who indwells it (verse 23). The *jasper* with which the wall is constructed also has a brilliance which reflects the glory of its Maker (see verse 11). The twelve jewels are closely related to those found in the breastpiece of the high priest (Exod. 28:17-20; 39:8-14). Eight are identical and the others are equivalent. The twelve stones of the breastpiece had inscribed on them the names of the twelve tribes, thus symbolizing the fact that the high priest represented the tribes every time he entered God's presence. But in John's vision, the foundation stones have written on them the names of the apostles, not the tribes (verse 14). What this means is that the symbolism applied to the twelve tribes in the Old Testament is transferred here to the twelve apostles, who are representatives of the church, the new Israel. The church is the foundation of spiritual Israel, which of course includes Jews as well as Gentiles.

Why are the jewels transferred from the Old Testament breastpiece to the foundations of the new Jerusalem? The answer is that the breastpiece was a replica (in miniature) of the holy of holies. It was square, and made of the same color of materials (gold, blue, purple and scarlet) as the veil guarding the entrance to the holy of holies (Exod. 26:31-32). The holy of holies itself, with its palm trees, pomegranates and cherubim, points back to the presence of God in the garden. But the holy of holies also points forward. The presence of God in the garden was provisionally and in a very limited way reintroduced into the holy of holies. But now it has been realized throughout the earth in an inaugurated way in the new temple of the church. This presence is to be restored in an ultimate sense in the new Jerusalem. Isaiah also prophesies that the latter-days Jerusalem will have its foundations and walls built with precious stones (Isa. 54:11-12). Ezekiel's similar list of precious stones, accompanied by gold, which were present in the garden (Ezek. 28:13), suggests that the new Jerusalem is a restoration of God's original creation. Ezekiel's stones were linked with the righteousness present in the garden. His prophetic words detail the loss of this righteousness through the picture of a prostitute (28:16-19, which is the model for John's portrayal of Babylon in chapters 17-18). But now this perfect righteousness is restored in the bride of Christ "adorned for her husband" (Rev. 19:7-9; 21:2).

Two further details are added. The twelve gates were pearls, each gate *made of a single pearl.* The street was *pure gold, transparent as glass.* The language is again figurative, for each pearl would have to be 144 cubits (216 ft. = 64m) in height. The previous mention of the *street of the city* was in 11:8. There the bodies of the two witnesses (the faithful church) were said to lay in the streets of spiritual Egypt. Now the street of their shame and defeat has become the street of their honor and victory.

4. THE FEATURES OF THE CITY (21:22-27)

The vision continues: *And I saw no temple in the city, for its temple is the Lord God the Almighty and the Lamb* (verse 22). By contrast with earthly Jerusalem, the new Jerusalem has no physical temple, for the Lord himself is the temple. Ezekiel gave a lengthy description of the eternal temple, but all that he said in chapters 40-43 is reshaped into this one phrase. Jeremiah prophesied that the latter-days Jerusalem would be called "the throne of the Lord" to which all the nations would be gathered (Jer. 3:17). Haggai said that "the latter glory of this house shall be greater than the former" (Hag. 2:9). Christ interpreted his resurrection as a rebuilding of the temple (Jn. 2:19-22; Mk. 14:58; 15:29). The New Testament pictures Christ as the cornerstone of the new temple (Mt. 21:42; Ac. 4:11, Rom. 9:32-33; Eph. 2:20). What was begun in Christ's earthly ministry and continued in his building of the church on earth is brought to fulfillment in the heavenly temple. If the saints, figuratively speaking, constitute the new Jerusalem, then God and the Lamb, figuratively speaking, constitute its temple. Judaism hoped for a final, material temple, greater in magnitude than any preceding it, but John understands this temple to be the presence of God himself. This is why he fails to dwell on Ezekiel's detailed descriptions, which are a prophetic foreshadowing of something Ezekiel himself did not fully understand. The prophet probably did understand that the structure he was seeing was symbolic in nature, and that the river flowing from it was more than just a physical or earthly reality.

The figurative language continues in verse 23: *And the city has no need of sun or moon to shine on it, for the glory of God gives it light, and its lamp is the Lamb.* This is a direct fulfillment of Isaiah's prophecy: "The sun shall be no more your light by day, nor for brightness shall the moon give you light; but the Lord will be your everlasting light, and your God will be your glory" (Isa. 60:19). The allusions to Isaiah 60 continue in verses 24-26: *By its light will the nations walk, and the kings of the earth will bring their glory into it, and its gates will never be shut by day -- and there will be no night there. They will bring into it the glory and the honor of the nations.* Here we have a clear echo of Isa. 60:3, 5: "And nations will come to your light, and kings to the brightness of your rising... the wealth of the nations shall come to you." The reference to *gates* takes us back to Isa. 60:11: "Your gates shall be open continually; day and night they shall not be shut, that people may bring to you the wealth of the nations, with their kings led in procession." The physical wealth of the nations referred to in Isaiah is fulfilled spiritually in the form of the honor and praise they now bring to God as those redeemed of every nation by the blood of the Lamb. The ungodly from every nation brought their literal wealth into earthly Babylon to conduct business with her (chapters 17-18). But the saved of every nation bring their praise and their worship, expressed in the dedication of their lives, into the eternal Jerusalem in order to give glory to God and to the Lamb. The "kings of the earth" here are not the wicked "kings of the earth" (referred to in 1:5; 17:2, 18; 18:3, 9), but represent in this text the righteous kings referred to in Isaiah's prophecy. This must be so, as only the saved will enter the eternal city (see verse 27). The kings themselves thus stand for the peoples of all the earth's nations who have given their lives to Christ.

Isaiah presents a picture of a literal city, a picture his listeners would have understood. John now sees that the fulfillment of this prophetic vision is eternal and spiritual in nature. It is not that at some future date pagan kings will enter a physically-restored earthly Jerusalem, but that the saved of all nations will enter the eternal city in which God himself will dwell. It would be just as ridiculous to see here a picture of people making their way into a literal city as it would be to assume that city extended to a height of fifteen hundred miles with walls two hundred and sixteen feet high, with gates of similar measurements made of a single pearl! The same is true with the picture of the open gates. The fact that the gates remain open does not mean that a ceaseless flow of people will physically enter it, but rather symbolizes open, unhindered access by the saved of every nation to the presence of God. It also signifies that the worldly security of literal gates is not needed when the eternal God himself is the Defender of the city, and has determined to exclude forever from its boundaries all that is evil. Direct access to the tree of life has been blocked by angelic beings since the fall (Gen. 3:24). Now, however, angels are stationed at the gates (verse 12) in order to allow those who "have the right to the tree of life" to "enter the city by its gates" (22:14). The redeemed may enter the city because of Christ's sacrifice on their behalf. They also constitute the city, for the new Jerusalem is itself pictured as the bride (verse 2). This is similar to the way in which the saved are both guests at the marriage feast of the Lamb (19:7-9), and are also his bride. All this further emphasizes the symbolic, rather than literal, nature of the language.

A different fate, however, awaits the lost: *But nothing unclean will ever enter it, nor anyone who does what is detestable or false, but only those who are written in the Lamb's book of life* (verse 27). Uncleanness links these people with the prostitute Babylon (17:4), who was full of abominations, impurities and sexual immorality (*porneia*, which as we have seen is a figure of speech for idolatry). The physically unclean could not enter the earthly temple, and neither will the spiritually unclean be able to enter the eternal temple. Only those whose names are written in the Lamb's book of life may enter. The phrase, the *book of life*, appears five times elsewhere in Revelation (3:5; 13:8; 17:8; 20:12, 15). In each case, it refers to the record, drawn up "before the foundation of the world" (13:8), of those who are saved and have been given the gift of eternal life through the sacrificial death of the Lamb and his enduring of God's wrath against human sin. Those whose names are not thus written will be excluded from the city.

5. THE SYMBOLS OF GOD'S PRESENCE IN THE CITY (22:1-5)

These verses form the conclusion to the picture of the new Jerusalem which began at 21:1. They focus on the river and the tree of life: *Then the angel showed me the river of the water of life, bright as crystal, flowing from the throne of God and of the Lamb through the middle of the street of the city; also, on either side of the river, the tree of life with its twelve kinds of fruit, yielding its fruit each month. The leaves of the tree were for the healing of the nations* (verses 1-2). Ezekiel's prophetic picture of the end-times temple has been in mind all through this section. The river pictured here is the same river Ezekiel saw flowing out from the end-times temple (Ezek. 47:1-9). Zechariah also prophesied that a day would come when earthly light would be no more, and on that day "living waters" would flow out from Jerusalem (Zech. 14:6-8; see also Joel 3:18 for a similar picture).

The river John and Ezekiel saw should be understood in relation to its original predecessor in Eden: "A river flowed out of Eden to water the garden" (Gen. 2:10). At the end of history, God will restore his creation in an even more perfect form. There, no presence of evil will be allowed (20:10; 21:27; 22:15). The living water represents our fellowship with God and Christ, as depicted in verses 3-5. It may also speak of the presence of the Holy Spirit, as Jesus taught (Jn. 7:37-39; see Ezek. 36:25-27, Jn. 4:10-24). This has the effect of placing all three members of the Trinity in the midst of the eternal city. The river flows down *the middle of the street*. This pictures the redeemed walking in the midst of the river, much as described by Ezekiel (47:3-5). The tree of life comes directly from Ezek. 47:12: "And on the banks, on both sides of the river, there will grow all kinds of trees for food. Their leaves will not wither, nor their fruit fail, but they will bear fresh fruit every month, because the water for them flows from the sanctuary. Their fruit will be for food, and their leaves for healing." John has only one tree in place of Ezekiel's many. However, John's tree grows on either side of the river, thus suggesting that the singular tree actually represents a group of trees. Because these trees are all of the same kind, they can be referred to as one. The tree of life in the eternal city is the tree of life which was in the garden. Its fruit, forbidden even to Adam, is now freely available to all the saints. The fact that the tree yields its fruit every month does not mean that the redeemed in the eternal city are in continual need of healing. The picture is figurative in nature. After all, literal months presume the existence of a literal sun and moon, which are no more (21:23, 22:5). The healing occurs once for all, as the saints enter the city. The reference to the twelve months is a figurative way of referring to complete healing for all God's people (of whom twelve is the number).

These verses picture the new Jerusalem as the ultimate fulfillment of the grand project God began in the garden. Originally, he put Adam in the garden to "work it and keep it" (Gen. 2:15). These same two Hebrew verbs are used to describe the work of the priests who "work [in] and keep" the tabernacle (Num. 3:7-8; 8:25-26; 18:5-6; 1 Chron. 23:32; Ezek. 44:14). The tree of life was probably the model for the tabernacle's lampstand. The carvings of Solomon's temple — gourds, flowers, cherubim, palm trees and pomegranates (1 Kgs. 6:18, 29, 32, 35; 7:18-20) — likely depicted the garden. The entrance to the garden was on the east – the same direction from which one entered the tabernacle (and the temple). When Adam failed to guard the temple and, by admitting the serpent, defiled it, he lost his priestly role. The two cherubim were stationed to bar the way into the garden (Gen. 3:24). That is why God commanded Moses to make two cherubim to guard the ark of the covenant in the holy of holies, which signified that the way into God's presence was still restricted. Only the high priest could enter, and he could only do so as a typological or prophetic forerunner of Christ. Adam was given stewardship over the whole earth (Gen. 1:28), which suggests that he was commissioned to extend the garden to the ends of the earth. What Adam failed to do, Israel also failed to do. As a nation, Israel was also charged with bringing the knowledge of God to the nations of the earth: "Is it too light a thing that you should be my servant to raise up the tribes of Jacob and to bring back the preserved of Israel; I will make you as a light for the nations, that my salvation may reach to the end of the earth" (Isa. 49:6; see Isa. 42:6; 54:1-3). This was the essence of the promise given to Abraham that in him "all the families of the earth" would be blessed (Gen. 12:3). But where Adam and Israel both failed, Christ succeeded. Through his atoning sacrifice, the gospel has gone to the nations of the world, and the saints of all ages are able to enter the eternal city. The promise given to Abraham is fulfilled on earth (Rom. 4:13-25) and eventually, in eternity. The extending and final establishment of the universal garden-temple, which runs like a thread through Scripture, is now completed.

The words of the angel continue: *No longer will there be anything accursed, but the throne of God and of the Lamb will be in it, and his servants will worship him* (verse 3). Zechariah prophesied (14:11) that in the days following the final battle against God's enemies, Jerusalem would be established forever under the eternal reign of God. At that time, there would be no more curse ("decree of utter destruction"). The destruction would instead come on those outside the city who attack it (Zech. 14:13). Christ has redeemed us from the curse by taking it upon himself (Gal. 3:13). The redeemed saints of all nations are delivered from all evils, spiritual or physical. They *worship* God before his throne as his servants. This is the same Greek verb used in 7:15, where the redeemed "serve" God day and night as priests in his temple. This fulfills the prophetic word of Isaiah: "But you shall be called the priests of the Lord....you shall eat the wealth of the nations, and in their glory you shall boast" (Isa. 61:6). Isaiah's prophecy is also fulfilled in the declaration of Rev. 21:26 that the glory and honor of the nations will be brought into the new Jerusalem.

The vision concludes: *They will see his face, and his name will be on their foreheads. And night will be no more. They will need no light of lamp or sun, for the Lord God will be their light, and they will reign forever and ever* (verses 4-5). The hope of the Psalmist, that "the upright shall behold his face" (Ps. 11:7) is now fulfilled. In the Old Testament, the high priest had the name of God (as part of the inscription "Holy to the Lord") written on the turban placed on his forehead (Exod. 28:36-38). The name of God signifies his ownership and protection of believers (2:17; 3:12). This is borne out by the fact that they will *need no light of lamp or sun, for the Lord God will be their light* (verse 5). This fulfills the prophecy of Isaiah: "The sun shall be no more your light by day, nor for brightness shall the moon give you light; but the Lord will be your everlasting light, and your God will be your glory" (Isa. 60:19). The hope of the Old Testament was that the Lord would shine the light of his countenance upon them (Num. 6:25-26; Ps. 4:6; 31:16; 67:1). There is a clear allusion here to Num. 6:27, where the light of the Lord's countenance shines on those who have his name placed upon them. In the old covenant, such a revelation of God's face would have brought death (Exod. 33:20). Now it brings life and eternal joy, as believers enter perfect fellowship with God through the blood of Christ. Even as Adam ruled over the garden, so now the saints *reign forever and ever* over the new creation.

The extended depiction of the new creation in 21:1-22:5 is intended to comfort and encourage believers to continue in faithful witness to Christ, in the face of suffering and temptations to compromise or renounce their faith. Whatever their earthly trials, their eternal reward is far greater. At the same time, this vision portrays the glory of God in the new creation. The vision, and the book as a whole, are designed as a pastoral encouragement to believers to persevere in the face of suffering. But even more significant than this is the portrayal of the glory of Christ and of God. We are to serve God because of the reward we will receive. But even more fundamentally, we are to serve him because, as the glorious God he is, he deserves our worship and the laying down of our lives.

11

THE END

(22:6-21)

The concluding section of the book is similar to the first verses of its introduction (1:1-3). Both contain allusions to Dan. 2:28-29, 45, which identify the book as a communication from God. Both present John as the witness to this revelation. Both state it is a prophecy communicated to its hearers. But while the introduction pronounces a blessing on those who heed it, the conclusion pronounces a curse on those who disobey it. The epilogue shows clearly that the purpose of the book as a whole is to inspire obedience among the saints. Eight of the final fifteen verses contain exhortations to obedience. These are accompanied by promises of blessing for obedience and warnings of judgment for disobedience. Both promises and warnings are based on events which remain in the future. The section contains five exhortations to holiness followed by one concluding verse.

THE FIRST EXHORTATION TO HOLINESS
(22:6-7)

The angel speaks: *And he said to me, "These words are trustworthy and true. And the Lord, the God of the spirits of the prophets, has sent his angel to show his servants what must soon take place* (verse 6). According to Dn. 2:45, the king's dream was certain (or true) and its interpretation sure (or trustworthy). Daniel announced that the events prophesied would take place "after this" (i.e. in the latter days, 2:45). But the angelic voice says to John that the Lord has sent his angel to show the things which *must soon take place.* What Daniel prophesied concerning the last days is declared here, as in 1:1, to be imminent or beginning to occur. These declarations of Daniel are quoted by John in 1:1, 1:19 and 4:1, at the beginning of the major sections of the book (understanding 4:1-22:5 to be one major section containing the various visions). The theme of the present establishment of God's kingdom in the face of attack and suffering (prophesied in Daniel) is thus present in the book from beginning to end. The same verse alluded to here shows that a new section — the conclusion — is beginning. God is identified here as the *God of the spirits of the prophets.* Daniel is very clearly alluded to, and the fulfillment of his prophecy is described. This means that the *prophets* are those of the Old Testament and of the church. This is different from 19:10, which describes the entire people of God as prophetic. God addresses John as a successor to Daniel in the prophetic office. The *servants* to whom this revelation is to be delivered, as in 1:1 and generally throughout the book, are all God's people, not just the prophetic community.

The things which *must soon take place* include Christ's own coming: *"And behold, I am coming soon. Blessed is the one who keeps the words of the prophecy of this book"* (verse 7). Here Christ himself, not the angel, is speaking. The present tense of the verb allows for a reference to all his comings, not just his final coming. The warning, given first to those John is addressing, is in fact to believers of all ages. In 2:5, 16; 3:3, 11, the "coming" of Jesus is clearly to the churches addressed, rather than to the entire world at the end of history. The same words in the same present tense, *I am coming soon* (Greek *erchomai tachu*), are used here as in 2:16, which clearly refers to a present coming in judgment: "Therefore repent. If not, I am coming to you quickly" [translated "I will come" in ESV]." The identical phrase reappears in 3:11, where it refers to a present coming of Christ to strengthen the church ("I will keep you from the hour of trial... I am coming soon"). Nevertheless, though Revelation presents many "comings" of Christ to his church, the emphasis at the end of the book, without excluding the previous "comings," is more heavily on his final coming. As Christians, we must always be ready for his final return, as Jesus taught (Mk. 13:32-37). In this verse, *soon* may also refer to the sudden and unexpected nature of Jesus' return (see below on verse 12). The main point of this exhortation is to *keep the words of the prophecy*, for it is even now beginning to unfold in our present lives, and will reach its sudden fulfillment in the return of the Lord, for which we must all be ready.

THE SECOND EXHORTATION TO HOLINESS
(22:8-10)

John witnesses the revelation contained in the book: *I, John, am the one who heard and saw these things. And when I heard and saw them, I fell down to worship at the feet of the angel who showed them to me, but he said to me, "You must not do that! I am a fellow servant with you and your brothers the prophets, and with those who keep the words of this book. Worship God"* (verses 8-9). John follows in the footsteps of the many prophets who preached faithfulness to God's covenant, and who reminded God's people of the blessings of obedience and the dangers of rebellion. Like the Old Testament prophets and Jesus, John directs his remarks first and foremost to the covenant community. The promises and warnings in the seven letters are directed to professing Christians. John, having repeated the same error recorded in 19:10, is rebuked by the angel, who tells him he is only *a fellow servant.* Although the Bible commands us to honor those in authority over us (1 Tim. 5:17; Heb. 13:17), we should never give to God's messengers (even angelic ones!) the worship due to God alone.

The contents of the book must remain open to all: *And he said to me, "Do not seal up the words of the prophecy of this book, for the time is near"* (verse 10). Witnessing the various heavenly revelations is not enough. John is to write down the words of the vision (1:10-11, 19; 2:1, 19:9; 21:5) and distribute them. The recording of the vision is thus as much under divine authority as is the vision itself. This again shows that John stands in the line of the Old Testament prophets. The record of his vision, passed down to us as part of the Scriptures, is just as authoritative as those of his predecessors. John's command is the opposite of that given to Daniel. Daniel was commanded to seal up the contents of the revelation he received: "But you, Daniel, shut up the words and seal the book until the time of the end" (Dn. 12:4; see also 8:26; 12:9). Daniel prophesied about kingdoms of earth and of heaven, but did not know how or when these events would happen, other than they were for an undefined time in the distant future (Dn. 12:13). The unsealing of the prophecy means that the prophecies of Daniel and other Old Testament prophets are *beginning to be fulfilled*, and their meaning can now be unfolded. Insight into these prophetic words is now given "which was not made known to the sons of men in other generations as it has now been revealed to his holy apostles and prophets by the Spirit" (Eph. 3:5). As Peter said concerning the prophets: "It was revealed to them that they were serving not themselves but you, in the things that have now been announced to you through those who preached the good news to you..." (1 Pet. 1:12). Both Paul and Peter thus make clear that *this fulfillment has already begun in the events commencing with the resurrection.* This reinforces the view that most of the events prophetically unfolded in Revelation occur throughout the church age, and are not restricted to occurrences immediately preceding Christ's return. This is also the meaning of Christ's unsealing of the book mentioned in 5:1. The contents of these books (that of 5:1 and the "book" of John's revelation) are not precisely identical, but would certainly have considerable overlap, both containing much material pertaining to the fulfillment of Old Testament prophecies. The prophecies are not to be sealed because *the time is near.* The meaning of *near* is the same as in 1:3: these events are beginning to unfold now, and will continue to do so until Christ returns and establishes his eternal kingdom in its completed form. The main point of the second exhortation is to worship God because of the unfolding of his prophetic purposes in Christ.

THE THIRD EXHORTATION TO HOLINESS
(22:11-12)

Verse 11 brings an apparently strange command: *"Let the evildoer still do evil, and the filthy still be filthy, and the righteous still do right, and the holy still be holy."* In verse 10, the angel has alluded to the sealing of Daniel's vision (Dn. 12:4). Now he alludes to the further angelic words recorded in Dn. 12:10: "Many shall purify themselves and make themselves white and be refined, but the wicked shall act wickedly." Daniel simply prophesies what he sees happening, but John's angel appears to suggest that evildoers should continue in their sin. To understand the meaning of this, we have to go back to the repeated exhortation of the letters: "He who has an ear, let him hear." This was based on Jesus' similar words, addressing the unfaithful in Israel (Mt. 13:9-17). Jesus in turn quoted Isa. 6:9-10, where God sends the prophet to a sinful people with a message that will cause them to be further hardened in their disobedience. Prior to Matthew 13, Jesus taught the people, but after that he began increasingly to use parables and prophetic sayings and actions which, like the similar prophetic declarations and actions of Isaiah, had the result of mystifying and offending un-believers and causing them to sink further into rebellion. Who would want to be identified with the unrighteous tenants or the proud older son? "Surely that cannot be the case," the Pharisees would declare. By contrast, genuine believers sought out the meaning of what Jesus was saying in order to enter into deeper repentance and obedience. Their attitude was, "If there is rebellion, pride or self-righteousness in me, then let God deal with me." The visions of Revelation serve the same goal as the prophetic actions of Isaiah and the parables of Jesus. They are not easy or transparent. In fact, they are hard and even offensive in the extreme nature of their presentation. Who would want to be portrayed as related to a Babylonian prostitute or foul beast? The ultimate root of the preaching and actions of Jesus and Isaiah are actually found in the signs Moses performed in the presence of Pharaoh. These powerful prophetic signs had the effect of angering and hardening the heart of Pha-raoh and those around him. Revelation paints a picture of a second Exodus, with the spiritual Red Sea serving as a barrier to freedom, and a spiritual dragon or Pharaoh seeking to destroy God's people as they enter the wilderness on their way to the Promised Land. The plagues of Exodus, therefore, are the model for the plagues of Revelation, and have the same effect. Thus God leaves the unbelievers and religious hypocrites in a place where they will inevitably do more evil yet. The abandoning of the lost to their own devices becomes in itself a further punishment for their sin, for a life of sin becomes its own punishment. The change from future prediction in Daniel (the righteous will purify themselves while the wicked will act wickedly) to a form of command in Revelation (let the unbeliever sink further into sin and the believer become more godly) indicates that the future prediction of Daniel is already beginning to happen in John's day, and will continue more and more until the Lord returns. *Let the evildoer still do evil... and the righteous still do right* is a prophetic declaration coming to fulfillment.

Christ speaks again: *"Behold, I am coming soon, bringing my recompense with me, to repay each one for what he has done"* (verse 12). As with Christ's words in verse 7, there is a double reference. As recorded in the letters, Christ comes to his church many times, either to judge or to bless. The same phrase, *I am coming soon*, is used in 2:16 to refer to Christ's imminent coming in judgment to the church at Pergamum. However, the words of Christ here also undeniably refer to his final coming, with their reference to final reward and judgment: *to repay everyone for what he has done*. We find both kinds of "coming" elsewhere in Revelation. Christ's words in 16:15 ("Behold. I am coming like a thief!") relate, in the context of the events of Armageddon, to his final return. Yet he uses similar words to warn the disobedient believers at Sardis of his imminent first-century historical coming to them in judgment: "'If you will not wake up, I will come like a thief, and you will not know at what hour I will come against you'" (3:3). If we take the emphasis here in verse 12 to be more on Christ's final return, how then are we to understand *soon*? It could be a reference to the suddenness of Christ's return — when it happens, it will be swift and unpredicted, just like his coming in judgment to the first-century churches must have been. Faithless believers are surprised by judgment, as much as faithful believers are surprised by revival. Yet both groups, in different ways (either through repentance or prayerful anticipation), are to make themselves ready. We could also understand this in the light of 2 Pet. 2:8-13. While according to human understanding, the delay in the Lord's return may seem lengthy, to God it is simply the next major event on the agenda. To him, "One day is as a thousand years, and a thousand years as one day" (2 Pet. 3:8). Writing in the context of an apparent delay in the Lord's return, Peter uses the same imagery of a thief: "But the day of the Lord will come like a thief" (2 Pet. 3:10). The picture of the thief runs backward from Revelation through 2 Peter all the way to Jesus himself. Jesus taught that the hour of his coming would be both unexpected and unknown, and that he would come like a thief (Mt. 24:36-44). Consequently, his followers are to behave and live as if he were returning at any moment (Mt. 24:44; 25:13; Lk. 12:35-40; 21:36). Malachi prophesied the sudden and unexpected manner of the final judgment: "And the Lord whom you seek will suddenly come to his temple... But who can endure the day of his coming, and who can stand when he appears?... Then I will draw near to you for judgment." (Mal. 3:1-2, 5). It is what is *soon* in God's eyes, not ours, that is to determine our perspective. God's eternal time frame dictates that Christ may return at any time. A delay of two thousand years delay is only two days to him. The point is we are to be ready as if he is returning tomorrow.

What does it mean for Christ to bring his *recompense* with him and *repay each one for what he has done*? The allusion is to Isa. 40:10: "Behold, the Lord God comes with might, and his arm rules for him; behold, his reward is with Him, and his recompense before him." What was attributed to God by Isaiah is now spoken by Jesus, thus again underlining his divinity. The text speaks of God rewarding the believer for what *he has done*. This does not refer to a reward given for works done through our own merit or righteousness. The reward Isaiah spoke concerns the forgiveness of sins by God's grace alone (see Isa. 40:2: "her iniquity is pardoned"). Salvation is bestowed solely on the basis of the pardoning of our sins. As the angel reminds John in verse 14, only the blood of Christ ensures our entrance to the eternal city. This verse, therefore, does not teach that we are rewarded or justified on the basis of our own independent works. The true meaning is that at the final judgment, the works of believers will be recognized *as the evidence of the fruit of the Spirit at work within them,* and thus as evidence they are truly saved. This is in line with what Jesus said: "Thus you will recognize them by their fruits" (Mt. 7:20). The main point of the third exhortation is that the unexpected time of the Lord's return should cause his people to live for him as they await that day.

THE FOURTH EXHORTATION TO HOLINESS
(22:13-17)

Christ continues to speak: *"I am the Alpha and the Omega, the first and the last, the beginning and the end"* (verse 13). The first two titles have been used in Revelation to refer to God (1:8; 21:6). The third has been used to refer to Christ (1:17; 2:8).

Now the three, all of which are Old Testament titles of God, are together used to refer to Christ. This once more highlights his divinity, and emphasizing his lordship over all of history, including its end. In response to Christ's words, John declares: *Blessed are those who wash their robes, so that they may have the right to the tree of life and that they may enter the city by the gates* (verse 14). The fact that Christ is Lord over all history gives believers courage to persevere in the assurance of the reward awaiting them. The washing of the *robes* refers to the standing of righteousness God has given them because of what Christ did on the cross. The *tree of life*, the *city* and the *gates* are images which speak of salvation and of God's eternal presence with his people. This verse looks back to the whole section 21:24-22:3, which speaks of the nations entering the eternal city and sharing in the tree of life. The imagery speaks of the restoration of what was lost when the gates of the garden were shut, and access to the tree of life was denied (Gen. 3:24). This verse also fulfills Isaiah's prophecy: "Open the gates, that the righteous nation that keeps faith may enter in" (Isa. 26:2).

John's warning continues: *Outside are the dogs and sorcerers and the sexually immoral and murderers and idolaters, and everyone who loves and practices falsehood* (verse 15). Similar warnings have already been given in 21:8, 27. The last group (liars) are identified in 1 Jn. 2:4, 22; 4:20; 5:10 (also Ac. 6:13) as false believers within the covenant community. Some church members accompany outward profession of faith with compromise with the world system. They are not true believers. Apostate or pseudo-Christian religious groups are sometimes in the forefront of attack on genuine believers throughout the world, cooperating with the second beast or false prophet in his evil endeavors. Jesus uses the word *dogs* to refer to unbelievers (Mt. 7:6; Mk. 7:27). Paul and Peter use the term to refer to false teachers (Phil. 3:2-3, 18-19; 2 Pet. 2:20-22). This relates them closely to the group of liars. The word "dog" is used in the Old Testament to refer to male cult prostitutes, whose offerings were not to be brought into the temple (Deut. 23:17-18). In the same way, the *dogs* here are excluded from the eternal temple. *Outside* refers to the lake of fire. There are only two possible destinations a person can face: the eternal city or the lake of fire.

Christ's words resume and come to a conclusion: *I, Jesus, have sent my angel to testify to you about these things for the churches. I am the root and the descendant of David, the bright morning star* (verse 16). The *you* is plural. It may represent a prophetic group within the churches who are commissioned to pass on the revelation. This would be in line with the statement in verse 6: "And the Lord, the God of the spirits of the prophets, has sent his angel to show his servants what must soon take place." However, it is not clear whether a specific prophetic group is in mind here. Further, if it is is a specific group, who then is charged *in future generations* to make sure the message is heard and understood? A better alternative is that *you* may simply represent all those to whom the book is addressed, that is, all believers throughout the church age. The Greek preposition *epi* (translated in ESV as *for*) might better be translated as "in" or "among." In other words, the angel is sent to *testify to you [all believers] about these things in [or among] the churches.* A parallel to this occurs in 1:4, where John first addresses "the seven churches" as recipients of his prophetic vision, and then immediately further addresses them as "you." Seeing as the seven churches are representative of the church throughout the ages (see on 1:4), the meaning in 1:4 would be that all faithful believers who read the book are exhorted to spread its true message among the churches they are part of. At the beginning and end of the book, its message is addressed to believers of all ages.

Two titles are given here to Jesus: *the root and descendant of David and the bright morning star*. These allude to two Old Testament prophecies describing the Messiah's triumph in the end times. In Num. 24:17, Balaam prophesies concerning the star that will come out of Jacob. Isaiah speaks of "the root of Jesse... of him shall the nations inquire" (Isa. 11:10; also 11:1). Jesus uses the present tense: *I am*. This indicates that these prophecies are already in process of fulfillment as Jesus is speaking to John. This is confirmed by the fact both titles of Jesus have already been used in Revelation in relation to his resurrection and the beginning fulfillment of his kingdom rule (5:5). *Root* seems to mean that Jesus is the origin of David, as well as being his *descendant*. However, it can also mean something sprouting out of the ground (Isa 53:2, where it is used, significantly, of the Messiah). David himself is described as the "root of Jesse" in Isa. 11:10, in that he was Jesse's son. Hence, the two words are probably synonymous.

Verse 17 contains four commands: *The Spirit and the Bride say, "Come." And let the one who hears say, "Come." And let the one who is thirsty come; let the one who desires take the water of life without price.* The *one who hears* encompasses all those throughout history who have obeyed the command given to the seven churches: "He who has an ear, let him hear what the Spirit says to the churches" (2:7, 11, 17, 29; 3:6, 13, 22). The church is even now the *Bride* of Christ, in spite of her imperfect condition. Those who hear and the Bride are one and the same, viewed from two different perspectives. The first "come" may express the Spirit-empowered prophetic preaching of the church. The second "come" may refer to Christians who hear the preaching and pass it on to the lost through their personal evangelism. All four commands are directed to the lost, urging them to come to Christ in faithful obedience. Most commands in any language are in the second person: "(You) do this or do that." Some, however, are in the third person ("Let someone do this or that"). The third-person command here (*let the one....*) urge those who thirst and desire the water of life to come. These commands may in a secondary way be directed to believers who need the continual empowering of the Spirit in order to remain faithful in the face of persecution and suffering. This verse fulfills the prophecy of Isaiah: "Come, everyone who thirsts, come to the waters; and he who has no money, come, buy and eat... without money and without price" (Isa. 55:1). Jesus issued a similar invitation in his earthly ministry: "If anyone thirsts, let him come to me and drink" (Jn. 7:37). He promised that from the hearts of those who believed would flow "rivers of living water" (Jn. 7:38). If even in this life we can enjoy the beginnings of the water of life, how much more shall we be satisfied by its infinite flow in eternity?

THE FIFTH EXHORTATION TO HOLINESS
(22:18-20)

John now gives an ominous warning: *"I warn everyone who hears the words of the prophecy of this book: if anyone adds to them, God will add to him the plagues described in this book, and if anyone takes away from the words of the book of this prophecy, God will take away his share in the tree of life and in the holy city, which are described in this book"* (verses 18-20). This warning is a precise parallel to a similar warning in the Old Testament. With the Israelites on the verge of entering the Promised Land, Moses gave these warnings: "And now, O Israel, listen to the statutes and the rules that I am teaching you, and do them, that you may live.... You shall not add to the word that I command you, nor take from it" (Deut. 4:1-2; also 12:32). Those who turned away from his commands were warned: "The curses written in this book will settle upon him, and the Lord will blot out his name from under heaven" (Deut. 29:20). At the end of Revelation (and of the New Testament as a whole), as Christian believers venture out on their journey to the Promised Land of the new Jerusalem, God gives a similar solemn warning.

Both Deuteronomy and the last chapters of Revelation deal with God's judgment on idolaters (Deut. 4:3; 12:30-31; Rev. 21:8, 27; 22:15). Both promise those who are obedient entrance into God's new land (Deut. 4:1; 12:28-29; Rev. 21:1-4; 22:1-5). Both use "plagues" to describe the punishment for unfaithfulness (Deut. 29:21; Rev. 22:18). According to Deut. 4:3 and 12:29-31, idolatry involves adding to or taking away from the words of God's law. Ancient Israel, like the Christians to whom John was writing, faced the continuous temptation to compromise with the pagan cultures and world system around it. For Christians, idolatry is at the heart of compromise with Babylon and the demonic powers behind it. Professing Christians can dilute their commitment to worship God alone by adding to the teaching of Scriptures what is not in it, and by taking away from that teaching what is clearly there. To add to or take away from this revelation means to undermine the authority of God's Word. Those who thus undermine the authority of Scripture do so in order to make way for worship of something other than God — whether that be a literal idol or today's cultural trends. It is a severe warning to those who suggest that the teachings of Scripture are culturally conditioned and no longer relevant for today. This suggestion is nothing more than a cover for compromising with pagan and idolatrous cultural values.

The Mosaic law was modeled on ancient near-eastern treaty or covenant documents which would have been well familiar to the Israelites. These treaties were imposed by triumphant kings on nations they conquered. Not one word could be altered in them. The Israelites understood that they could not tamper with the covenant God had made with them. The New Testament as a whole is the new (or renewed) covenant or treaty. We could thus consider the words of warning here to refer to tampering with *any part of the New Testament*, in the same way that Moses' words of warning dealt with tampering with *any part of the Mosaic law* (which, by extension, included the whole Old Testament). The ancient treaty documents always contained curses on those who added to or took away from the words of the treaty (covenant) in order to dilute the commitment of the conquered people to the conquering king. As in the days of ancient Israel, these words of warning are particularly addressed to those who profess to be believers but are not. The phrase "everyone who hears the words of the prophecy" (verse 18) is almost identical to the phrase "those who hear [the words of the prophecy]" in 1:3. At its beginning and end, Revelation shows itself to be a document written to believers — both genuine and merely professing.

It is those within the visible, professing community of faith who hear and are warned in these closing verses. Sadly, there are those within the visible church whose names are not written in the Lamb's book of life, and these are the very ones who attempt to draw the church off into idolatry. Of course, countless unbelievers who never made any profession of faith will also perish in the lake of fire, but these particular words of warning are directed first and foremost to those who profess to be believers but are not, or to those who are compromised or wavering in their faith.

In verses 16 and 18, Jesus (through the angel he has sent) and John have given testimony to the truthfulness of the words of the book. If we look at the concluding verse of each of the seven letters ("let him hear what the Spirit says to the churches"), we see that the Spirit also testifies. In verse 20a, Jesus adds this: *He who testifies to these things says, "Surely I am coming soon."* The weight of these combined witnesses is insurmountable (the Bible requiring two witnesses to verify an accusation), and emphasizes the legal character of Revelation. *Those who read it are legally accountable for what they have read.* Jesus testifies to *these things*. The same phrase ("these things") is used in verse 8 to refer to the "words of the prophecy of this book" (verse 7). Jesus is thus testifying here to the entire content of Revelation. This is in line with the warning in verses 18-19 against adding to or taking away from any portion of the book. Jesus adds his testimony to the truthfulness of the entire revelation given through his angel to John. He repeats what he has said in verses 7 and 12: *I am coming soon.* Believers are to remember that God's timing is not their own, and the Lord may return at any time. They are always to be ready. In response to this, John utters the prayer, *"Amen. Come, Lord Jesus"* (verse 20b). *Amen* ("so be it") is an expression of his sure hope and trust that, as Christ has proven faithful throughout John's long life, so also will he be faithful in returning for those he loves.

CONCLUSION (22:21)

The section and the book as a whole conclude with John's words, *The grace of the Lord Jesus be with all. Amen* (verse 22). The closing words of Revelation are in line with the closing words of most other New Testament letters. This demonstrates again (as in 1:4) that Revelation is a *pastoral letter addressed to Christians.* Just like the other New Testament letters, it deals with problems and issues in the life of the churches. Those reading the letter need the grace of God in order both to understand the things said in it, and to obey its commands. However, their experience of God's faithfulness and the many ways he has blessed them, as well as their assurance of future reward, strengthens and motivates them to further obedience, even in the face of challenge and hardship. The five exhortations to holiness found in this last section encapsulate this theme of persistence in obedience in order to inherit the promises. From its very beginning in chapter 1, Revelation unfolds the theme of the fulfillment of Old Testament prophecy. Christians must continue in obedience if they are to share in the blessings this fulfillment has already begun to bring. The main *pastoral point* of the book as a whole is that faithful endurance in the face of suffering will result in eternal blessing and reward. The main *theological point* of the book is that this faithful obedience by Christians will ultimately result in the glory of God and of Christ.

Soli Deo gloria. To God alone be the glory.

Amen.

ABOUT THE AUTHOR

From the Toronto region. David holds three degrees in theology. He and his wife, Elaine, have planted churches in the UK and Canada. David also teaches internationally in churches, Bible colleges, leadership training centers, and Hillsongs TheosU. David and Elaine have eight children and six grandchildren which, let's be honest, is an accomplishment.

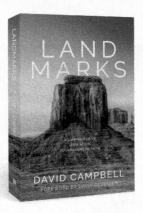

Landmarks
*A Comprehensive
Look at the
Foundations of Faith*

By David Campbell

FIND THE WONDER IN HIS INCREDIBLE PLAN

Landmarks by David Campbell charts our course from the Word of God to our everyday lives. Each marker on this trail of bread crumbs reminds us of an essential truth that has shaped our knowledge of God and his plan. This is not a history book or an opinion piece; it's a compendium of foundational belief that celebrates monumental breakthroughs in christian understanding. Reading through Landmarks will leave you enlightened, grateful and strengthened in your faith.

Other titles by David Campbell

No Diving
*10 ways to avoid
the shallow end of your faith
and go deeper into the Bible*

By David Campbell

The Book of Revelation
A Shorter Exegetical Commentary

By G.K. Beale
With David Campbell

CPSIA information can be obtained
at www.ICGtesting.com
Printed in the USA
LVHW100933250421
685283LV00027B/1299